A PLAGUE OF CORN

The Social History of Pellagra

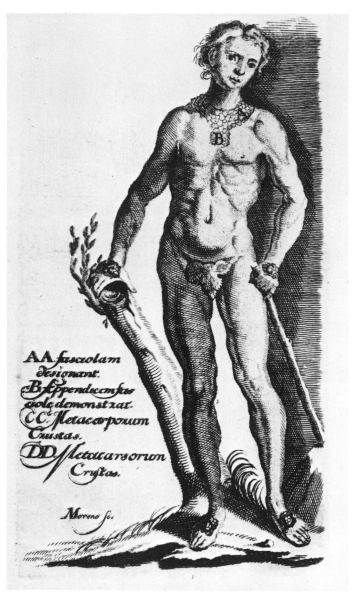

Mal de la Rosa. Copperplate of an antique figure. From Gaspar Casal, *Historia natural y medica de el principado de Asturias: Obra posthuma* (Madrid: Martin, 1796).

A PLAGUE OF CORN

The Social History of Pellagra

DAPHNE A. ROE

Cornell University Press | ITHACA AND LONDON

First published 1973 by Cornell University Press.
Published in the United Kingdom by Cornell University Press Ltd., 2–4 Brook Street, London W1Y 1AA.

International Standard Book Number 0–8014–0773–7
Library of Congress Catalog Card Number 72–12408

Printed in the United States of America by Vail-Ballou Press, Inc.

Librarians: Library of Congress cataloging information appears on the last page of the book.

Contents

Illustrations

Preface

Some may share with me an attraction to books that are out of date, pictures that are out of fashion, and diseases that no longer ravage the earth. My present concern is with pellagra, a disease which was unknown to ancient scholars and which has become unfamiliar to most modern physicians. I was introduced to pellagra when I was a medical student in London, but I can remember seeing only one case during the entire period of my clinical clerkship and my years as an intern. As a matter of fact, this was the first case of pellagra I saw until I went to Pavia, Italy, in 1951 and was shown a group of old women with the disease. Since then and since I have been resident in the United States, I have occasionally seen pellagra but have only twice had cases under my care.

How is it then that I have the temerity to write a book called *A Plague of Corn,* about pellagra and its victims? For over twenty years I have been interested in medical bibliography, and for the last five I have been preoccupied with all the literature on pellagra. My literary journey began in the stacks of the Flower Veterinary Library at Cornell University, where I chanced upon little-known monographs on the causation of the disease as well as upon the transactions of the first congress on pellagra held in the United States. The scientific merit of some of these books is negligible, but in reading them I gained insight into the social impact of pellagra. Indeed, I was stimulated to pursue the social history of the pellagrin. With this as my major goal, I located the voluminous writings on pellagra and analyzed the works of men who saw the disease during the great epidemics in Europe, Africa, and the United States. Although the majority of the accounts were in monographs, theses, or standard medical texts written by physicians, I also found a number of descriptions of pellagra in diaries of famous travelers and a novel by Edmond About, *Maître Pierre* (1858), in which the tragedy of pellagrous peasants in the Landes region of France provides the introductory theme.

As I read, I became aware that there were two general types of observers: those who believed that pellagra was a man-made disease, the result of the inhuman practice of restricting the poor to a diet that cannot support health in a dog; and those who thought that it was the fault of the afflicted. The origins of these divergent opinions can repeatedly be traced to contemporary dissertations on the causes of poverty and malnutrition. As long as men have believed that human bondage is an inescapable partner of civilization and material progress, they have ascribed destitution to the inferior qualities of the destitute. Pellagra has been variously accepted as a disease of those with an inborn taint, a susceptibility to infection, or an unwillingness to live on a diet of foods other than corn-meal mush. Conversely, those who have held fast to the credo that freedom from want is an integral human right have been among the pioneers who have elucidated the cause of pellagra and have striven to conquer it.

As well as recounting the social history of pellagra, I explain how the disease originated and how, through a thousand human and animal studies, its cause became known. This is an adventure which has been told in part before and which I now bring up to date. Since, however, I do not want this book to seem like the end volume of a defunct journal, I make it plain that all is not yet known about the disease. Pellagra-like illnesses go unexplained, and the biochemist is still unsure of all the answers. This malady is still endemic in parts of the world.

In preparing this book, I have been dependent on the research, aid, and criticism of many people. My colleagues in the Graduate

School of Nutrition at Cornell University have been particularly helpful in guiding me to source materials I would otherwise have missed. Among them, I would like to mention my special indebtedness to André van Veen and Michael Latham, who have facilitated my contacts with international nutritionists who have a wide experience of pellagra. The late Leonard A. Maynard, Professor of Biochemistry and Nutrition and first Director of the School of Nutrition, generously allowed me access to his personal files of the Food and Nutrition Board, so that I was able to learn the story of the fortification of the American loaf and how this World War II emergency measure contributed to the conquest of the disease. Another associate, Louise Daniel, guided me along the biochemical pathways of pellagra research in her wonderful lectures as well as in private conversations.

Elisabeth Linusson, a student in the College of Human Ecology at Cornell, was until recently a field worker with the United Nations Food and Agriculture Organization (FAO) in Lesotho, Africa. She supplied me with published and unpublished data on pellagra, especially the account I give of the socioeconomic and dietary factors responsible for the spread of pellagra among women, herd boys, and older men in that country.

My efforts to obtain information on the current incidence of pellagra in formerly endemic areas have met with success because of the precise information supplied to me in letters from heads of public health and nutrition departments in a number of European countries. I am particularly grateful to Dr. Ratko Buzina, of the Institute of Public Health of Croatia, for data on the decline of pellagra in Yugoslavia during the last fifteen years. Similarly, Dr. Francesca Ronchi Proja, Nutrition Officer of the World Food Program of FAO in Rome, gave me authoritative evidence that pellagra is no longer an endemic disease in Italy. Both Dr. Buzina and Dr. Ronchi Proja gave me to understand that pellagra may still be seen in their respective countries among chronic alcoholics subsisting on a faulty diet.

I am delighted to acknowledge the help afforded me by the

family of the late Dr. Joseph Goldberger. Beatrice Goldberger, his niece, directed me to little-known newspaper accounts of her uncle. Dr. Joseph H. Goldberger also assisted me in locating published accounts of his father's life and many contributions to pellagra research.

Data on the current distribution of pellagra would not have been available if it had not been for the information generously provided me in unpublished reports of observers outside the United States. I am particularly indebted to Dr. Coluthur Gopalan, director of the National Institute of Nutrition of the Indian Council of Medical Research in Hyderabad, who sent me an account of endemic pellagra in India with detailed information on the dietary and socio-economic factors that determine its incidence in the Deccan Plateau region. Aaron Lebona, Permanent Secretary for Health and Education in the Ministry of Health, Education and Welfare in Maseru, Lesotho, kindly supplied a description of the diet of the working people in his country, among whom pellagra is still prevalent. This report included a detailed list of the edible wild plants consumed, some of which are known to cause light sensitivity and thus influence the clinical picture of the disease. My good friend Lalit Bhutani, head of the Department of Dermatology at the All India Medical Institute in New Delhi, gave me important information on his own experience of pellagra and the associated light sensitivity.

I am also indebted to Dr. William Darby for letting me see in manuscript the data on the history and incidence of pellagra in Egypt, from the book *The State of Nutrition in the Arab Middle East,* by the late Dr. Vinayak N. Patwardhan and himself, published by Vanderbilt University Press in 1972.

Some of the writings on pellagra that I quote came to my notice in unusual ways. Theodore Brown, of the Department of the History of Art at Cornell University, was assembling the photographic works of the late Margaret Bourke-White for an exhibition when he learned of my interest in the pellagra problem. He lent me a copy of the book *You Have Seen Their Faces,* by Erskine Caldwell and Margaret Bourke-White, published by Viking Press in 1937; illustrations from that book, reprinted here, provide excellent documentation of the social deprivation of pellagrins in the South during the last years of the Depression. W. O. Caster, Professor of Nutrition at the University of Georgia, talked pellagra with me after I had given a closed-circuit television program on this subject at the 1971 Western Hemisphere Nutrition Congress in Bal Harbor, Florida. He directed my attention to the Ph.D. dissertation of one of his students, Elizabeth Williams Etheridge, who entitled her work "The Strange Hunger: A Social History of Pellagra in the South." She says in her preface, "It is concerned not so much with science and medicine as it is with a way of life that fostered a disease." Her description of quack "cures" for pellagra gave me a new conception of the depravity of those who snatch the last cent from the afflicted.

My deepest thanks go to all who have helped me write this book and prepare it for publication. Beverly Hastings, my secretary, has done a splendid job of typing and retyping the original manuscript. My family have sustained me at all times and have egged me on with the chant "When will it be finished?" David and Laura, my children, have also greatly assisted in checking the text and notes. Above all, I must express gratitude to my husband, Albert Sutherland Roe, not only for his supportive role, but also for the active part he has played in collecting literary sources and helping to translate French, German, and Italian works at home, in London, and even when I was lying blindfolded in the New York Hospital under the care of a retinal surgeon.

DAPHNE A. ROE

Ithaca, New York

A PLAGUE OF CORN

The Social History of Pellagra

1 | The Disease Pellagra

Pellagra was first observed in Europe in the eighteenth century by a Spanish physician, Gaspar Casal, who found that it was an important cause of ill-health, disability, and premature death among the very poor inhabitants of the Asturias. In the ensuing years, numerous Italian authors described the same condition in northern Italian peasants, particularly those from the plain of Lombardy. By the beginning of the nineteenth century, pellagra had spread across Europe, like a belt, causing the progressive physical and mental deterioration of thousands of people in southwestern France, in Austria, in Rumania, and in the domains of the Turkish Empire. Outside Europe, pellagra was recognized in Egypt and South Africa, and by the first decade of the twentieth century it was rampant in the United States, especially in the southern states.

Wherever the disease appeared, it attacked those whose precarious livelihood was drawn from the soil, the miserable peasants who had no choice but to work under the sun and to eat the cheapest and least varied diet. In each country and in each district, the local people coined names to identify the disease, names describing a common symptom or names referring to the district of maximum occurrence. Physicians and other scholarly authors often adopted these local names in their writings, leading to considerable confusion as to the unity of the disease manifestations. Despite the semantic difficulties, however, pellagra was easily identified in en-

1

demic areas by a triad of symptoms: a rash, intense diarrhea, and mental disturbances.

Recognition of pellagra has not always stimulated the study of causal relationships. Although Casal himself believed that this is a nutritional disease, political and economic considerations prevented people from accepting the thesis. It was more reassuring to believe that the victims had some hereditary taint, akin to congenital syphilis, or that they had an infection. Who would want to believe that thousands upon thousands of indigent families lived on a diet which caused both physical and mental degradation?

In this book we shall trace the story of pellagra, considering its origins and how it has been associated with maize-eating peoples. We shall follow the sun and attempt to find out why it burned the pellagrins. We shall open old texts and look into the strange detective story that ultimately resulted in our present knowledge that pellagra is a specific deficiency disease. The conquest of endemic pellagra will be described. Yet this book cannot end on a note of triumph. Pellagra still exists and in some countries is still widespread. New problems concerning a congenital pellagra are currently under investigation. Even now the relationships between the nutritional deficiency and the clinical features of the disease complex are ill understood.

Medical students or young nutritionists asked to describe the clinical features of pellagra will answer that this is the disease of the three D's: dermatitis, diarrhea, and dementia. Usually they are hesitant to enlarge upon this description, because they have never seen a case. Indeed, this would also be true of many physicians who work in any but the few remaining world areas where endemic pellagra persists. In the United States and in most countries in Europe, pellagra is rare, occurring only as a secondary complication of gastrointestinal disease or in alcoholics, psychotics, or occasionally in food faddists. The best discourses on the signs and symptoms of pellagra were published at a time when the disease was rampant among impoverished corn-eating people.

Armand Marie, in 1908, quoted a saying of the pellagrins of

Venetia, who had a long and unhappy familiarity with the affection: "Pellagra can give rise to seven kinds of ills. . . . It drives one crazy, it drives one into the water, it draws one backwards, it makes one walk bent, it gives one vertigo, it gives one ravenous hunger and it causes rashes on the skin." [1] Two contemporaries of Marie expressed the belief that this was not a very accurate description of pellagra.[2] On the other hand, a great student of pellagra, Dr. Fleming Sandwith, was confident that he had seen variants of pellagra which would fit each of the peasants' diagnostic criteria.[3]

Reputable accounts of pellagra tend to be a synthesis of the author's experience and that of his mentors and the renowned teachers of a previous generation. The description of the disease by Dr. Edward Jenner Wood, commendable for its accuracy, can be summarized in lay terms. Clinical manifestations of pellagra are usually divided into four stages: (1) a phase in which the patient feels unwell but has no definite symptoms; (2) the stage of redness of the exposed areas of the skin, during which there occur, in addition to the skin changes, various digestive disturbances and some central and peripheral nervous disturbances; (3) the stage of severe neurological disturbances, with psychic phenomena and a downhill phase of wasting sickness; and (4) the cachectic stage, which is usually terminal. The first stage usually begins soon after Christmas in the Northern Hemisphere, and is characterized by very indefinite symptoms such as loss of appetite, abdominal pain and flatulence, and usually diarrhea, though the reverse condition of constipation may occur or the two conditions may alternate. Sometimes, there is an insatiable thirst or, on the other hand, an aversion for water. The tongue is thickly coated. Even in this early stage of the disease there occur certain nervous symptoms, which usually first manifest themselves as headache, pain in the neck and back, hypersensitivity to touch, dizziness, and muscle weakness, especially of the legs. This first stage may last only a few weeks, or it may be prolonged for several years.

Coincident with the appearance of such mouth symptoms as a sore tongue or soon after there appears a redness of the light-exposed skin which gave the name *mal de la rosa* to the disease and which is usually accounted the most important symptom. All authorities do not agree that this is the most important symptom. Sandwith thought it the least important and that it received an undue amount of attention. In Wood's opinion, the skin changes of pellagra should be regarded as characteristic, and the diagnosis was never justified without them or a history of their past occurrence. The skin lesions appear in the spring after the weather has become warm and sunny. Distinctive features are redness, symmetry, location on exposed portions of the body, pigmentation, and peeling. A skin lesion which does not occur on the exposed areas or is not accompanied by such a lesion of the exposed portions must not be considered pellagrous, for the selection of such locations is a definite peculiarity of the disease. The first appearance of redness strongly suggests simple sunburn, and for the first few days cannot be distinguished from it. Following this, there occurs peeling of the skin, which usually proceeds from the center to the periphery, leaving a border of brownish pigmentation that is the last remnant of the skin condition. In America two types of skin lesions were recognized: the wet and the dry, the former accompanied by exudation of serum. At the height of the attack, nervous symptoms have commonly already developed.

These symptoms usually last from three to four months. The skin of the affected areas often remains for some time darker in color and sometimes rough and dry. Finally every vestige of the affection seems to have disappeared. Wood points out that many physicians with a limited experience in this disease have assumed that the treatment instituted by them has been successful and make unjustified claims for certain drugs as a result. But the next spring brings a recurrence of all the symptoms mentioned. Another repetition usually occurs each succeeding spring, and with each recurrence the severity of the symptoms is increased and a more indelible impress is left, especially on the nervous system.

The next stage of the disease is characterized by the appearance of severe cerebrospinal disturbances. The patient complains of many abnormal sensations in the skin—among which are itching of the backs of the hands and occasionally of the feet—and burning in the stomach, shoulder region, feet, hands, and arms. This burning is said to cause the tendency of the sufferers to plunge into water. This weird performance was never observed by Wood, though, he tells us, it is mentioned by a number of Italian pellagrologers. A dull headache is often a constant symptom, but probably the most constant complaint is dizziness. Psychical symptoms are very prominent in this stage of the disease, usually those characteristic of melancholia. In milder cases there are interference with thought, slowness of ideas, mild irritable depression, and an aversion to any form of activity. When the disease is more severe, there is often the firm conviction of unpardonable sin. Then the mental attitude is always one of profound depression or delusions of persecution. The patient will often refuse food to the point of starvation, not because of inability to take food occasioned by the sore mouth, which occurs earlier in the disease, but purely as a result of mental disturbance. Some writers describe a definite suicidal tendency. Weakness of the muscles, especially of the legs, is sometimes found. Spasms and painful cramps sometimes occur. The decrease of muscle power may progress to partial paralysis.

The fourth stage is the stage of wasting. It manifests itself with increasing weight loss, disappearance of subcutaneous fat, diminished strength, and an inability to resist intercurrent diseases. Weakness is so great that the patient is often bedridden. Diarrhea is usually very severe. Death often results from a weakened heart muscle; sometimes death is due to tuberculosis, to which pellagrins are peculiarly susceptible.[4]

Wood's description has not been bettered by more recent authors. Indeed, accounts of the clinical features of pellagra have often been made confusing by the inclusion of symptoms which are due, not to pellagra per se, but to coexisting deficiency diseases. Virgil Sydenstricker pointed this out in his review of the history of pellagra in the United States. He noted that even after the specific cure for pellagra had become available and the dermatitis, dementia, and diarrhea could be made to disappear by giving a patient the vitamin niacin, some symptoms would persist. These symptoms included a magenta discoloration of the tongue, cracks at the corners of the mouth, scaling around the nose, burning of the throat, and redness of the eyes. Such lesions were found to be due to a deficiency of the vitamin riboflavin, and they only cleared when this nutrient was supplied in adequate amounts.[5]

Minute description of the signs and stages of disease culminated during the nineteenth century in a nomenclature of debased Latin and Greek. Little was known of the causes of infection, degeneration, or atrophy of skin, gut, brain, or any other tissue. Predisposition to a specific illness was believed to be dictated by "diathesis" —a term applied to constitutional peculiarities not far removed from the humors of Aristotelian philosophy. Ignorance and rigid adherence to classical nomenclature combined to perpetuate vague disease categories. Thus pellagra was described by the well-known British dermatologist Malcolm Morris as a "trophoneurotic" disease.[6] It passed through a premonitory phase, "pellagra *sine* pellagra," and might proceed through "herpetic" and "typhoid" stages. In their clinical study of pellagra included in their translation of Marie's *La Pellagre*, Claude Lavinder and James Babcock commented:[7] "To give any clear and succinct clinical description of a disease like pellagra is a task beset with no little difficulty. The malady is so protean in its manifestations and often so varied in its evolution as to make a clear and logical description of it by no means easy. Almost all writers and clinicians seem to have been impressed by this fact and hence Lombroso's use of the epigram 'There is no disease, only the diseased.' "[8]

The protean character of pellagra has given rise to the idea that it is not one disease, but this concept is not easy to rationalize, since it has been found that the signs disappear when a single vitamin, niacin, is given. One of our contemporaries, Theodore Gillman, who had extensive experience of pellagra in South Africa, brought forward an ingenious theory to explain the spectrum of clinical manifestations. In 1965 he wrote: "It is reasonable to suggest that the food we consume actively precipitates specific requirements for additional nutrients. If these new metabolic needs are not met promptly, then a series of physiological adaptations rapidly supervenes. The latter may in turn lead to profound metabolic dyscrasias which are likely to be expressed in various organs and tissues." Gillman essentially believed that in pellagra, as in certain other nutritional diseases, one deficiency creates a number of secondary deficiencies and that the symptoms are compounded of the multiple deficiencies.[9] Modern knowledge of dietary interrelationships has tended to support this idea, but it must not be overlooked that most pellagrins are hungry, protein-deficient and low in many vitamins of the B complex because they live on poor-quality cereal diets.

Perhaps the most logical explanation of the varied symptomatology of pellagra is that niacin deficiency, secondary deficiencies created by a lack of niacin, and a lack of other dietary factors operate together to produce the total clinical picture.

2 | Pre-Columbian Maize Culture and Its Consequences

Archaeologists and agronomists have for many years been interested in the origins of American agriculture and have reached the conclusion that maize (corn) was one of the chief crops grown in ancient times. Zelia Nuttall, in her writings on the Aztecs, developed this thesis further: "The history of the development of maize is inseparable from the history of the origin and development of civilization on the American continent." [1] As Paul Mangelsdorf and Robert Gatlin Reeves pointed out in a monograph on the origin of Indian corn, this is not surprising, because all the great civilizations of all times have based their economy on the cultivation of cereals.[2] Since we are particularly concerned with the disadvantages of maize culture, it is of some significance to review and discuss the words of Edward J. Payne in *History of the New World Called America,* published in 1892:

Whether, if the wild form of maize had not existed, cereal agriculture would have had any place whatever in aboriginal American advancement is extremely doubtful. . . . A narrow wooden or bronze spade was the most advanced agricultural implement of the New World: and, in the absence of the ox and the horse, the tillage of the soil had to be universally accomplished by the unassisted labour of man. In such circumstances, the wide prevalence of maize-agriculture suggests that this cereal must be especially suitable for cultivation by slightly advanced populations; a suggestion which is at once confirmed by an examination of its nature. The chief characteristic of maize is the

8

extraordinary size both of the plant and of its grain. . . . This gigantic size directly facilitates its cultivation by limiting the number of plants that can come to maturity in a given space; while smaller cereals require the laborious tillage of the entire surface of the field, maize can be successfully cultivated without this process, and by means of the fire-hardened stake alone. All that is necessary is to burn the trees and wild plants on the surface of the plot, to make holes at proper distances, to drop in the seed, to stir the earth around the young plant, and to keep it clear of weeds, and in two to four months' time, according to the quality of the soil and the degree of rain and sunshine, the seed yields from one to fourhundredfold. Two crops can be grown in a year on the same plot: and in some places three or even four successive crops are taken. While the ease with which the unrivalled crop is produced placed cereal agriculture within the reach of man at a comparatively early stage of advancement, the large returns which it yielded greatly stimulated its cultivation; and at the time of the Discovery it had already spread over most of tropical and temperate America, where no animal capable of agricultural labour existed, and in many parts of which the idea of reducing the soil to tilth was wholly unknown. Thus did nature to some extent compensate America for the want of the great domestic animals by endowing it with an unique cereal, the largest and most productive known, and capable of being profitably cultivated without them.[3]

Whether this is a precise account of why the American Indians came to raise and eat corn is doubtful. As Mangelsdorf and others have shown, strains of wild maize grew in the Americas, and it seems that the availability of these plants decided the direction of primitive agriculture. Interesting in Payne's account is the nineteenth-century view that man at the dawn of civilization purposefully chose to cultivate an indigenous plant because of the economic advantages that might accrue. This theory is about as credible as the account of the Elephant's Child in Rudyard Kipling's *Just So Stories,* who acquired his trunk by having his nose pulled out by an irate crocodile. There is a definite suggestion in Payne's writing that he attributed to the pre-Columbian inhabitants of the American continents the same motives for maize cultivation that were extant in his own day and go back to the time when maize first became a commercial crop in Europe. By making maize available, untutored man can easily increase the agricultural wealth of nations; this is why peasants and day laborers have been encouraged to grow this crop. Indeed, they can even cultivate maize with the farmer relaxing in the shade or the landowner away.

It is worthwhile to consider how the Indians believed maize culture began. Paul Weatherwax has summarized their traditional stories, which generally show that they believed maize was brought to them as a miraculous gift. Thus the Navajos say that they first knew of corn when a turkey hen came flying from the direction of the morning star and shook from her feathers an ear of blue corn. The Cañari Indians of Ecuador told of a great flood which destroyed all the people on the earth except two brothers who climbed a high mountain. After the water subsided and the men came down to the lowlands, they were visited by two parrots, which gave them food and drink made of maize. When one of these birds was captured, it changed into a beautiful woman, who gave the men the seed of maize, taught them how to grow and use it, and eventually became the mother of the Cañari race.

Many of the stories are creation myths expressing the belief that man was formed from maize. In one such fable of the Quiche Indians, the branch of the Maya race inhabiting the highlands of Guatemala at the time of the discovery of America, the gods made several unsatisfactory attempts to create a man. Thus the man made of clay fell apart when it got wet, and the men carved of wood had no minds or souls, so they were condemned to die. Finally, the body of a man was modeled from a dough made of white and yellow corn. The first four beings created in this way became the ancestors of the human race. The gods found them to be good, and the men gave thanks to their creator. Even so it has come about that man continues to be made of the same substance, which he eats in tortillas.[4]

Two recurring themes appear in all the Indian corn myths, whether or not they are embellished with complex imagery. Maize was considered a tangible evidence of the gods' beneficence and also a sacramental element. In other words, the Indians recognized from an early time that corn was the bread of life. It provided the basic sustenance for the body and the soul.

Such stories have a nobility not altogether in keeping with the practical aspects of the ancient Mexican religions. Maize deities, who we presume were created by the ancients as their protectors, were believed to become capricious in their requirements, wanting all kinds of sacrifices, from birds to girls, to insure a bountiful harvest. How else could the ancients explain the constant battle with nature or account for failure of the corn crop except by the belief that the greedy gods had not been appeased?

The all-pervasive influence of this cereal on the culture of the Indian peoples is amply demonstrated in pre-Columbian art where the maize motif is constantly in evidence in conventionalized form. It also decorates the utensils of everyday life.

We have looked at the origins of maize culture from the point of view of a nineteenth-century pragmatist and through the eyes of those who lived in America before Cortes. Since this is not a book of myths, let us give attention to the scientific theories which attempt to explain the origin of this cereal.

Mangelsdorf referred to the idea that cultivated forms of maize are derived from pod corn (*Zea tunicata*), a plant superficially resembling ordinary corn but in which the grains are surrounded by husklike structures. There is some evidence that pod corn once grew in the wild state, though very little is known of its occurrence in pre-Columbian times. Some of the remains of corn found in New Mexico are thought to represent a form of pod corn.[5] For genetic reasons, Weatherwax cast doubt on the theory that maize could have evolved from pod corn: "We are disposed to mark it off the list of likely candidates for the role of the ancestor of cultivated maize." He believed that a more likely ancestor was teosinte, or wild maize, though he was not convinced that this undomesticated plant was the single direct ancestor of corn as we know it. He escaped the necessity of naming a plant which developed into maize by proposing a promaize species which changed its character in a series of mutations. In the development of the domesticated varieties of corn, it is thought that the Indians of Central America played a major part. Their accomplishments in this regard were not deliberate, because they certainly knew nothing about heredity. Nevertheless, they became corn breeders and must have improved the plant by the isolation of varieties and simple selection. The Indians must also have learned the wisdom of saving part of their crops for seed and using the seed best suited to their purposes.

Campaigns against Hunger, published in 1967, presents archaeological proof of the very early domestication of maize in Mexico. Fossil corn pollen, estimated to be at least eighty thousand years old, has been identified from remains found in drill cores two hundred feet below the present level of Mexico City. This fossil pollen has given evidence that modern corn was derived from a cornlike plant.[6] Excavations of once inhabited caves in the valley of Tehuacán by Richard S. MacNeish revealed tiny corn cobs, which Mangelsdorf and his colleague Walton Galinat identified as cobs of prehistoric wild corn. This was the first wild corn to be discovered. Radiocarbon dating has shown that some of these cobs are of the 5000 B.C. era. Other corn remains in the Tehuacán caves have distinguished an evolutionary sequence of domesticated corn from the wild plant. By 3500 B.C., corn had been cultivated, though the cobs of the period are still small. About 2300 B.C., a more modern type of corn evolved, apparently by hybridization with one of its wild relatives.[7]

This development of a grain which could provide a plentiful food supply was undoubtedly an important factor in conditioning the rise of the early civilization in America, but a surmise that an agriculture based on corn alone dictated the rise of a complex culture in this area would be unjustified. More acceptable is the premise of Elizabeth Kennedy Easby and John F. Scott that perhaps because maize was difficult to domesticate and required care to grow and because it was the "staff of life," it became associated with one of the major deities of the Mesoamerican pantheon.[8]

For our purposes, it is more important to remember not only that corn was first domesticated in Central America, but that it continued to be a most important source of food in Mexico and in Guatemala long after Pitao Cozobi, the God of Abundant Sustenance, Lord of the Fields of Maize, was forgotten, and down through the centuries to the present day. Despite their corn eating, the Mexicans and their neighbors seem to have been protected from the plague of corn. As far as we know, pellagra has been a problem in Central America only in times of famine, and there is no definitive evidence that it occurred in pre-Columbian times.

In the past, while the argument was still raging as to whether pellagra was associated with maize eating, those opposing this theory pointed up the situation of the Mexicans. How was it that these people, who had lived on corn for countless centuries, had not succumbed to pellagra? Théophile Roussel, the great French authority on pellagra, answered the doubters by giving his readers in a nutshell the culinary secrets of the Indians with respect to the preparation of corn.[9] He obtained his information from reading the thesis of a young Mexican physician which was presented in Paris in 1863. Ismael Salas wrote his dissertation on the utilization of maize in Mexico, where pellagra was unknown, comparing the practices there with those in countries where pellagra was common.

Salas emphasized that the principal article of diet of the Mexican peasant was the tortilla instead of the corn bread that was eaten so widely in France and Italy by pellagrins. He said that in the preparation of tortillas the grains of corn were mixed with slaked lime and water in earthenware pots and heated for eighteen hours. At the end of this time, the limewater was drawn off, the corn washed and then pressed in a primitive grindstone till it formed a glutinous paste. This paste was made into round, flat cakes which were baked on a heated iron griddle and turned frequently to avoid undercooking.[10] This is the way tortillas are made today, but what is more interesting is that the technique seems to have been developed in remote times. We know of the ancient process through the survival of essential implements which differ little if at all from those used by Indian peasants today in the making of tortillas.[11]

Starting with the husked corn grains and finishing with the flat cake ready to eat, the tortilla maker requires utensils and implements for four distinct processes. The lime treatment imposes a need for large earthenware pots to contain the quicklime or wood ashes and water which can be boiled with the corn to soften the hulls (pericarps) of the grain. Perforated clay pots are required to wash the corn and sieve off hulls after the lime treatment. The resultant hominy paste has to be worked in a grinding device which may take the form of a pestle and mortar or a metate, which consists of hand-operated grinding stones. Finally, the tortilla has to be baked on suitably large, flat griddles.[12]

These objects were all in use in pre-Columbian times, as we know from grave furnishing and other artifacts which have survived. A hollow monkey figure, an Olmec work of the preclassic period, 1150–550 B.C., found in Las Bocas, Puebla, Mexico, shows the use of the pestle and mortar to grind the prepared corn. Numerous prehistoric grinding stones have been found, and numerous forms of the metate have been preserved, some without decoration and others, which had ceremonial significance, elaborately carved to show the distinctive head of a bird-monster or monkey and legs fashioned in animal forms. Whereas there is evidence that these curved table-like objects were adapted for use as altars, their original use for working the hominy into flat dough cakes is evident from the mano, or heavy rolling pin, sometimes found with the metate, which exactly fits the hollow of its upper surface.[13]

The Indians' age-old process of corn preparation was known to the Spanish conquerors. Of the foods used by the Indians of Yucatan about 1550, Diego de Landa says: "Their principal subsistence is maize, of which they make various foods and drinks.

. . . The Indian women place the maize in lime and water to steep the night before, and in the morning it is soft and half-cooked, and in this way the hulls and nibs are separated from it; and they grind it on stones." [14] In the seventeenth century, breads and gruel were made by a similar method in Guatemala, and the method has held its own among the poor of Mexico and countries in Central America until the present day. The metate is still their most important household implement, though some relinquish its use in favor of the local mill, where their corn is also treated with lime before it is ground.[15]

Roussel was not able to explain why countless generations of American Indians had been able to subsist on a maize diet and remain healthy, whereas for European peasants, high consumption of the cereal was associated with pellagra. He realized, however, that the difference might lie in the method of preparation and that the lime treatment of maize was somehow beneficial. It is obviously ridiculous to suggest that the pre-Columbian Indians introduced the lime treatment in order to improve the nutritional qualities of the maize. The method probably evolved because the Indians found that lime-treated corn could be better preserved and also because chemical removal of the hulls was less tedious than scraping them off by hand.

Almost a century after Roussel learned of the lime treatment of corn from Salas, American nutritionists were able to offer an explanation of why pellagra is and has been rare among the Indians of Mexico and Central America. The relative absence of pellagra in the corn-eating countries of this area has been attributed to the greater availability to the consumer of the vitamin niacin from alkali-treated corn.[16] Maize is low in this pellagra-preventing vitamin; corn which is not lime-treated has the added disadvantage that a part of its niacin content is unavailable to man, because it exists in a chemically bound form. The alkali or lime treatment frees the bound niacin, and there is evidence from studies of experimental pigs that the amount of niacin so freed can be just sufficient to prevent pellagra.[17] It must be admitted, however, that when Grace Goldsmith studied the efficacy of lime treatment in converting corn to an antipellagragenic food, she did not find that tortillas had any pellagra-curing activity.[18] Both Goldsmith and her critics have suggested that in these investigations insufficient lime-treated corn was given to demonstrate its special effect.[19]

While we now have evidence that lime treatment may increase the nutritional value of corn with respect to the provision of utilizable niacin,[20] there is every reason to believe that the native peoples of Mexico and Central America have escaped pellagra for other reasons. Since the very early time when corn was first domesticated, other food crops have been widely grown. Remains of beans, squashes, and chili peppers have been found in the same sites in the Tehuacán caves where corn specimens have been identified, and it appears that these vegetables were also grown about 3500 B.C. Not only was there a varied agriculture from an early date in Mexico, but the proximity of various vegetable remains, particularly corn and beans, in archaeological sites has suggested also that these were grown together. While it is impossible to conceive that the Indians living in remote times knew that beans would enrich the soil by nitrogen fixation, they may well have learned through experience that beans growing in the cornfields would improve the yield of grain. Lawrence Kaplan, after studying the cultivation of edible legumes in the Andean region and in Mexico, has intimated that wherever beans and corn were grown, these two plants were used as food crops, not by accident, but as a result of "adaptive combination" based on human nutritional requirements. In essence, he believes that human survival and development in these areas have been determined by the complementary nutrients supplied by beans and corn. He generalizes this concept thus: "The evolution of human diet is marked by synergistic combinations perhaps to a greater extent than by small increments in the food value of individual nutrient sources."[21] Corn and bean agriculture was established in Middle America about six thousand years ago. An attractive and scientifically tenable theory is that feeding habits based on these two staples developed as a result of innate recognition that they were needed together for health. Conversely, early man, when deprived of animal protein, could not live on corn alone but only by supplementing his diet with legumes. A great deal has come to light about the subsistence of the prehistoric inhabitants of the Tehuacán Valley. Richard MacNeish, summarizing the findings of the members of the Tehuacán Archaeological Botanical Project, has emphasized changing trends in the principal sources of food. Meat began as the dominant food and then decreased from about 4500 B.C., when the consumption of wild plants was very extensive. Subsistence based on agricultural plants, including maize, squash, and corn, became more important than a diet of either wild plants or meat from 1500 B.C. until the time of the Spanish conquest. MacNeish has speculated that the changes in food habits may have taken place in response to an awareness that the number of man hours required to obtain food from the domesticated plants was substantially less than the number needed to hunt wild animals or collect wild fruits, grains, and roots. Furthermore, the yield of food from maize and beans was greater than from other sources. In other words, people got increasing quantities of food by expending decreasing amounts of energy and obtained more protein and food energy with less work. Throughout the pre-Columbian period, when domestication of animals for food consumption was rare, the significance of cereal and legume agriculture for man's sustenance cannot be overestimated.[22]

In seeking the reasons why pellagra has not been a major problem in Middle America and Mexico, we have considered the lime treatment of the maize and the food habits of the people, who have eaten corn and beans together since ancient times. The continuance of these practices from the time of the Aztecs to the present suggests that they have a protective function. In remote times, before the domestication of corn, when men depended on hunting game and collecting wild edible vegetation, they either survived or died of starvation. Later, when agriculture had been developed, the corn staple could be supplemented by beans, a little meat, and the same wild vegetables and fruits that were eaten at an earlier time. Since, however, this phase was also associated with the growth of a civilization in which some Indians were subservient to others, we can assume that there was unequal distribution of food. It is known that domestic slavery soon developed, but whether the slaves received gifts of food from their masters or could grow and collect food for themselves has not been established. By analogy with other slave economies, it seems likely that the master would see that his slave was fed, much as the farmer feeds his domestic animals, because this was the only means of getting him to work hard. At the time of the Spanish conquest, domestic slaves were sold to Europeans, as were other Indians who had previously been freemen. The newly enlarged slave population was compelled to work in the mines, where we know very many died of physical maltreatment coupled with disease, some of which may have been malnutrition. According to David Brion Davis, this frightful mortality in the mines eventually caused the slave owners to reconsider the employment of Indian slaves, whom they replaced by black slaves, because Africans were considered more expendable.[23] Whether the slaves served a Mayan chieftain or a Spanish overlord, it appears unlikely that pellagra would have occurred among them as long as they were able to include protein foods in their daily diet. There is documentation from fecal remains that cave-dwelling Indians who are believed to have been slaves prior to the conquest ate the meat of small animals such as mice, bobcats, and kangaroo rats.[24] Furthermore, the writer Oviedo mentions that in the sixteenth century in Mexico, the "Christians" used green corn to feed their horses and their Indian and black slaves.[25] Green corn was unripened corn which was cooked in the husks together with the grubs which infested it. It is therefore justifiable to assume that the slaves as well as the horses had a source of protein.

The Indian peasant has continued to like green corn. He has gone on making tortillas and eating them with fried bean mush.

He has supplemented his cereal diet with a number of unusual protein sources such as corn pests and toasted locusts. In an instinctive way he has warded off pellagra, the disease of the corn eaters who have received no supply of the pellagra-preventive vitamin or of protein.

The moral to this story is that endemic vitamin deficiencies, such as that which causes pellagra, have occurred only when men have been fed an unnatural diet not of their own choice. We shall see how such diets have been forced on men as our narrative unfolds.

3 | *Grano Turco*

The first man from Europe to report the cultivation of Indian corn was probably Columbus. The journal of his first voyage to the New World was taken back to Spain, but the original was lost and only an abridgment remains, consisting of seventy-six handwritten folios compiled by the priest Bartolomé de Las Casas.[1] In his book *Indian Corn in Old America,* Paul Weatherwax has pointed out that some of the existent folios may be almost verbatim copies of the journal, but other portions, written in the third person, are discursive and may differ considerably from the original.[2] Las Casas reported that on October 16, 1492, as Columbus looked out over the green fields of Haiti, he said he had no doubt that the people there grew millet, and the chronicler added that this assumption was correct, because in that area they did plant and harvest "the green maize, which the Admiral called panizo." The significance of this statement has been doubted, because Las Casas did not begin his rendering of the journal until long after this event. Perhaps Columbus did see maize during the first week he spent in the New World, but even if he did and called it *panizo,* the term suggests that he thought it was a kind of millet. *Panizo* is the Spanish for panic grass or millet, a cereal type with which he was familiar. Anyway, by November 5 of that year, when the explorers landed on the northeastern coast of Cuba and proceeded inland, where they were welcomed by some very friendly Indians, they not only saw Indian corn or maize, but ate it boiled, roasted, or made into a porridge.[3]

Perhaps at the end of Columbus's first voyage samples of the plant were brought back to Spain to demonstrate the fertility of the soil in the newly discovered land. Documentation of such an event, however, is meager, to say the least.

The earliest record of the appearance of maize in Spain, which Weatherwax believes to be reliable, is in the first volume of Peter Martyr's *Decadas del Nuevo Mundo* ("Decades of the New World.") [4] Martyr began writing his books on this subject in 1493, and the first book of the series was published in 1511. Martyr explains that the Indians make bread from the roots of the yucca and that "they also make bread in the same way from a grain like the millet which is abundant among the Milanese and the Andalusians. The ear of this is more than a palm in length, somewhat pointed and as thick as a man's arm. The grains are naturally arranged in a marvellous order. In form and size they are like peas. While immature, they are white and they become very black when they ripen. Break them open and they are whiter than snow." In the next edition of the same book, which appeared in 1516, the account ends with the sentence, "This kind of grain they call maize." [5]

Another very early mention of maize in European literature occurs in a Latin pamphlet about America, by Nicolo Syllacio, published in Pavia December 13, 1494. In a paragraph dealing with the foods of the Indians, the author writes: "There is here also a prolific kind of grain, the size of a lupin, rounded like a chickpea. When broken, it produces a fine flour, and it is ground like wheat. A bread of excellent flavor is made from it. Many who have little food simply chew the grains themselves." [6] It is believed that part of this document derives from observations made by Guglielmo Coma, who was a member of the party with Columbus on the second voyage. Coma wrote a letter about his experiences from somewhere in the West Indies and sent it back to Spain when twelve of the ships returned early in 1494.[7]

Maize was reported as growing in Europe very early after the discovery of the New World. Columbus, in his report on the third voyage, wrote that the plant was then growing in Spain.[8] The 1525 edition of Oviedo's *Historia* mentions maize growing near Madrid.[9]

Shortly thereafter, maize began to attract the attention of the herbalists who were chiefly interested in the uses and medicinal properties of plants. The Renaissance herbalists, knowing nothing of the reports of the Spanish explorers that maize had been seen in the New World and had been brought back to Europe, believed that the new grain came from the Orient. The first herbalist to mention maize was the German Jerome Bock, in 1539. He calls the plant *welschen Korn* ("strange grain"), and he explains that it is new in Germany and probably came from India.[10] The next reference in a herbal was in Leonhard Fuchs's *De historia stirpium,* first published in Latin in 1542; it contains the first illustration of a maize plant to appear in Europe. Fuchs reported that maize had become quite common in Germany and in 1542 was growing in all the gardens. He called the plant *Frumentum turcicum* and believed that it had been brought to Germany from Asia by the Turks.[11] John J. Finan, discussing references to maize in the great herbals, alluded to the sixteenth-century use of the word *turcicum* to mean anything foreign; he mentioned that from a similar misconception the turkey got its name.[12] The term *grano turco* persists as the modern Italian name for maize.

The mid-sixteenth-century herbals of the Low Countries essentially follow those of German authors in insisting that the grain came from Asia, though late editions of these works sometimes concede a New World origin. One of the most distinguished of the Italian herbalists, Petrus Matthiolus, the first herbalist to see the literature of the explorers, denied the Oriental origin of maize. In the first edition of his book, which appeared in 1565, he states: "This type of grain, which they wrongly called Turcicum, can be numbered among the varieties of wheat. [It has been named] incorrectly I say, because it ought to be called Indicum, not Turcicum, for it was brought from the West Indies, not out of Turkey and Asia as Fuchs believed." [13]

While the herbalists continued to argue, a naturalist-missionary,

José de Acosta, visited Peru in 1570 and Mexico in 1583. He published descriptions of maize which became known to the herbalists who were active in the latter part of the sixteenth century.[14] His studies of the grain made these European botanists understand that whether or not maize came from the Far East or the Near East, it certainly did originate on the American continents.

At the end of the sixteenth century, there was still a belief that maize came from the east, although herbalists realized that it came from the New World. John Gerarde, in the first edition of his herbal, published in 1597, states these beliefs as if he had both scholarly and firsthand information about the plant. He describes the different sources of maize as follows: "These kinds of Graine were first brought into Spaine and then into other provinces of Europe, out of Asia which is in the Turkes Dominions, as also out of America and the Ilands adjoyning from the east and west Indies, and Virginia or Norembega, where they use to sowe or set it, and to make bread out of it, where it groweth much higher than in other countries. It is planted in the gardens of these northern regions, where it cometh to ripenes when the summer falleth out to be faire and hot, as my selfe have seen by proofe in myn owne garden." The names of the plant are the subject of some philosophical remarks in this book, but the treatment of this subject points up Gerarde's indecision about the plant's origin. Thus he goes on: "Turky wheat is called by some Frumentum turcicum, and Milium indicum. Strabo, Eratostenes, Onesicritum, Plinie and others, have contended about the name heereof, which I minde not to rehearse, considering how vaine and frivolous it is. . . . In English it is called Turky corne and Turky wheate: the inhabitants of America and the Ilandes adjoyning as also of the east and west Indies do call it Maizium and Maizum and Mais." [15]

The second edition of Gerarde's herbal, which appeared in 1633, was a magnificent volume that contained much more accurate information about maize, as about other plants. The title page suggests that Gerarde may have obtained this knowledge from a colleague: "The Herball or Generall Historie of Plantes . . . Gathered by John Gerarde of London, Master of Chirurgerie—very much enlarged and amended by Thomas Johnson, Citizen and Apothecarye of London." Under the heading "Of Turkie Corne," is an emended account of the plant with a number of subheads. A description reads: "The graine is of sundry colours, sometimes red, sometimes white or yellow as my selfe have seene in myne owne garden where it hath come to ripenesse." Discussing the plant's place of origin, the author asserts that it was first brought into Spain and then into other parts of Europe, not, as some supposed, out of Asia Minor, but from America and the adjoining islands. "It is sowen in these countries in March and April and the fruit is ripe in September." The author has changed his mind about the ancients: "It in all probabilitie was unknown to the antient Greek and Latin authors." The Virginians, he says, call the plant "Pagatowr."

The section of this chapter most closely related to our theme is entitled "The temperature and vertue." It is quoted in full because of its nutritional implications. Gerarde declares his antipathy to corn in these words:

Turky wheat doth nourish far less than either wheat, rie, barley or otes. The bread which is made thereof is meanly white, without bran: it is hard and dry as Bisket, it hath in it no clamminesse at all; for which cause it is of hard digestion and yeeldeth to the body little or no nourishment; it slowly descendeth, and bindeth the belly as that doth which is made of Mill or Panick. We have as yet no certaine proofe or experience concerning the vertues of this kinde of Corne; although the barbarous Indians, which know no better, are consrained to make a vertue of the necessitie and thinke it a good food: whereas we may easily judge, that it nourisheth but little, and is of hard and evill digestion; a more convenient food for swine than for men.[16]

In spite of the repeated allusion to the growing of corn in "myne owne garden," Gerarde apparently did not make his own illustrations of the plant. The first edition of his herbal contains figures of two varieties which, in keeping with the supposed origins of maize, are called "Turkie Corne" and "Corne of Asia." Finan has pointed out that these are the same figures used by Jacobus Tabernaemontanus of Frankfort, who published a herbal in 1588 and who also accepted the theory of the dual origin of maize.[17] It has further been suggested that Gerarde and Tabernaemontanus

¶ *The kindes.*

OF Turkie cornes there be diuers forts, notwithftanding of one ftocke or kindred, confifting of fundry coloured graines, wherein the difference is eafie to be difcerned, and for the better explanation of the fame, I haue fet forth to your view certaine eares of different colours, in their full and perfeꞔt ripeneffe, and fuch as they fhew themfelues to be when their skinne or filme doth open it felfe in the time of gathering.

The forme of the eares of Turky Wheat.

3 *Frumenti Indici ſpica.*
Turkie wheat in the huske, as alfo naked or bare.

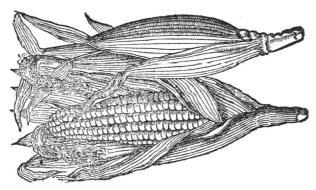

¶ *The temperature and vertues.*

Turky wheat doth nourifh far leffe than either wheat, rie, barley, or otes. The bread which is made thereof is meanly white, without bran: it is hard and dry as Bisket is, and hath in it no clamminefle at all; for which caufe it is of hard digeftion, and yeeldeth to the body little or no nourifhment; it flowly defcendeth, and bindeth the belly, as that doth which is made of Mill or Panick. We haue as yet no certaine proofe or experience concerning the vertues of this kinde of Corne; although the barbarous Indians, which know no better, are conftrained to make a vertue of neceffitie, and thinke it a good food: whereas we may eafily iudge, that it nourifheth but little, and is of hard and euill digeftion, a more conuenient food for fwine than for men.

Figure 1. Woodcut of ears of corn and reproduction of original text. From J. Gerarde, *The Herball or Generall Historie of Plantes* (2d ed.; London: Islip, Norton, and Whitakers, 1633).

used the same blocks for printing, a common practice occasioned by the lengthy and expensive process of wood-block production. The second edition of Gerarde's herbal has figures borrowed from other sources.[18]

Later herbals provide several descriptions of the untoward effects of eating corn. John Parkinson's *Theatrum Botanicum: The Theater of Plants,* published in London in 1640, says in its discussion of the "Vertues": "Acosta saith that by feeding too much on maize it engenders grosse blood, which breedeth itches and scabbes in those that were not used to it." [19] Caspar Bauhinus' herbal, published posthumously in 1658 at Basel, describes the ill effects of eating corn experienced by natives of the New World: "Indeed, the boys of the Guineas who often eat it in place of bread, shaking the grains out of the ears and roasting and burning them, if they take it a little too often cannot rid themselves of the itch, since the plant produces blood that is too hot and virtually burned." [20]

Apparently these seventeenth-century authors had some idea that the eating of maize in large quantities was injurious to health, but even with the widest stretch of the imagination we cannot accept any suggestion of a reference to pellagra. Indeed, it may well be that there was delayed acceptance of maize as a food by some Europeans living in the Old and New World and that their prejudices engendered the stories. At best, there may be a grain of truth in these anecdotes.[21]

The appearance of maize in the great herbals documents the fact that this cereal was known to a number of educated people in western Europe during the period between its original importation and the middle of the seventeenth century. They give no evidence, however, that the plant was grown elsewhere than in botanical gardens. Furthermore, since the illustrations in these books were not always original, we cannot be sure that every herbalist had more than a cursory or perhaps second-hand knowledge of the cereal.

Our information concerning the spread of maize cultivation in

Europe comes from other sources, mainly from early books on agronomy. Haphazard reading of such manuals gives the impression that maize was introduced into certain countries or certain areas of one country because of some whim of a landowner or because the climate was auspicious for its growth. While the former theory is sometimes valid, the latter is erroneous. Large-scale cultivation of maize was dictated more by political geography than by any particular attribute of the land or weather.

Although corn was grown in Spain from the time of its importation into that country from America and the West Indies, we know little about its early history there as a cereal crop or about its use for human consumption. Fortunately, however, factual accounts exist of the introduction of corn into Italy. A book by Agostino Gallo published in 1775 says that corn was first brought into the area of Rovigo about 1560, and from there its cultivation spread gradually through the Venetian states and into Lombardy.[22] This assertion seems to have a reliable basis, because Matthiolus, writing in 1571, states that maize was already known in Italy and that the peasants used it as food.[23] According to the economist Antonio Zanoni, who looked carefully into the Venetian archives, the cultivation of corn began in Belluno and in the Friuli region in 1610. He further stated that it was from this area, just south of the Carnic Alps, that a maize economy spread into the Veneto and then into Lombardy. Maize was imported into Bergamo for the first time in 1682 and was cultivated in villages within the province.[24]

In the documents collected by the physician Vincenzo Sette from the archives of a number of abbeys in the Venetian states, there is proof that maize began to figure among the agricultural products that brought in an annual revenue about 1700. Théophile Roussel, who had access to Sette's memoirs, mentions that in the years just prior to this date there was a rapid increase in the production of maize which was encouraged by the Venetian government. This government may have foreseen great financial gain from the maize, because the harvest was more prolific than that of other cereals. In order to prove that production greatly increased, Roussel quotes from Sette:

In the archives of an ancient monastery in the Venetian provinces, in the place where the malady (pellagra) was first discovered, I have ascertained that Turkish wheat did not begin to figure among the annual revenues until the beginning of the seventeenth century but then only in such small quantities that even in 1688, at the monastery of Correzzola, in the province of Padua, they harvested 1682 hogsheads of wheat, 217 of millet, 205 of buckwheat, 212 of barley, and 788 of Turkish wheat [corn]. However, by the end of the eighteenth century, they had abandoned the cultivation of barley, buckwheat, and millet and had reduced the production of wheat, but the Turkish wheat crop amounted to more than 4000 hogsheads. The predominance of this grain over all the others was stabilized toward the middle of the last century at the precise epoch when pellagra began to be observed.[25]

About 1710 the American grain began to figure in the commodities sold in the Broletto market in Milan, at which time the registers began to show the price of cereals. Subsequently, corn made its appearance in the records of other cities, as in Brescia, where it is mentioned for the first time in the public register of the town in 1774.[26]

The idea and the application of maize culture as an important agricultural venture spread widely from Italy, where it had been shown to be successful. It spread directly into Carinthia, to the valley of the Gail River, which is separated from Italy only by the Carnic Alps, and from there into the whole region which is now Yugoslavia. It was cultivated in Austria, not only in the gardens of noblemen, but also as a field crop, and from there it was taken into Hungary.[27] All this happened in the eighteenth century, and not by chance. Maize cultivation was actively fostered at that time by the Hapsburg rulers because the yield was great and they could extort tithes to bolster their revenues and fill their coffers. Also, they sought stability in their domains by encouraging local despotic landlords and suppressing the peasantry. Here was a grain that seemed tailored to their needs; its great economic potential, combined with its obvious usefulness as a staple food for the indigent, justified their efforts to promote production. As we shall see, when corn began to be grown as a major cereal in other areas of Europe, as also in Egypt, South Africa, and the United States, the motives of those who made agricultural policy were not dissimilar.

4 | *Mal de la Rosa*

Diseases are discovered through the experience of the afflicted; only later, physicians win laurels by bringing the condition to the attention of their colleagues. Thus, when in 1735, Dr. Gaspar Casal, of the town of Oviedo in the Asturias, began to see patients with a strange and terrible new ailment, he was told by the sick that this was *mal de la rosa*.[1] The peasants of that area of northwestern Spain recognized that the disease was heralded by a red discoloration of the skin and applied the name accordingly. Casal made careful observations of the various symptoms and signs of the condition and recorded case histories with meticulous detail, indicating that he was familiar with the skin changes, the fluxes of the bowels, and the severe mental changes which appeared with relentless regularity. Apparently, he felt no urgency about publishing his findings but was content with the expedient of writing to at least one other Spanish physician about his observation. In response to such correspondence, he received a letter from Dr. Benito Feijoo written December 2, 1740, which mentioned that *mal de la rosa* had also been seen in Galicia.[2]

Several years later, when Casal was residing in Madrid and had been appointed to the Royal Academy of Medicine and as physician to the court of King Philip V, he was visited by a French physician, François Thiéry, who was in the service of the French ambassador.[3] Thiéry had the chance to read Casal's medical diaries, and after he returned to France he published a brief account of Casal's disease in the medical *Journal de Vandermonde* in

1755 [4]—an act which might be interpreted as plagiarism except that Thiéry was honest enough not to claim the observations of *mal de la rosa* as his own.

On August 10, 1759, Casal died; three years later his magnum opus was published under the title *Historia natural y medica de el Principado de Asturias*. In this book of modest size the epidemic and endemic diseases of northern Spain are described in relation to the climatic environment. *Mal de la rosa* is the third endemic disease considered,[5] but to Casal it must have had great importance, because the only illustration in the entire volume pertains to this section. A copperplate print shows an antique human figure on which is drawn a conventionalized presentation of the skin lesions of pellagra, including the lesion around the neck which subsequently became known as the "collar of Casal." [6]

The Latin text gives the clear impression that Casal recognized *mal de la rosa* as a multisymptom disease which affected the poorest laborers in the Asturias, who lived on a maize diet varied only by the addition of turnips, chestnuts, cabbage, beans, nuts, and apples. Casal mentions that maize flour was made into a kind of bread. According to Edouard-Adolphe Duchesne, the usual corn bread of these Asturians was a very unattractive comestible. They made thick flat cakes of the flour and water and left them in the cinders all day, covered with leaves and straw, and finally ate the half-cooked smoky mass that was left.[7] Although Casal does not go into culinary details, he emphasizes that the "rose" can be effectively treated by changing the inadequate and unattractive diet to provide milk, cheese, and other foods seldom eaten by the poorer segments of the population. Definite evidence that *mal de la rosa* continued to occur in this area of Spain later in the eighteenth century has been obtained from the journals of Dr. Joseph Townsend, a British traveler who was in Oviedo in 1786. Spanish physicians showed him cases of the disease in the local hospital; it was apparently not considered a rarity.[8]

It is important to consider why this new malady appeared in northern Spain during those years. In a nutshell, the outbreak may be explained as the result of increasing poverty and the reliance of poor people on an inadequate maize diet. The cultivation of corn was and is an important part of the economic life of the Asturias. By the time of Casal, the grain had been grown there for over a hundred years, yet apparently corn eating had not caused any serious problems before the time he came to Oviedo. By then, corn was being eaten by the Asturian peasants because they could afford little else. The reason for their poverty in the eighteenth century have been discussed by Julius Klein in *The Mesta: A Study in Spanish Economic History*. This author gives a full account of the rise and fall of the Mesta, a most powerful guild, which was founded in the twelfth century to promote and control the raising of Merino sheep and the sale of their wool. By the eighteenth century, this organization had lost its controlling influence, so sheep owners and shepherds had no union to which they could address their grievances. The king, as well as local authorities, was free to impose innumerable taxes; the herdsman paid for the privilege of grazing his animals, and the proprietor of the sheep paid tolls on migrating flocks. In 1758, it was recorded that in the Asturias, 321 different sheep taxes were in effect, completely crippling a once prosperous industry. As a result, many of the rural people of this region moved to the cities or emigrated to the Spanish colonies. Those who were left were dependent on the large-scale landowners, who cared little for their humble shepherds and farm laborers. The old medieval way of life was at an end. Peasants could no longer depend on their masters for paternalistic support. They picked up the crumbs from the rich man's table, but the landlord consumed more and left fewer crumbs.[9] Penury, destitution, and disease among the Spanish peasants of the period are strikingly depicted in Goya's frescoes in the church of San Antonio de la Florida in Madrid. The interior of the dome shows St. Anthony healing the sick; a ragged crowd, some with bandages of rags on their legs; a blind man; a starving beggar; and in the middle, a tall figure with the signs of the "rose" on his neck.[10] Whether Goya ever saw pellagra is entirely unknown, and indeed, from the quality of his painting, we cannot be sure that he intended to represent a case of Casal's disease. It is, however, believable that on such people the scourge of *mal de la rosa* would fall.

The spread of *mal de la rosa*, or pellagra, in Spain at the end of the eighteenth century and during the early years of the nineteenth century has been disputed, because few written accounts of the disease appeared. Certainly the diet and the way of life of the working people in northern Spain improved very little in those years. Fréderic Le Play published an account of a Spanish tenant farmer and his family who lived in the village of Revilla, near Santander, during the years 1840–1847. Despite the author's assurance that these people lived a life of temperance, thrift, and religious fervor, which supported health and natural dignity, the existence described was one of grinding poverty which would not be tolerated in western Europe today.[11] Le Play obviously believed in nineteenth-century principles of class distinction as satirized by Dickens: "Bless the squire and his relations . . . / And always know our proper stations." [12] The Spanish peasant lived as God had ordained and apparently also ate the humble food appropriate to his lowly estate. This family in Revilla subsisted chiefly on puchero, a type of corn bread, and ferrapas, a sort of corn-meal mush. To this basic diet were added some beans, a little milk, and a few sardines or salt cod, cooked over charcoal. Cheese and butter were eaten occasionally. The man and his wife were essentially sharecroppers, while the children herded sheep or goats —services for which they might be paid with pocket money or with a handful of food. We are told that the children did go to school and could read and write to some extent. Medical services were said to be of a high order. A second- or third-class physician or physician's assistant was available without fee to all the villagers; his only remuneration was twenty kilograms of maize per annum.[13]

Roussel was in touch with Spanish colleagues in 1840; he was informed that pellagra was still seen in the Asturias but not in other parts of Spain—a statement which strained his credulity.[14] In the next seven years he made a thorough search of Spanish medical literature and found published reports of pellagra-like diseases from widely separated regions of the Iberian Peninsula. Outbreaks of a strange illness, known commonly as *mal del higado,* were seen in the district of Alcañiz in 1809 and during the succeeding years in Daroca, Teruel, and Morella. It affected a large number of the inhabitants of the pueblos, or villages, and was characterized by chronicity, annual recrudescence of symptoms, liver dysfunction, and gastroenteritis.[15] A Dr. Gimeno, writing in 1826, believed this condition to be synonymous with *mal de la rosa,* though this was purely guesswork on his part, based on the fact that the description of *mal de la rosa* in the dictionary of Boliano had many features in common with *mal del higado.*[16] In 1835, Dr. Francisco Mendez-Alvaro saw a group of women in Villamajor de Santiago, in the province of Guenca, who had scaly red lesions on the backs of their hands and forearms. These women, who were very poor, attributed their skin condition to the use of a form of lye in place of soap. Mendez-Alvaro soon realized that this could not be the cause, since he saw identical lesions in men who had not handled lye. He further noted that many of these people had gastrointestinal symptoms and exhibited delirium and a form of dementia. The same condition was observed by physicians working in the villages between the Tormes and Duoro rivers, where the disease came to be known as *flema salada* (literally, "salty phlegm").[17] Although Mendez-Alvaro thought his patients had a form of *mal de la rosa,* this diagnosis was disputed by his colleagues.

Another endemic disease known as *mal del monte* or *mal el monte* was described as occurring among peasants living near the frontier of Portugal and in the province of Zamora about 1847. This condition had clinical features which resembled those of pellagra in every particular.[18]

When Roussel had analyzed the writings of the various doctors who had reported these conditions, he drew up the following synopsis: (1) Pellagra, up to the year 1847, had received no careful study in Spain; no aspect of it had been the subject of careful observation sufficient to provide a reliable description or consideration of cause. (2) In addition to the endemic pellagra of the Asturias, there existed other endemic diseases which so nearly resembled it that, in the present state of knowledge of the disease, it was very difficult to designate them with other names. (3) Endemic pellagrous districts were found in a large number of places far from each other; the disease occurred in the north as well as in the central part of Spain. (4) All the endemics, however imperfectly studied, have the appearance of pellagra; despite local variations the unity of the various Spanish diseases with pellagra cannot seriously be doubted. (5) In all cases the pellagra-like diseases appeared in very poor country people.[19]

It is curious to realize that, in the 1840's, not only was there doubt that the pellagra-like diseases of Spain were one and the same, but also that there was no consensus of opinion that *mal de la rosa* was the same disease as pellagra, which was rampant in northern Italy and southwestern France. From his reading alone Roussel felt sure that the two diseases were the same, but in order to prove his theory, he traveled to Spain in 1847 and embarked on a seven-month tour to investigate cases of *mal de la rosa* in the area of the Asturias where Casal had worked. On his return to France, he made a report to the Academy of Medicine in Paris, in which he was able to give evidence for the correctness of his earlier assertions.[20] Endless discussion and dispute followed the publication of this report. Spanish physicians resented the fact that a Frenchman had meddled in their medical affairs. Arnault Costallat, one of Roussel's colleagues, agreed with Roussel in the main but denied the identity of *flema salada* and pellagra, because the afflicted did not live on maize and because certain symptoms of the two diseases seemed to him dissimilar.[21] In June 1860, Costallat went to Spain and spent some time in the districts where *flema salada* was seen. From a letter written by him in 1861 to the French specialist on pellagra Hector Landouzy, it is apparent that he considered *flema salada* to be a form of acrodynia, a disease then believed to be due to ergot poisoning.[22]

Whether or not *flema salada* was a form of pellagra can never be decided because it no longer exists. It is more important to understand that Roussel's theory of the unity of all endemic pellagra-like diseases was a great step forward. Today, we believe that though this theory has some limitations, for the most part it is valid.

What happened to Casal's disease? A modern author, Dr. Jaime Peyri, in a preface to a 1956 edition of Casal's work, remarks that by 1905, the number of cases in Spain had greatly diminished; he attributes this to improved diet and health standards.[23] On the other hand, Triller, in his thesis on pellagra written in 1906, stated that despite public health measures aimed at the prevention of the disease, pellagra still affected 20 per cent of the inhabitants of certain provinces.[24] Such a difference of opinion is worth remembering, because the essence of the pellagra problem over the years has been that so many men have been led to believe that because the pellagrin does not ring his bell, like the leper, he does not exist.

5 | The Polenta Eaters

In the library of the New York Academy of Medicine, there is a typescript copy of an important monograph, *Animadversiones in morbum vulgo pelagram,* by Dr. Francisco Frapolli of the Ospedale Maggiore in Milan, which was published in Italy in September 1771. Bound with this document is a rough English translation by the distinguished American authority on pellagra, James Babcock, for his friend and colleague Claude Lavinder, who was presented with the combined English and Italian versions of Frapolli's work in February 1925. For Babcock and Lavinder, as for us today, this work has special significance, both because it refers to the disease for the first time as pellagra (misspelled *Pelagra*) and because it gives a vivid picture of the plight of the Italian field laborers whose pitiable way of life made them pellagrins. Babcock's translation begins as follows:

There is now raging among the farmers . . . around Milan a strange malady not rarely fatal which verily stirs the feelings of everybody by the variety of its symptoms and by its novelty, but most of all, of the physicians and stimulates them to search out more prompt remedies with which to counteract its effects and to vouchsafe the precious safety of the peasantry who are assiduously intent upon the questions of fertile fields, larger crops and public good.

When upon the approach of Spring, the peasantry . . . settle down . . . all day long to farming . . . , it often happens that the color of their skin changes suddenly to red, like erysipelas and sometimes reddish spots (which the peasants call "The Rose") appear upon the

37

epidermis and frequently small tubercles of varied color rise up; then the skin becomes dry, the surrounding coats burst, the affected skin falls in white scales just like bran: finally the hands, feet, chest, rarely even the face, and other parts of the body exposed to the sun become repulsively disfigured. This then truly wonderful series of external changes, which up to the present we physicians have treated only lightly, constitutes that disease which the people commonly call Pelagra. . . . When the summer time has passed every affected part is restored to its former condition; the natural constitution of the skin returns and unless there is a change for the worst, the peasants do not trouble themselves about Pelagra and for the time being suffer no further ill. But in truth, the disease rages recurrently until at length the skin no longer desquamates [peels] but becomes wrinkled, thickened and full of fissures. Then for the first time the patients begin to have trouble in the head, fear, sadness, wakefulness and vertigo, mental stupor bordering on fatuity, hypochondria, fluxes from the bowels, and sometimes to suffer from mania, then the strength of the body fails, especially in the calves and thighs and they begin to lose motion of those parts almost entirely, to emaciate in the highest degree, to be seized with a colliquative diarrhoea most resistant to all remedies and consumed with a ghastly wasting, they approach the last extremity.[1]

There is reason to believe that pellagra had existed in Italy a number of years before Frapolli's paper appeared. The author Jacopo Odoardi has informed us that his teacher Dr. Giuseppe Pujati saw the disease when he was practicing in Feltre about 1740 and that it was also seen by Dr. Nascimbeni and Dr. Anton-Gaetano Pujati in Friuli about the same time.[2] There was also the claim that it was observed by a certain Antonio Terzaghi on the shores of Lake Maggiore about 1750.[3] Giovanni Albera, writing in Italy in 1784, emphasized that the terms *mal rosso* and *mal della rosa* had been used by at least two generations of poor people in the Milan area to describe the early symptoms of pellagra. He commented further that the local peasants, in his own day, reserved the terms *mal rosso* and *mal della rosa* to indicate the early stage of the disease, characterized by a light sensitivity, and used the term "pellagra" when the condition was more advanced and affected internal organs.[4]

Undoubtedly, once the disease had appeared in northern Italy, it spread rapidly. Gaetano Strambio, Sr., who wrote extensively on the subject, calculated that by 1784 nearly one-twentieth of the population of Lombardy was pellagrous. In the districts worst affected, there was estimated to be one pellagrin in every five or six individuals.[5] By the second decade of the nineteenth century, the morbidity statistics were increasing daily. Dr. Henry Holland, visiting the hospital for the insane in Milan in 1817, found that of five hundred lunatics of both sexes confined in this establishment, more than two-thirds were there because of pellagra.[6]

The affected areas were not only in the Lombardy plain but also in the mountainous areas to the north. Goethe described the pathetic condition of the hill people when he was traveling in Italy in 1786.

At dawn, a quarter of an hour after crossing the Brenner Pass, I came, near Colma, to a marble quarry. . . . Of the inhabitants, I have little to say and that unfavorable. After crossing the Brenner, I noticed as soon as it was daylight a definite change in their physical appearance. I thought the sallow complexion of the women particularly disagreeable. Their features spoke of misery and their children looked as pitiful. The men looked little better. Their physical build however is well-proportioned and sound. I believe that their unhealthy condition is due to their constant diet of maize and buckwheat, or as they call them, yellow polenta and black polenta.

These are ground fine, the flour is boiled in water to a thick mush and then eaten. In the German Tirol they separate the dough into small pieces and fry them in butter, but in the Italian Tirol the polenta is eaten just as it is or sometimes with a sprinkling of grated cheese. Meat they never see from one year's end to the other. Such a diet makes the bowels costive, especially in children and women, and their cachectic complexion is evidence of the damage they do themselves. They also eat fruit and green beans which they boil in water and dress with garlic and olive oil.

Goethe learned that well-to-do peasants fared no better. When he asked an innkeeper's daughter what they did with their money, she replied, "Oh, they have their masters all right, who relieve them of it again." He believed that his theory about the peasants' diets as the cause of their poor health was "confirmed by the fact that the women in the towns all looked healthier." He also commented: "The people I met around Lake Garda were very dark-skinned without the least touch of red in their cheeks. . . . Their complexion is probably due to the constant exposure of the rays of the sun, which beats so fiercely at the feet of their mountains." [7]

It is interesting that Goethe correctly associated the malnutrition and, specifically, the pellagra with the fact that the poor of this region lived on polenta. This polenta, their daily food, was a corn-meal porridge, flavored with salt, butter, and cheese when these commodities were available. Usually the yellow corn meal was just cooked with water in a large pot and eaten without the addition of anything. Since the peasants could not often afford a fire, polenta was sometimes replaced by corn-meal cakes. A number of these cakes were baked or half-baked at a time, but before they could all be eaten, they became so stale and moldy that they were inedible except to these Lombardy peasants who lived in a constant state of famine. Polenta, together with corn cakes, made up almost the total winter diet, while in the spring and summer frogs were also eaten and fruits and vegetables consumed when they could be obtained at little or no cost.

In order to understand the outbreak and prevalence of pellagra in Lombardy, it is important to know that there was economic depression in this region which was very severe in the eighteenth century when that part of Italy was under Austrian domination. According to Livio Marchetti, growing poverty resulted from the fact that large revenues were extracted from landowners through taxation; these were in no way balanced by the sums spent by Hapsburg overlords on their dominions. The poor peasants became poorer than ever because the land proprietors and farm owners could not or would not remunerate them for their toil in the fields. However, the financial distress of landowners does not fully explain the destitution and malnutrition which existed among laborers both during the period of general financial insecurity and later when relative prosperity returned to the area.[8]

From the sixteenth century onward, the system of land tenure known as *mezzadria* was as widespread in Italy as the corresponding *métayage* was in France. Under this system a portion (usually half) of the crop harvested by the peasant cultivator was paid over to the landowner as a means of discharging ground rent on a piece of land. In impoverished areas, the farm owners considered *mezzadria* a good system because the peasantry had no money to lease land and because they wanted cheap field labor. In practice, the poorer peasants became utterly dependent on their masters for their dwellings, their tools, and their food. The worse the harvest, the less the laborer received, but even in good seasons, he could never raise animals or grow food for himself, since he did not possess a plot of his own, nor did he have the right to common land.[9]

These conditions and mode of life of the Italian peasant continued virtually unchanged throughout the nineteenth century. In 1881, an editorial appeared in the *Medical Record* of New York entitled "The Scourge of Italy." The author described the cause of pellagra in terms of the economic plight and inadequate diet of the Italian peasant:

The disease prevails in the most fruitful and beautiful parts of Italy. But this beauty and fruitfulness are at the expense of those who labor to produce it. The farmer of Italy is one of the most ill-paid, ill-housed, underfed and overworked creatures in the world. . . . He works ten or eleven hours a day; his home is filthy and unwholesome; the water he drinks is bad; his food consists mainly of maize. The maize is often imperfectly ripened, and becomes the seat of the growth of a fungus (Sporiosorium maidis). . . . The overwork and famine will not induce pellagra; neither will the diseased corn; but the two together are sufficient.[10]

Maurice Neufeld, in his history of the Italian labor movement, has documented attempts to alleviate rural poverty which were initiated in the 1870's and 1880's. In June 1872, the deputy Agostino Bertani proposed to the Italian parliament that there should be a systematic inquiry into agricultural practices. Although on this occasion Bertani described the terrible social conditions endured by the peasantry, his proposal was defeated. Four years later, when the government instituted an agrarian investigation, a commission studied each province of the country and published reports between the years 1881 and 1886. It was then known that everywhere in northern Italy the prevalence of pellagra was dependent upon the economic deprivation of the laborers. The worst situation was found in the province of Rovigo, in the Polesine district. Here, in the marshy lowlands, malaria as well as malnutrition took its toll. Around 1880 two political groups existed in the Polesine: the conservatives, who controlled the whole province, and the progressives, who constituted a small minority. The progressives set up mutual benefit societies among the peasants and encouraged political assemblies where the peasants could voice their grievances. During the June harvest of 1880, the Polesine peasants went on strike, but to no avail. Their revolt was promptly terminated when the police arrested several hundred people. The strikers received severe sentences, the liberal leaders who were believed to have instigated the strike were persecuted, and the status quo was maintained.

Conditions were little better in the Lombardy province of Mantua. Here, peasant farmers became bankrupts as a result of high taxation and antiquated farming methods. Large landowners acquired the small farms, and although hundreds of peasants emigrated, chiefly to Brazil, those who were left behind to face penury lived on polenta and fell easy victims to pellagra.

Two workers' organizations were formed in 1884, each with its own newspaper, and in these publications, as well as in a third paper, *Il Pellagroso* ("The Pellagrous One"), demands were made for wage improvements. The hungry people, however, grew impatient; they could not wait for constitutional action; they rose in revolt, clashes with the police followed, and the peasant organizations were brought to an end in the spring of 1885. Wages remained the same as before, and there was no decrease in the incidence of pellagra.[11]

From Frapolli's time until the first decade of the twentieth century, efforts that were made to control endemic pellagra in Italy were unsuccessful because they failed to change social conditions or even to relieve the ever present famine. In 1902, a law was passed for "the prevention and cure of pellagra." Under the provisions of this act, supposedly curative and preventive measures were instituted; these included the free distribution of salt, the provision of food either at the homes of the patients or at sanitary stations (*locande sanitarie*), and the treatment of severe cases in hospitals for pellagrins (*pellagrosarii*). Directives aimed against the use of spoiled corn included regulations for corn inspection, the exchange of spoiled for good corn, the desiccating of plants, cheap cooperative kitchens, the improvement of agriculture, and the education of the people. An official census of pellagra incidence and the death rate was instituted.[12] The effect of the act was to reduce the mortality from pellagra, but the incidence of the disease was not materially altered.[13]

During the first decade of the present century, endemic areas of pellagra decreased in the north but extended into the southern parts of the country. In 1909, Assistant Surgeon Wollenberg of the U.S. Public Health and Marine-Hospital Service, reporting to his department, stated that pellagra continued to spread in some regions of Italy, in spite of a vigorous campaign against the disease: the enactment of laws, improved methods of grain cultivation, improved sanitation. Although very large sums were annually expended for salt, proper food, and hospital accommodations for the care and treatment of the poor affected with pellagra, the number of pellagrins decreased slowly.

In the preceding twenty-five years, the incidence of pellagra declined markedly in northern Italy—Piedmont, Lombardy, Venetia,

Table 1. Number of pellagrins in Italy, 1881–1905 *

	1881	1889	1905
Piedmont	1,328	1,223	1,012
Liguria	56	30	56
Lombardy	36,630	19,557	15,746
Venetia	55,881	39,882	27,781
Emilia	7,891	4,617	3,357
Tuscany	924	1,125	1,137
Marches	406	920	1,436
Umbria	872	5,103	4,250
Latium	32	146	195
Abruzzo and Molise			59

* There is reason to believe that Italian statistics on pellagra are inaccurate.
Source: A. Marie, *Pellagra* (Columbia, S.C.: State Co., 1910).

and Emilia—but spread persistently in central Italy, especially in Tuscany, the Marches, and Umbria. It was "appearing in alarming proportions in Latium and in Abruzzo and Molise, compartments in which it was unknown some years ago." It had "invaded southern Italy in 1908"; cases had occurred in the neighborhood of Naples and in Calabria. Pellagra seemed "to be firmly established in the lower as well as in the upper portion of the Italian peninsula. The reason for this better showing in the north is not altogether plain, but is partly attributed to the economic, social and sanitary improvements that have been effected there in recent years." Wollenberg's report continues:

The mortality seems to be lessening. It changed very little after the law of 1902 came into effect until the years 1906 and 1907, when there was a fall in the number of total deaths to less than one-fifth of those during the preceding years. . . .

The hoped-for results and salutary intent of the law—to prevent the consumption of maize of poor quality—have hardly been realized. The law permits the milling of low-grade maize in case it is not to be used as aliment for man, but this provision is held to be difficult to enforce, proper sanitary supervision of country districts being very difficult.[14]

At length, by the 1930's, pellagra was largely brought under control in Italy. According to Wallace Aykroyd, in his 1933 review of the disease, pellagra was ceasing to be a serious menace in the areas of Italy it had formerly ravaged. In 1928 there were only 91 new notifications of pellagra cases in Italy, and the death rate was 0.2 per 100,000. The sale of spoiled maize as human food had been strictly prohibited since the passing of the law of 1902, and the local authorities had been forced to acquire municipal reservoirs in which the maize could be kept in good condition.[15] From the study of pellagra by Vincenzo de Giaxa we learn that in 1910 there were 546 public maize desiccators in Italy. Rural bakeries were set up, whose purpose was the furnishing of cheap wheat bread to those whose staple food was maize, and by 1910 there were 1300 of these bakeries. Charitable kitchens of two kinds were established. One type, which supplied soup and sometimes bread and meat free or at very low prices during the whole year or before and during the pellagra season, was designed for preventive action; the other supplied similar fare free to persons in the initial stage of pellagra. In 1910 there were 127 of the former, 533 of the latter. Further, as a result of the 1902 ordinance, *pellagrosarii,* or pellagra hospitals, and asylums for the children of pellagrins had been founded.[16]

Aykroyd was uncertain about the extent to which the diminution of pellagra in Italy could be ascribed to legislative measures or to changes in the diet of the people brought about by rising standards of living. As we shall see, the latter is more likely, because of what is known of the economic development of Italy during those years.

6 | Evils of Maize in the French Economy

"Turkish Wheate"

In the later years of the sixteenth century, maize was grown in France; it was sown for pleasure rather than for the provision of a staple crop. Even at this early date the nutritional value of corn was questioned by the authors of *Maison rustique,* Charles Etienne and Jean Liebault. Richard Surflet's English translation, first published in 1600, gives a description of "Turkish wheate" (a synonym for maize):

The meale thereof is whiter than that which is made from our wheate, but the bread made thereof is more grosse, thicke, or close and of a more slimie substance, in such sorte as that nourishment made thereof is likewise more grosse, and apter to ingender obstructions; wherefore if the dearth of wheat and famine doe force and compell you to sowe of this Turkish wheate, to make bread thereof, it will doe better if you mingle it with the flour of our wheate, then if you should use it by it selfe all alone. The meale of this wheat in as it is thicke and clammie, will be good to make cataplasmes of, to ripen impostumes withall: for being apt to stop the pores of the skin by his clamminess, it cannot choose but work such effect.[1]

Maize remained an exotic crop for a century after its introduction into France. Antoine-Augustin Parmentier described the principal reasons for this limited growth of corn. It was an unpopular cereal with both titled landowners and farmowners because corn was exempt from the tithe (the dime) which was collected on all other crops.[2] It was also believed that the growth of corn impoverished the soil so that succeeding grains grown on the same ground would fail to reach their full potential. Further, a suspicion arose that diseased corn lying in the fields turned wheat black.

In the late seventeenth century maize began to assume some importance as a crop in the Midi; in 1698, Guyet mentioned that in the region of Pau, more corn was gathered than either wheat or rye and that the local people lived on corn.[3] It was only during the latter part of the eighteenth century, however, that corn became an important crop. By then it was growing extensively in the Lauragais plain ("le veritable pays du mais"—"the real corn country"), and maize products became the staple of the populace. Little by little maize was also substituted for other crops as the principal cereal grown in all the departments of the Pyrenees. Maize was also grown largely in eastern France, in the areas of the Vosges, in the Jura, and throughout Burgundy. In 1790, Arthur Young traced an oblique line across the map of France to divide the northern areas, where corn would not ripen, from the southern areas, where corn was easily produced. This line cut through the mouth of the Garonne, across the plain of Berry, through Nivernais, Champagne, and Lorraine, and ended on the Rhine, close to Landau.[4] But some maize was grown also in the north and even around Paris.

In 1829, the French Horticultural Society sought to encourage the development of the corn crop in the environs of Paris. Louis-Philippe, then the Duke of Orléans, planted a tremendous acreage of maize on his land at Neuilly and was given a medal by the society for his example.[5] That same year pellagra was reported in southwestern France.

Misery in the Landes

In the year 1818, the French physician Jean Hameau began to observe "une maladie nouvelle" among the poverty-stricken inhabitants of the Bassin d'Arcachon, near Teste-de-Buch. He described cases of this disease at a meeting of the Société Royale de

Médecine of Bordeaux in 1829, pointing out that although the condition was known locally as *mal de la Teste,* it resembled pellagra. He reported, "This disease attacks individuals of both sexes and all ages, but I have not yet seen it in any but the poor and uncleanly who subsist on coarse food." [6] Hameau's report was quickly followed by others from physicians in surrounding areas, and a commission was appointed by the medical society of Bordeaux to investigate the new disease. They found that the condition was the same endemic pellagra then rampant in northern Italy. The public health doctor of the Gironde was also charged to study the problem; from his survey it became apparent that pellagra was a major cause of disability and death among the rural poor, not only in the Bassin d'Arcachon, but also in other areas of southwestern France, including the departments of the Gironde, the Landes, the Haute-Garonne, the Pyrénées-Orientales, the Hautes-Pyrénées, and the Aude.[7]

Although this extensive outbreak of pellagra created local attention, in Paris the most distinguished physicians failed to mention its existence. Thus, as late as 1838, Dr. Alphée Cazenave and Henri Schedel published a description of pellagra as it had been seen by their colleague Dr. Biett of Lombardy, but confessed that they had no personal experience of patients suffering from this illness.[8] The reticence of such writers concerning pellagra in their own country may have been purposeful. Would they want their readers to know that a disease clearly associated with poverty and a bad diet had come to the country of prosperity, progress, and learning? Duchesne, in his book *Traité du mais ou blé de Turquie,* which was published in 1833 and dedicated to Louis-Philippe I, extolled the agricultural and culinary advantages of corn but also refrained from any mention of pellagra—a strange omission, because it is quite clear from the book that the author was familiar with members of the Academy of Sciences of Bordeaux and with other notables in this city who may well have heard Hameau's report or who at least were experienced in detection of the disease.

The course of events and the economic background which determined the occurrence of pellagra at that time in France were best explained by Edmond About in his novel *Maître Pierre*. By the time this book was published in 1858, pellagra had existed in the Landes for at least thirty years and probably for several years before it was described by Hameau. W. F. Rae commented on About's literary achievements: "Maître Pierre is but an essay, in disguise, on the best way of reclaiming that uncultivated district in the South of France called the Landes." [9] For our purposes, this book has much more to offer: it gives a vivid account of the plight of the peasants who fell victims to pellagra.

Maître Pierre himself and his little protégée, Marinette, tell the story. According to these villagers, the Landes was ever threatened by encroachment from the sea. The soil, mostly sand, was impregnated with salt, and few crops would grow in this harsh environment. Attempts were made to prevent soil erosion by planting trees, but most of these were unsuccessful. In the winter the earth was soaked with water, and in the summer it was burned dry by the sun. Only gorse and heather would grow on the barren earth, and only a few sheep could find enough to eat.

A hectare of land fed one sheep for a year. At the end of the year, the owner of the sheep paid the landowner ten sous; of this sum, the proprieter paid a fifth to the government. It was a bad state of affairs for France, for the landowner, for the shepherd, and for the sheep. Although the sheep could provide wool to stuff mattresses, the meat was poor, and nobody felt it worth while to try to make cheese from the sheep's milk. Rather, the shepherd sold his sheep. If times were bad, he would succumb to the disease pellagra, which might have been invented, as Maître Pierre remarks, especially for this wretched population. Marinette recalls that her father, who was a shepherd, earned twenty francs and ten hectolitres of mixed grain a year. The girls started to lose their teeth at the age of fifteen. All the unfortunate people in her village had swollen and macerated feet that looked like the roots of trees that had been in water.

Apparently, 1844 was a hard year. That year, when she was six, the whole family became sick. Where did the illness come from? That was the question on people's lips. It might be due to the air, to the brackish water, or to the food. Some would blame the millet, others the rye or the corn. A few thought it came from eating sardines or salted eels. Only one thing was certain: it never attacked wealthy people. The disease began in the stomach, but almost immediately it also affected the skin, like a weed that spreads everywhere at the same time. The skin darkened, broke out in blemishes, and showed scaly patches. Sometimes the hair was involved.

Marinette's mother's health failed rapidly, and she finally succumbed to the disease. Her father consulted the doctor in the village, who ordered wine and roast meat but could not give it to them. The child was sent to stay with a neighbor during the day, but her father continued to work in the fields though he was sick and easily tired. His nerves and his mind were so deranged that often, wishing to go out early, he would nevertheless arrive late at work. In the evening he returned home weaker, and the family tried to eat but had appetite for nothing. He was like a boat adrift when the oars are gone. Marinette sensed that his courage was at an end, because when he sat on a bench he rested his head between his hands and she could see despair in his eyes. She did not know what to say to console him. Finally, his depression went beyond all bounds. His grave illness persuaded him to shorten his remaining days. She awoke, as if from a bad dream, to find his dead body suspended from a beam in the roof.

Maître Pierre rescued Marinette and nursed her back to health. He would shoot wild birds and in spite of her protestations would insist that she eat the wings of baby pigeons and morsels of duck. Many were not as fortunate as Marinette. As the winter approached, every time Maître Pierre heard of a death in the neighborhood, he knew that it was caused by pellagra. Whenever he chanced on a burial, he would raise his hat in honor of the dead and shake his fist at the pellagra. Over and over again, he would repeat the local proverb:

Tant que Lande sera lande
La pellagre te demande.[10]

(As long as the Lande remains a waste land, pellagra will get you.)

Though the characters in About's story are fictional, his account of the physical and mental devastation caused by pellagra was taken directly from contemporary documents.[11] He certainly had access to Lalesque's account of pellagra in the Landes. This author, writing in 1846, cites a number of instances illustrating the conditions of misery under which pellagra occurred.[12]

Contagion from Sheep

Most French physicians of the early and mid-nineteenth century who saw and treated endemic pellagra did not subscribe to the view that the disease was primarily associated with poverty and a poor corn diet. They preferred to support the concept that it was a peculiar infection transmitted from sheep, to which people with a bad hereditary trait were susceptible. Thus Jean-Marie Hameau, the son of the man who first described pellagra in France, could dismiss nutritional causes of the disease in an acceptable doctoral thesis in the year 1853. He defended the peculiar concept that pellagra occurs only in places where the peasants tend or live close to sheep. The sheep have an infectious disease known as *pelle,* which is associated with intractable diarrhea, redness of the thighs, loss of wool, staggers, and a progressive loss of locomotion. This condition affects the sheep each spring and is eventually fatal. The shepherds sleep in the barn with the sheep and wear untanned and unwashed sheepskins. This seemed to him a rational cause for pellagra which should be seriously investigated. Hameau, *fils,* could not get proof of his theory, so he goes on in the text of his thesis to remark that whether pellagra is caused by a virus transmitted from sheep to man or whether it is due to the mold on corn as suggested by his colleagues, it is certainly transmitted by heredity. "Omnes fere pellagrosos ab alios ortos cernas" ("You see that almost all pellagrins are descended from others"). He found many examples of familial pellagra in his practice; of 124 cases, there was a family history of the disease in 50. Who could deny such evidence? Treatment was aimed at controlling infection, so the victims, who were already nutritionally bankrupt, were bled and given quinine, arsenic, and other toxic drugs which undoubtedly hastened their demise.[13]

France Demands Bread

Real progress in controlling pellagra in the Landes and in other areas of southern and southwest France came about through recommendations made by Théophile Roussel.[14] Roussel held the opinion that pellagra was due to eating maize—not just any maize diet but rations composed largely of moldy corn. Despite his support of this theory, which had been propounded by Italian pellagrologists, he realized that pellagra was a handmaid of social misery and that it was hardly ever seen in those who had a mixed diet containing adequate amounts of meat or other animal protein. Further, he knew that those who ate corn meal mixed with wheat or rye were largely exempt from the disease. In his book *De la pellagre* of 1845, he comments that the lot of the peasants in Spain, Italy, and France changed little between the time of Casal and his own day. Further, he points out that the history of the spread of maize cultivation in Europe can be well correlated with that of pellagra incidence. Pellagra, called by the French peasants *mal de la misère,* came not from the increased consumption of corn as such but from the fact that the economically deprived rural people ate an exclusively vegetable diet, in which the absence of "animal" food predisposed them to pellagra. For the prophylaxis of pellagra, Roussel proposed that measures should be taken to perfect maize culture so that a more wholesome product would become available, that country folk in the deprived areas should be provided with more food of animal origin, and that reforms should be instituted to improve working and living conditions among the peasants.[15]

In 1848, Roussel sent a report to the Minister of Agriculture in Paris in which he asserted that pellagra could be prevented by changing the peasants' diet. In his second book, *Traité de la pellagre et des pseudo-pellagres,* published in 1866, he came to the conclusion that the pellagra problem would not be solved through scientific discovery but through social progress.[16] He believed correctly that this book, which won the prize in medicine of the Academy of Sciences of France, would bring about legislation to improve the living conditions and diet of the rural poor.

Marie, in *La Pellagre,* writes: "At the time of the journey of Roussel (1844) and the researches of Costallat (circa 1857), aggravating agricultural blunders were seen in the French provinces of the southwest, as in upper Italy; the crop rotation which every two years permits the replanting of corn upon the same field; the cultivation of white corn, and of slow growing varieties; the same relations between the proprietors and laborers, the share system of farming and the estivandiers (boss-hands); the most numerous class were compelled to eat the cheapest food, and consequently of the worst quality." [17]

Roussel's recommendations, supported by the pleas of Arnault Costallat, of Bagnères-de-Bigorre, led the French government to decrease maize cultivation for human food. The substitution of potatoes and other cereal crops, as well as the official encouragement of animal husbandry, contributed to the gradual disappearance of pellagra from France. The disease persisted only in a few small areas of southern France where continued poverty and ingrained food habits limited the peasant's diet. When, in 1908, Dr. Regis of Bordeaux and Dr. Mairet of Montpellier surveyed pellagra in their respective districts, they found only a few survivors of the "terrible pellagrous insanity" in the asylums of Auch, Montpellier, and Pau.[18]

Roussel's cry of alarm had been answered. By the first decade of the twentieth century the division of the landed estates in France had allowed the peasants to acquire individual ownership, so they were no longer dependent on the landowner for every morsel of food. In the conquest of pellagra in France, the earlier transformation of the Landes also played a significant role. Marie says:

They made of a marshy waste a rich and fertile country by the exploitation of sea-coast pines, and by the cultivation of better cereals, even of the vine, all accomplished by the marvelous works of drainage, which are the glory of the government of that region. . . . Corn is still cultivated, and is even still eaten; but it is in part given to stock; and even if it is used for human food, there is added wheat or other cereals, legumes, and also meat and wine. . . . Today the Landes has railroads, which guarantee the transportation of foodstuffs of all sorts. Intelligence, the will of individuals, the aid of the local government, such are, if not the entire prophylaxis against pellagra, at least the instruments of this great work.[19]

In 1907, a monument to Théophile Roussel was unveiled in the Avenue de l'Observatoire, and on that occasion many speakers extolled his distinguished career.[20] It was recalled that his influence led to the passing of laws to control drunkenness, to protect children, and to give free medical aid to the needy. His battle against pellagra was not remembered, no doubt because the terrors of the disease, thanks to him, had been forgotten and the plague of corn was an outdated problem within the French republic.

7 | The Zeist Controversy

Corn Theories and Theorists

From the time of Casal through the eighteenth and nineteenth centuries, it was repeatedly noticed that pellagra occurred among corn-eating peoples. Harriette Chick pointed out, however, that knowledge of nutritive values available before the end of the nineteenth century provided no reason why maize should be less nutritious than wheat or other cereals.[1] Hence, to explain the ill effects of its consumption as a staple food, recourse was made to theories involving a toxic material either originally present in the grain or developed when it was harvested or stored under damp conditions resulting in infestation with molds or fungi. Actually, before these theories evolved, it had been suggested that maize was an insufficient source of nourishment. The first to put forward this idea was Francesco-Luigi Fanzago, who published his first observations of pellagra in 1789 [2] and read a memoir before the Academy of Padua in 1807 in which he stated that maize was the sole cause of the disease.[3]

Three years later, another Italian pellagrologist, Giovanni Battista Marzari, set forth his ideas on the causation of pellagra—ideas which were to be elaborated by the proponents of the "zeist theory" (the belief that pellagra is caused by a maize diet). Observation of the disease for twenty years had given him ample evidence that outbreaks of pellagra always followed long winters when the Italian poor lived solely on boiled corn meal. Working in Treviso, close to the Italian Alps, he noted that maize was often

55

picked before it was ripe, that it was allowed to become moist and was then stored undried. While he believed that these improper methods of corn harvesting may have contributed to the development of pellagra, he also thought that the corn diet was inadequate because the cereal was deficient in gluten; he apparently meant that corn was low in nitrogenous material. His observations on the ill effects of the corn diet are best summarized in a translation of his own words:

The appearance of the disease is preceded by the continual use of a vegetable diet throughout the winter season. This diet is composed of Turkish wheat which is almost entirely of the cinquantino type, never quite ripe, sometimes moldly, which in our locality is made into polenta, often without even salt for seasoning. This monotonous food forms at least 95 per cent of the total diet of the peasants throughout the winter, and in the spring they may have in addition a few vegetables, such as cabbage, cooked in water, skim milk, but practically never any eggs, because they are too expensive. They may have lettuce or chicory which grows wild. During the long sub Alpine winter, the laborer stays at home and goes neither to the markets nor to the inns, because even if he goes to such places he knows he will get little or no meat or wheaten bread. He keeps a small reserve of provisions for the summer, which is the time of heavy work in the fields; these he eats mainly on feast days. If he eats salted fish, then it is only during the Lenten fast, which he keeps scrupulously, and he never eats more than an ounce of fish per day. The alderman and the Carmelite nun eat fish and "fast" constantly, but they never get pellagra like the field laborer; their rations are twenty times more ample than those of the peasant, and they live on them without any health problems. This diet, which is unvaried among the pellagrous people of the kingdom and which is more inadequate than that suggested by Pythagoras, is taken more often than not with water alone, or during certain months they will drink a very sour wine which is known here as "aquariola." It must be seen besides that during the long and cold season of winter, field laborers, living on this debilitating regime, lead an idle, miserable life, lying down for many hours of the day and during the long nights in the stables with the animals, thinking of their debts and of what will become of their jobs and of the necessities of each day and of the impossibility of meeting their commitments and particularly of their complaints against all men who disturb, menace, and oppress them. I have many times observed that if a villager passes rapidly from a state of comfort to one of misery, then this is soon followed by a crisis, a cachexia or period of withering away in which the pellagrin, in addition to his other ills, fails in the last degree and comes to a sad end. You will find that two things constantly precede the appearance of pellagra: the first is the continual use of corn or Turkish wheat, where the diet is only of vegetable sources; the second is the idleness of winter, which I have described and which is the time of growth of the germ of this disease which is regularly developed by the light or the heat of the springtime.[4]

Marzari concluded that the exclusively cereal diet eaten by the peasants during the winter engendered pellagra and that exposure to sunlight caused development of the disease. He also believed that the economic distress which condemned the peasants to this fatal regime was the primary cause of all their troubles.

In spite of the strength of Marzari's convictions, his arguments were contested by contemporary physicians who objected that pellagra had been seen in people who lived well and did not subsist entirely on a maize diet. Some blamed the disease on bad water, excessive use of sea salt, too great an intake of dairy foods, consumption of raw meats, eating sour rye bread or bread made of millet. Marzari, in a bitter attempt to support his theory that the poor corn diet was causally related to the appearance of pellagra, remarked, "Thus when a million facts have caused me to think that this particular food forms the cause of pellagra, two or three things which would appear to oppose should not be sufficient to disprove this view."

A book entitled *Saggio di ricerche sulla pellagra,* written by Vincenzio Chiarugi and published in Florence in 1814, asserts that though the cause of pellagra may always be doubtful, what is overwhelmingly evident is the wretchedness of the poor peasants with pellagra, who are reduced to malnutrition by a debilitating diet, lead a life of work that is too hard, and have too little in the way of clean homes or even beds. The industrial and farm laborers are as dependent on the rich peasants who bake good bread and drink wine as are the poor mountain dwellers who live on chestnuts. They have to sustain themselves on Turkish wheat, the principal cause of pellagra that cannot be eliminated.[5]

The same year Chiarugi's book appeared, Pietro Guerreschi suggested that pellagra was due exclusively to moldy corn. He pointed out the marked resemblance between pellagra and ergotism and the strong probability that the two affections were the result of related agents. It was then known that ergotism was caused by the toxins produced by a fungus growing on rye; by analogy, Guerreschi concluded that pellagra could be produced by a mold growing on corn. He did not try to prove his hypothesis by direct experimentation, but his ideas were soon taken up and developed by other workers and writers in the field.[6]

There were three great proponents of the theory that pellagra was caused by the toxins from moldy corn. The first of these, Ludovico Balardini, started in his early writings by accepting Marzari's ideas. In 1845, he commented:

Maize gradually drove out the older cereals, and the poor peasants subsist almost entirely on polenta. This constitutes nine-tenths of the entire daily food. In order to understand the method of living in this region, let us enter the house of a peasant. We will see placed in the middle of the table a large mass of yellow dough cut into large slices, the entire family eating in a circle, with a few legumes and green things which the season allows, with very little cheese, rarely or never fresh meat or other more nourishing aliment. Coming to the later meals, we find that polenta plays the same important part, it constituting practically the only food; with it water is usually drunk, wine being only rarely added to the feast.[7]

Balardini was impressed, as were others before him, by the close relationship between the consumption of corn, particularly moldy corn, and the incidence of pellagra. He examined the corn and found a greenish discoloration on the grain that came to be known as *verderame* and that was subsequently found to be due to the fungus *Sporisorium maidis*. When Balardini and his colleagues fed maize infested by this parasite to chickens, the birds lost their appetites, lost weight, became droopy, and exhibited great thirst. They also showed some roughening and scaling of the skin. After twenty-eight days they died of progressive exhaustion. In men, Balardini produced gastritis and diarrhea by feeding the moldy corn. The symptoms in the birds and in human subjects were thought to resemble those of pellagra,[8] and although they may not seem very convincing to us, they were enough to give impetus and support to those who subscribed to the corn-toxin theory and to Dr. Cesare Lombroso in particular.

Lombroso was born in 1836 at Verona. He studied at Padua, Vienna, and Paris. In 1862 he became professor of psychiatry at Pavia, then director of the lunatic asylum at Pesaro, and later holder of the chair of criminal anthropology at Turin. His chief interests centered on the relation between mental and physical disorders, and his principal claim to fame was that he contended that criminals could be identified by certain physical characteristics. During the last twenty-five years of his life, he devoted himself almost exclusively to the study of pellagra.[9] He published voluminous writings supporting the idea that the disease was caused by spoiled corn; indeed, he wrote so much on this subject that this view is frequently spoken of as Lombroso's theory.[10]

In his experiments, he found that a tincture of bad corn contained three substances: a red oil, a bitter toxin which he named pellagrosein, and a third product which was resinous in character and had the odor of burned polenta. Lombroso and his co-workers also conducted a number of animal studies in which they either injected cultures of bad polenta into dogs or gave the same animals injections of the alcoholic extract of the corn. They found that the alcoholic extract was rapidly fatal but that the cultures of polenta were well tolerated, though they contained *Sporisorium maidis* and penicillia. Injections of extracts of sound corn were also harmless. Lombroso's final conclusion was that pellagra was an intoxication produced by the action of certain organisms on maize. These organisms in themselves were harmless, but they possessed the property of producing a poisonous ptomaine when they came in contact with the kernel of the maize. He did not believe that the *Sporisorium maidis* per se was harmful or that it caused pellagra.[11]

Undoubtedly the most important advocate of the moldy-corn theory, a self-styled zeist, was Théophile Roussel, who despite his theories succeeded in conquering pellagra in France. He developed his ideas concerning the etiology of the disease over a period of twenty years and made a formal summation of his beliefs in his treatise on pellagra, which was published in 1866. In this book, he propounded the theory that pellagra was the result of both extrinsic and intrinsic factors. According to Roussel, a diet of damaged or rotten corn products would cause pellagra only in poor people whose bad heredity gave them a peculiar susceptibility to the disease. In those who had such "bad blood," the germ of pellagra could develop, and their weakened state would aggravate the disease and cause the involvement of the nervous system.[12]

The zeists gained much support during the nineteenth century in Italy and in France. While the idea that maize diet itself was dangerous met with considerable opposition, physicians, public health officials, and even the poor pellagrins themselves could believe that moldy corn might be detrimental to health. One may judge how seriously the French and Italians regarded the eating of spoiled corn by the words used in various dialects to describe its odor: *scagn, padul, muffito, paù, sobbollì, verdet, buttà, arbollì, smaserido, romatico, mofflet.*[13] As time went on, those in authority took comfort from the belief that good corn, the pride of their country and a major source of national and personal income, could be exonerated as a cause of pellagra. Either, they argued, unwholesome imported corn was responsible for the trouble, or the lazy peasants brought the disease on themselves by storing corn before it had dried or by allowing corn or corn meal to get moldy before they ate it.

Precise documentation of instances in which pellagra occurred for the first time in populations that received imported corn abounded, and it was said that these people had remained healthy as long as they stuck to the home-grown product. In 1866, Dr. Pretenderis Typaldos, professor of medicine at the University of Athens, reported an outbreak of pellagra on the island of Corfu. On this island, the poor had been subsisting on a bread, prepared from maize, which was called *barbarella*. Typaldos commented, "When cooked it is soft and pleasant to the taste, but when dry it is very heavy and indigestible." In spite of the shortcomings of the bread, it was apparently eaten with impunity for many years; the first case of pellagra was seen in 1839. After that no cases were observed until 1858, but thereafter a great many pellagrins were seen. At the time of the report the incidence in villages varied between 1 in 1218 and 11 in 480 members of the local population. Maize was cultivated locally, but from 1857 onward, the grain was imported from Albania, Romagna, Naples, and from the Danubian area. According to Typaldos, this imported corn was imperfectly ripened and unwholesome.[14] This account was much quoted as a classic example of the dangers of bad imported corn. It is quoted verbatim in the account of pellagra, or "Italian Leprosy," in the third edition of Tilbury Fox's book on skin diseases and mentioned by a number of American authors, including Harris, in support of the zeist theory.[15]

Geoffrey Gaumer's description of pellagra in Yucatan was considered further corroboration of the evils of spoiled corn. This author, who was an eyewitness of the outbreak, described the circumstances in which the disease occurred in that part of Mexico:

In 1882, in Yucatan, locusts destroyed vegetation, especially Indian corn. Corn being the only cereal used in Yucatan for bread, famine seemed inevitable, until the merchants began to import it from New York. This importation continued until 1891, when the country had recovered from the devastation of the locusts. The imported corn was brought in the holds of vessels as ballast. By reason of exposure to heat and humidity on the voyage, the corn underwent fermentation and became unfit for food. The constant eating of this spoiled corn led to the slow development of pellagra.

The disease was confined to the lower and middle classes, who were obliged to purchase the cheapest corn in the market. The wealthy class escaped, as they did not eat the imported corn. For the next ten years, 1891 to 1901, Yucatan produced enough corn for home consumption, and cases of pellagra no longer developed. The old cases ran their course fatally. From 1901 to 1907 the corn crops were almost total failures, and corn was again imported in larger amounts than ever before. Mobile and New Orleans were the chief sources of supply, but some came from Vera Cruz—all by water. Again pellagra became epidemic, but was not confined to the middle and lower classes as before. It had been found more profitable to raise hemp than corn, so all classes used the imported cereal. Consequently pellagra spread alike among the rich and poor. At the close of 1907, ten per cent of the inhabitants were victims of pellagra, and in August, 1909, not less than eight per cent of the population had the disease.[16]

By the beginning of the present century, the beliefs of the early zeists like Marzari were either forgotten or replaced by a blind adherence to the concept that imported or foreign corn was the cause of pellagra in whatever country it appeared. Those who thought that imported corn presented a peculiar health hazard failed to realize that it was bought and eaten because it was the only cheap food and also that in such instances as the Yucatan outbreak of pellagra, the people who ate the corn from abroad were already malnourished owing to the existing famine.

Bad Heredity

Antizeists, as well as some of the supporters of the corn theories, insisted that corn played a subsidiary role in the induction of pellagra and that such other factors as heredity were equally or more important. In 1853, Jean-Marie Gustave Hameau remarked, "La pellagre est une diathèse particuliere," by which he meant that the disease was determined by predisposition.[17] This idea had been previously advanced by a number of Italian authors; it had been mentioned first by Jacopo Odoardi, in 1776, and later distinctly advocated as a theory of causation by Giovanni Albera.[18] It was upheld by Gaetano Strambio, who stated that hereditary influences were operative in more than half the cases of pellagra he had seen.[19]

Carlo Calderini in 1843 suggested the possibility that the affection was always inherited: "Saria quasi indotto a credere che questo sia quasi l'unico ed esclusivo mezzo di sua diffusuone" ("I am almost disposed to think that this heredity is almost the one and only means of its diffusion").[20] He made a statistical study of pellagrins and their families and found that of 1319 persons who were members of 184 pellagrous families, 671 were healthy and 648 were victims of the disease. Similarly, in an investigation of 1005 pellagrins—449 men and 556 women—admitted to the city hospital of Milan from 1844 to 1846, he found that there were family histories of the disease in 618 cases—a finding he believed pointed to a definite hereditary influence. In the group of 1005, he thought that a hereditary pellagrous taint existed in an additional 380 people; in fact, there were only 7 in whom he could find no evidence of bad blood. He came up with some curious data suggesting that a male pellagrin was more likely to have pellagrous sons, that a female pellagrin was more likely to have pellagrous daughters, and that pellagra was particularly common among the siblings of pellagrins.[21]

These figures, though very interesting, hardly merited the attention they received as evidence of hereditary influences in the etiology of pellagra. They could, and do, support the opposite conclusion that pellagra occurs among members of families exposed to the same set of environmental factors.

Lombroso, no doubt influenced by his beliefs about criminal types and their recognition through a particular physiognomy, revealed his ideas about congenital pellagrins in 1898:

There are pellagrous and nonpellagrous conditions which are even harder to diagnose than complicated pellagra, because the pellagra, while it is present, has not been able to develop fully. Here belongs the type which I designate hereditary pellagra. It occurs in a very severe and a very mild type. It is noticeable at the end of the second year of life, rarely with desquamation, more frequently with pains in the epigastrium, pyrosis [heartburn], voracious appetite [*Heisshunger*], uncertain gait, timidity, diarrhea, yellowing of the skin as in malaria-cachexia, retardation and cessation of development; but later all the symptoms of pellagra appear and resist strongly any treatment. . . . In many cases, I find a bad formation of the skull, exceptional brachy-cephaly [a disproportionately short head] or dolichocephaly [a pecu-liarly long head], a receding forehead, badly set ears, asymmetry of the face, and abnormalities of the genitalia.[22]

Undoubtedly Lombroso did see young pellagrins who were suffer-ing from mixed protein and vitamin deficiencies which would ac-count for impaired physical and even mental development, and perhaps the skeletal changes were due to rickets, though one is tempted to believe that even this prominent physician and anthro-pologist was influenced by dabblers in phrenology.

If a famous man promulgates an idea, the ripples on the sea spread a long way. The belief that there were pellagrous types per-sisted and was elaborated in Europe and then in the United States. As recently as 1916, two papers were published in a prominent American medical journal on the subject of the hereditary factor in pellagra, and these were incorporated in the report of a Federal pellagra commission and reprinted as a bulletin of the Eugenics Record Office. The author of one of these papers, Dr. Charles Davenport, set forth complex and fantastic ideas: "It appears that certain races or blood lines react in the pellagra families in a spe-cific and differential fashion that will go far to prove the presence of a hereditary factor in pellagra." Davenport, who had no medical training, went on to describe "biotypes" who differed in the rela-tive susceptibility or resistance of their tissues to a hypothetical pellagrous toxin. He concluded that there were skin-susceptible biotypes, intestine-susceptible biotypes, nerve-susceptible biotypes, and other biotypes resistant in each of these respects. He believed that pellagra was communicable and that the progress of the germ in the body depended on constitutional factors.[23] His notions con-cerning the infectivity of pellagra were undoubtedly derived from those of early antizeists who had put forward this theory to explain the grouping of cases and the familial occurrence of the disease.

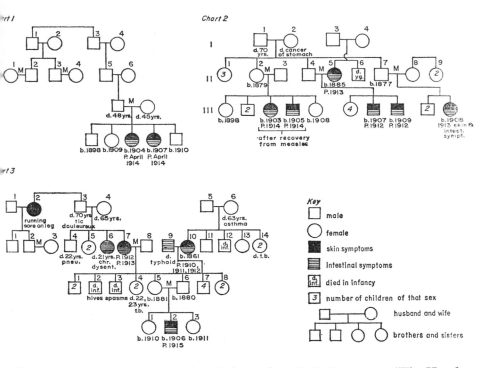

Figure 2. Family trees of pellagrins. Redrawn from C. B. Davenport, "The Hereditary Factor in Pellagra," *Archives of Internal Medicine,* 18 (July 15, 1916), 16–17.
P.: Attack or recurrence of pellagra in the year indicated.
M: Matings of persons with pellagrous traits.

Antizeist Beliefs

Opposition to the zeist concepts stemmed originally from descriptions of pellagrins who ate corn only occasionally or not at all. The antizeists were influenced also by authors who had developed etiological theories based on traditional ideas about the causes of epidemics. Among the latter, Pierre Thouvenel seriously believed that pellagra was caused by bad air. In a book entitled *Traité sur le climat d'Italie,* published in Verona in 1797, he explained that the extensive formation of irrigation canals in the Lombardy plain had produced huge areas of stagnant water and caused a mist to cover the area. This in turn led to a "dephlogistication" of the atmosphere, and when this was breathed by debilitated peasants, pellagra resulted. Thouvenel was not entirely averse to the idea that the eating of corn played some part in causing pellagra, but he thought that diet was subsidiary to the effects of the air.[24] Perhaps he was influenced by Casal, who believed in the importance of meteorological phenomena and was inclined toward the opinion that excessive humidity can play an important role in causing *mal de la rosa*. But the general concept that foul air or some miasm in the air can cause epidemics goes back to Hippocrates and persisted until, in the late nineteenth century, bacteria were definitely shown to cause infection. Even after this time, diseases without an easily demonstrable agent were ascribed to vague air-borne particles.

Roussel was scornful of Thouvenel's ideas relating to bad air, dismissing them with the quip: "Il suffit de remarquer combien Thouvenel se trompait sur les limites géographiques de la pellagre, pour montrer sur quelles bases debiles reposait sa théorie." ("It suffices to say that Thouvenel deluded himself many times about the geographical distribution of pellagra in order to find support for his weak theory.") [25]

Roussel was equally unhappy about other theories which strove to prove that pellagra was due to local or phasic changes in weather conditions. The seasonal development of pellagra had been noted by all observers who had seen the endemic disease; the changes in the skin after exposure to sunlight were plain to see. Frapolli, in his monograph of 1771, attributed pellagra to the sun's rays and believed that the disease was a variant of sunstroke.[26] His ideas were strongly opposed by the experts on pellagra of both the zeist and nonzeist camps. Thus Strambio commented: "Si quis pellagra, morbo laborans, a sole omnino abstinet, desquammationem quidem evitat, non morbi progressum. Ergo insolatio non est causa morbi." ("If, as pellagra develops, there is no exposure to the sun, then scaling of the skin is avoided, but the internal disease progresses. Therefore insolation or sunlight exposure is not the cause of the disease.") [27] The twin facts that pellagra could continue even when the patient was not exposed to the sun and that the skin lesions made their appearance in the spring rather than in the summer when the light was most intense created powerful opposition to the theory of insolation. Years later, the idea of sunlight as the cause of pellagra was revived and developed into a more sophisticated photodynamic theory, in which it was claimed that maize contains a light-sensitizing substance.

The zeists, as we have seen, varied in their beliefs. Some thought that corn itself caused pellagra; others supported the idea that the disease was due to a maize toxin derived from a mold. Each of these groups had reservations about the extent to which such factors as heredity and hygiene played a part in causation. The out-and-out antizeists refuted any concept that included corn as an etiological agent. Such a school of thought was prevalent in France in the mid-nineteenth century. Some of the men who subscribed to these ideas described a pellagrous syndrome and spoke of the disease as the *morbus miseriae*. They believed that pellagra developed in alcoholics, in the insane, in those whose lives consisted in all manner of wretchedness, and that misery itself was productive of the disease. Others, such as Jean Hameau and his son, preferred the concept that pellagra was a contagion due to some unseen infective organism which they termed a virus. The latter group accounted for those cases of pellagra that had been observed among people who were not corn eaters by suggesting that they had caught the disease. Argument was so fierce between the zeist and antizeist camps that the zeists invented the term "pseudo-pellagra" to designate a pellagrous condition in non–corn-eaters. This term was rather unfortunate in that it provoked jibes from the opposite camp, and the idea became the object of ridicule. The famous British physician Sir Patrick Manson spoke of the comfortable term "pseudo-pellagra" and scornfully remarked, "The disease is pellagra when it fits in with the orthodox theory and when it can be connected in any way with maize but when it is not possible, the disease becomes pseudo-pellagra." [28]

Triumphs of Zeism

It would be fair to generalize that during the nineteenth century the zeists won out over their opponents. Furthermore, it is obvious that despite the fact that the supporters of the corn theories did not understand the precise cause of pellagra, their convictions and their pleas aroused the governments of Italy and France to consider whether peasant mortality from pellagra could be decreased by dietary change. Just as Dr. John Snow stopped an epidemic of cholera in London in 1854 by taking the handle off the communal Broad Street pump, so legislation prompted by Roussel to provide French peasants with wheat instead of corn bread curtailed pellagra in France. Snow was ignorant of the cholera vibrio, but his observations of the cholera epidemic gave him the idea that it was transmitted by infected water. Similarly, Roussel and his followers, knowing nothing about pellagra as the result of a vitamin deficiency, nevertheless controlled the disease by their advocacy of a regime which would limit consumption of corn products. Italy lagged behind France in its conquest of pellagra, not because there was less knowledge of the disease among Italian than among French physicians, but because the Italian governments were not persuaded to change the food of the polenta eaters.

8 | Sandwith's Experience

A strange and recurring feature in the history of pellagra was the slow recognition of its existence in endemic areas. Thus the magnitude of the pellagra problem, outside of Europe, was not realized until very late in the nineteenth century. Before this time, a handful of doctors had seen the disease in Africa and in the United States. Franz Pruner, in his book *Topographie médicale du Caire,* published in Munich in 1847, under the heading "Leproses" wrote, "Pellagra is sporadic in Egypt and such as we have studied it in Milan." [1] Eighteen years later, an Egyptian physician, Dr. A. Figari Bey, writing of the appearance of venereal disease in Lower Egypt, mentioned that he had seen a "kind of leprous pellagra." [2]

Systematic evaluation of the geographical, economic, and nutritional factors which determine the incidence of pellagra in Egypt was not undertaken until the British epidemiologist, Fleming Sandwith, met the challenge when he was on the medical staff of the Kasr el Ainy Hospital in Cairo. At the annual meeting of the British Medical Association in 1898 he told his audience:

Eight years ago there was no English literature and no great interest in tropical disease, and I went myself to Egypt quite ignorant of the diseases of the country. In 1893, while collecting a few records for publication, I became aware that a large number of my anchylostomiasis [hookworm] patients showed a symmetrical eruption which sunburn, chapping and dirt could not explain. I eventually decided that some of them had pellagra in addition to their anaemia, and though there was no one in Egypt who could give any information on the subject, I was confirmed in my suspicion by Italian physicians visiting my hospital wards.

He went on to relate that since 1893 he had seen more than five hundred cases in his hospital wards, besides many in other sections of the hospital and in the lunatic asylum. Apparently, by that time the peasants had discovered that an interest was being taken in the disease, and the word went from one to another that they should go to Cairo for treatment. In analyzing the demographic data for the cases under his care in the year 1897, Sandwith found that there was a great preponderance of the disease in Lower Egypt; of 164 patients, 127 came from districts in Lower Egypt and only 37 from parts of Upper Egypt. He quickly came to the conclusion that the distribution of the disease could be accounted for by the feeding habits of the people: in Lower Egypt the peasants lived chiefly on maize, whereas in Upper Egypt they subsisted on millet. Sandwith was particularly interested to find that in the Fayum, where no maize was eaten, there was no pellagra. He was also told by his former students that pellagra was rare in the neighborhood of Luxor for the same reason, but when he visited this area he saw several cases in the hospital and among beggars. Obviously, experience with pellagra heightened the ability of physicians to recognize it: Surgeon-Captain Myles, fresh from seeing Sandwith's cases, found four pellagrins among six thousand starving Arabs at Tokar on the Red Sea, in 1891 after a famine.

Another important aspect of pellagra in Egypt that Sandwith appreciated was its rural distribution. He called it "a country-bred disease" that occurred in laborers living on a monotonous diet and exposed to the sun. In Cairo and the other large cities, it was mainly seen in those living in the utmost poverty. At that time the peasant had two names for the pellagrous skin eruption: *qushuf*, often pronounced *ushuf*, which means "chapping"; and the term *gofar*, which was used for an eruption which attacked camels and sometimes horses.

The pellagrins seen at this time were mainly men and boys, all of whom were suffering from hookworm infestation; about a third of them had schistosomiasis, a parasitic disease spread by snails. Sandwith believed that the preponderance of males among his cases could be accounted for by the fact that they, rather than the women, worked in the fields, which in some way made them more vulnerable to the disease. He believed, however, that if he had had time to go into the country district, he would have seen female pellagrins, who because of poverty or traditions affecting women could not get as far as a Cairo hospital. His cases were all Egyptians, not Nubians or Sudanese, whose living conditions were in some ways different from those of the Egyptian fellaheen, or peasants. Of the pellagrins whom Sandwith listed as seen in 1897, 88 per cent were farm laborers, and the others were either masons, laborers, readers of the Koran—who were practically beggars—boatmen, policemen, or brickmakers. There were one potter and one servant. Sandwith says of these people: "They were invariably men of the poorest class, who had been out of work, and therefore out of food for some time."

In discussing the cause of pellagra, Sandwith states that he had no evidence that among his cases there was a hereditary predisposition to the disease. In July 1895, he had visited Dr. Enrico Locatelli at the *pellagrossario* at Mogliano, near Venice. Here he had been shown cases of so-called hereditary pellagra, even children at the breast, but he was not impressed, since he had learned that very young children in Italy were fed polenta. He therefore thought that it would be difficult to prove that in any given case the etiology was hereditary rather than acquired. Sandwith accepted the views of the latter-day zeists; he thought the essential causes of pellagra were bad maize, poverty, and exposure to the sun, with bad maize the essential factor. On this point, he quotes the well-known British physician Clifford Allbutt, who in his *System of Medicine* of 1897 says that the fungus attacking the maize was *Reticularia ustilago* [3]—a statement Sandwith is inclined to take with a grain of salt. Undoubtedly the maize of the

Egyptian fellah and his family was rotten stuff, for as we are told by this author, "The poorer peasants sell the best of their maize at the market and keep the worst to eat at home." In Egypt a staple cereal was always alluded to as durra. Among the staples were *durra beledy,* which was *Sorghum vulgare;* great millet, or Guinea corn, which did not cause pellagra; and *durra shamy,* which was *Zea mays,* or Indian corn, which Sandwith says was introduced into Egypt about sixty years before the time of his writing. It was grown mainly in Lower Egypt and did cause or seem to cause pellagra. Two-thirds of his patients ate their corn durra in the form of bread, while others had it roasted or ate it raw in the green state. The last Sandwith thought the least dangerous, as the fungus would not have time to grow as it would when the corn was stored.

Some of the most astute of Sandwith's observations pertain to the concomitant diseases of the pellagrous fellaheen. It seems that not only did they have intestinal parasites, but many also had malaria and untreated syphilis, so the debility caused by these infections could have rendered the poor population more susceptible to pellagra. Pellagra was long-standing before treatment was sought. Sandwith says, "Speaking generally, the fellah does not make up his mind to journey to Cairo for treatment until pellagra has become chronic, and he is too exhausted by that time and other troubles to earn his bread." [4]

The natives had their own methods of treatment. A pellagrin would be taken by his friends to a neighboring wise man or wise woman, who was sometimes the village barber and vaccinator. Any painful parts of his body would be burned with red-hot irons. If that did no good, setons were tried. These were threads which were drawn through the skin to act as counterirritants, but which in fact caused chronic fistulous tracts. A journey was often made to a mosque or sheik's tomb to pray for recovery. Last of all, the patient would apply for relief at a government hospital, or he would be brought there by the police, starving and homeless and unable to answer questions intelligently.

Sandwith's treatment of pellagra was in part innovative and in part traditional. He debarred his patients from eating corn in any form and provided them with a good mixed diet. Tonics were given, as well as cod-liver oil and iron. In addition, he prescribed fresh but compressed bone marrow, which he found to be efficacious, particularly in causing a weight gain.

When a medical congress was held in Cairo in December 1902, Sandwith, then professor of medicine at the medical school, presented a paper describing his further experiences with pellagra and recommending a plan that he believed would prevent or eradicate the disease in Egypt. His account of the incidence of pellagra among working peasants gives insight into the economic deprivation of the fellaheen. He told of some of the findings:

In June 1902, I examined 315 men living in 11 different villages in the province of Gharbieh; 114 of them, or 36 per cent, showed signs of early pellagra. In one village, where the inhabitants are especially well-to-do because they get regular pay throughout the year from the Domains Administration, there were only 15 per cent of pellagrous men, while among the men of the village which has the reputation of being the poorest the percentage rose as high as 62. Yet all these men stoutly denied they had anything the matter with them and the overseers in charge of them stated that the pellagrous could do a fair day's work. On the same day I examined 23 young girls who were working at the threshing floor or picking eggs off the cotton plants and again I found that 30 per cent of them were already pellagrous. On a previous occasion I had examined 139 presumably healthy peasants in the province of Sharkieh and had found 50 per cent of them to have pellagra. If these figures are in the least typical of the state of the male inhabitants in Lower Egypt, it is quite time that something should be done to disseminate information on the subject and gradually to teach employers of labour and peasants that the early symptoms of the disease can easily be recognized, that they will then yield to treatment, but that, if neglected, the symptoms are of a progressive nature and will end in insanity or in general debility which entirely unfits an individual for work.[5]

Sandwith was a keen observer of humanity, particularly of poor humanity; he was not a research worker except in the clinical sense. Thus his plan to control pellagra in Lower Egypt depended almost entirely on government control of the importation, distribution, and sale of maize. In other words, he was still imbued with the idea that pellagra was caused by diseased maize. His students and colleagues followed in the master's footsteps; if they added anything to information about Egyptian pellagra, it was only some notation of local environmental factors or customs which modified the clinical picture.

Their experiences were conveyed to the French pellagrologist Armand Marie when he visited Cairo hospitals and the asylum at Abbassia in 1907. Reporting on his visit, Marie mentions the peculiar distribution of the skin eruption which was localized because of the costume worn by the Egyptian peasant: the short wide sleeves made the pellagrous arm lesions or "glove" more extensive, and the *grandoura,* opened wide at the neck, caused the redness to extend down to the breastbone. Marie also tells of the pellagrous children and of how he had seen scores of them from ten to fifteen years old dwarfed, wizened, anemic, displaying pellagrous rashes and usually mentally disturbed. Some of these children, he said, "look like little mummies." [6]

Sandwith "found" pellagra in Egypt twenty years after the country had been opened to European visitors who wanted to see the Pyramids. In 1870, the Egyptian government appointed J. M. Cook, son of the founder of the firm of Thomas Cook and Son, passenger agent on the Nile; largely through his efforts, well-dressed English and French tourists made the journey in the utmost comfort. In the years immediately before this, guided tours to Egypt were beginning to be the vogue.[7]

A satirical account of one such journey, which is not lacking in social overtones, is given by Edmond About in his novel *Le Fellah.*[8] The French narrator of the book, which is doubtless about himself, travels with Mr. and Mrs. Longman and their daughter Grace through the length of Egypt during the winter of 1868. Their young guide, Ahmed ibn Ibrahim, shows them the antiquities, mosques new and old, the inside of a harem, the more refined elements of Arab life, and above all the marvels of modern technology. Everything is exotic, romantic, and painted in the colors of About's friend Léon Gérôme, the artist, to whom the book is dedicated. Then, one memorable day, they are granted an audience with "the viceroy," or Ismail Pasha himself, at his palace at Kasr-en-Nil. The prince receives them with great cordiality and generously offers them assistance with their journey and a chartered steamboat to sail along the Nile. Throughout the meeting he takes pains to describe for their benefit the problems of the rural economy, referring to himself as the prince of fellahs. Ismail is anxious for them to visit both Upper and Lower Egypt to see the life of the people, whom he professes to understand so well. When Ahmed hears of the scheme, he tells them that although the viceroy is a fine agriculturist, he has no conception of the life of the Egyptian peasant. Ismail has described a labor shortage to them, but Ahmed explains that actually a great many foreign laborers have been brought in, especially skilled artisans for whom the government provides modern transport and all kinds of work incentives, which are denied to the fellaheen. The fellaheen still work all day in the fields, though certainly advances have been made by the new ruler; now each fellah can free himself of forced labor at a price—a freedom that used to be guaranteed if the money was forthcoming for the landowner.

While our traveling companions were waiting for the train at the Bena station, they saw several veiled women running along the platform selling food for the ride. Ahmed bought them some thin soft cakes, telling them, "You must try the de luxe bread of our peasants." Our narrator describes the cake as powdery on the outside, soft within, badly made and badly cooked, seemingly made of flour mixed with sand, tasting sour and with a musty smell. "Dear friends," said Ahmed, "the sad repast which you have had is forbidden to most of my fellow citizens; they only eat maize or millet flour, which is badly ground between two stones. Neither the millet nor the maize includes an atom of gluten; they only furnish starch to human beings, that is to say, unfit fuel for bodily repair. Even our wheat, which you are tasting at present, is poorer in nitrogen than other grains. This is sad, but it is true."

Obviously, this is an improbable fragment of nutritional knowledge to be produced by an uneducated Egyptian guide, but it documents the fact that prior to Sandwith's investigations, a French author long interested in the economic implications of malnutrition understood that the toiling fellah was chronically debilitated by his horrible diet. It is curious that About, who had been familiar with pellagra in France, did not comment on the disease in Egypt.

Whatever the contributions of About in publicizing the feeding habits of the Egyptian peasant and in describing his vile way of life, it was Sandwith who discovered pellagra in the country of the pharaohs. His writings on pellagra were the first major contributions on this subject in English. His reports in their day had a great impact, influencing American physicians who were to find pellagra so frequently in the southern states. During the Boer War, when he found himself surrounded by poor Bantu people living on maize, he expected to meet with pellagra among them, too. The medical men of South Africa apparently knew nothing of this ailment, for they assured him that no such disease had ever been seen. When, however, he examined the insane patients of Robben Island, near Cape Town, he found cases of pellagra, as he anticipated.[9]

9 | King Corn in the Ascendant

When pellagra first appeared on the North American continent is unknown. A number of writers have suggested that it may have occurred in pre-Columbian times, but there is no real evidence to support this contention. Indeed, claims that pellagra existed in America prior to the nineteenth century have not been substantiated.

In 1864, Dr. John Gray of Utica, New York, reported a case of pellagra. Dr. Tyler of Somerville, Massachusetts, in discussing this case, referred to a similar case of his own. Both these cases were among the insane; they were described at a meeting of the American Asylum Physicians in Washington, D.C.[1] Dr. Charles Wardell Stiles, in conversation with his friend Dr. W. J. W. Kerr, a firsthand observer, said that he was confident that the causes of the high death rate among the Federal troops imprisoned in the Confederate prison at Andersonville, Georgia, in 1864 were hookworm infestation and pellagra. Lacking sufficient information, we cannot really say whether or not this is true. It was claimed by H. N. Sloan that pellagra was diagnosed in the South Carolina Asylum for the Insane at Columbia in the early seventies, but it was not reported or recorded. Certainly the disease existed among the inmates of this institution in the eighties, but it was attributed at that time to sunburn. According to Dr. Edward Jenner Wood, a certain Dr. Pope saw at least two cases in the South Carolina penitentiary in the middle eighties.[2]

A few cases of pellagra were reported between 1883 and 1889.

In the latter year, a patient of Dr. Thomas Mask in Wilmington, North Carolina, presented a skin disease which was believed at the time to be atypical psoriasis. In 1907, when a large number of cases of pellagra were noted in the same area, Dr. Mask described the case at a meeting at which Edward Wood was present. The case history convinced Dr. Wood that Dr. Mask's patient had originally been misdiagnosed and that the correct diagnosis was pellagra.[3]

In 1893, when Sandwith noted the occurrence of pellagra in Egypt and became interested in the geographical distribution, he wrote to many physicians in the United States, but was unable to elicit any evidence of its presence there at that time or any history of past occurrences.[4] Cases of pellagra were unrecognized. Dr. James Babcock, in the opening remarks at the first National Conference on Pellagra in 1909, cited evidence that the illness had occurred in Louisiana, Alabama, Georgia, North Carolina, and South Carolina before the disease reached epidemic proportions in these southern states.[5] The same author mentioned elsewhere that after pellagra had been generally recognized in the United States, he had examined the records of the State Hospital for the Insane in Columbia, South Carolina, of which he was superintendent, and had satisfied himself that cases of pellagra dated back to the time of the establishment of the institution in 1828.[6]

The incidence of pellagra in the South was brought to the attention of physicians and public alike in 1906 when an epidemic developed in the Alabama Institution for Negroes, situated at Mount Vernon. It is interesting that one of the physicians in this hospital, Dr. Emit L. McCafferty, had seen a case of pellagra presented by Edward Wood to the students of the Atlanta College of Physicians and Surgeons in February 1902. Whether Dr. McCafferty communicated any recollection of this case to his colleagues at the institution is not known. It was McCafferty who, with his senior associate George H. Searcy, studied the cases of pellagra in the Alabama mental hospital. In 1907, Searcy reported a group of 88 cases, of which 57 had died. Through the help of this report, which was published in the *Journal of the American Medical Association,* other physicians in Alabama and in neighboring southern states came to recognize the existence of the disease in their own practices.[7]

The following year, Dr. Joseph J. Watson and Dr. James Babcock of Columbia, South Carolina, went to Italy to find out whether the disease seen in the United States was the same as the endemic pellagra of Lombardy. They soon concluded that the disease was identical in the two countries. On their return home, they set about determining the incidence of pellagra. Babcock began by organizing a national pellagra conference. Watson and Babcock together communicated with the South Carolina State Board of Health and brought the matter to the attention of Claude Lavinder and Charles F. Williams, both of whom were employed by this health department.[8]

Williams used the following questionnaire to obtain statistics on pellagra:

1. Have you seen any cases of pellagra in your institution or in your State?

2. How many cases have you seen?

3. How long since you recognized the disease?

4. If at all, how long do you think the disease has existed in your section?

5. What proportion were male? . . . female?

6. What was the occupation of these affected? . . . Nationality?

7. Do the products of Indian corn (hominy or meal) form a part of the dietary of the patients and are those products derived from native or shipped corn?

8. Were your patients from the poor, . . . moderate, . . . or well-to-do classes? . . . And were they from the city, . . . town . . . or country? [9]

He addressed this letter of inquiry to the superintendents of state hospitals for the insane in the United States. To 164 inquiries, 120 replies were received, showing that about a thousand cases had been recognized by the medical correspondents in 13 states.

The states reporting the largest number were South Carolina (500), Alabama (200), Georgia (235), and North Carolina (75). A few were also reported from New York, Pennsylvania, Maryland, Virginia, Florida, Louisiana, Mississippi, Tennessee, and Kansas. More than half were reported from asylums or similar institutions, in which there was a large preponderance of female cases. Unfortunately, the method of collecting data was totally inadequate; while some physicians responding to the questionnaire described cases under their care, others reported numbers estimated in their state, town, or hospital. It is of interest that although most reports showed that the disease was first recognized after the publication of Searcy's report, it was believed to have existed for up to thirty years. Very little was learned about the environment, occupation, or diet of the patients mentioned.

The first National Conference on Pellagra was held under the auspices of the South Carolina State Board of Health at the State Hospital for the Insane, Columbia, South Carolina, on November 3 and 4, 1909.[10] Governor Martin Ansel, who welcomed the delegates, referred to Dr. Babcock as the discoverer of pellagra in the United States—a slip Babcock immediately corrected.[11] Numerous papers were delivered by physicians who had had actual experience with pellagra. The first scientific communication was presented by Dr. Babcock for Sandwith, then vice-president of the Society of Tropical Medicine and Hygiene in London. A summary of Sandwith's knowledge, as well as that of contemporary Italian investigators, was given in order to prove to the members of the congress that certain general axioms which had been found to be true in Italy and Egypt would probably hold good in America. In districts where no maize is cultivated or habitually eaten, pellagra does not exist. Well-to-do people in pellagra districts, living on varied diets and consuming maize as an occasional, not a staple cereal, usually escape pellagra. Furthermore, "it is not good maize or good maize flour which produces pellagra but the disease for its production requires the habitual use of damaged maize in some form." Sandwith cautioned those who were relatively inexperienced with pellagra against certain misconceptions.

Thus, in concluding, he pointed out that while it was true that the world area of maize cultivation was greater than the area of incidence of pellagra, the regions of pellagra distribution did appear to correspond with the regions in which people habitually ate damaged maize or products made therefrom. Lastly, he emphasized that whereas pellagra had been overlooked in the United States in the past, now there was an almost equal danger that pellagra might be diagnosed incorrectly in those who had disorders which superficially resembled pellagra.[12]

Whether or not Sandwith's paper was available to delegates before the meeting is unknown, but certainly his discussion of the role of maize in the causation of pellagra seems to have excited Ebbie J. Watson, the commissioner of the Department of Agriculture, Commerce and Industries in South Carolina. He delivered a speech which might have gone down better at a political meeting than at a medical congress. Entitled "Economic Factors of the Pellagra Problem in South Carolina," his contribution was a very "corny" talk about corn, in which song and verse were interspersed with vital statistics. His words built up to a climax:

I am not here to attempt to discuss the etiology of pellagra, to attempt to say whether pellagra has its origin in impure Indian corn—the original wild grass of the Mayas of Central America, brought to us centuries after our country was discovered, via Mexico by the Toltecs and the Aztecs, given to us by the Indians and sent by returning explorers to Spain, Italy and other countries. I know that within the heart of the corn kernel, carefully encased in a cylinder of oil, are life-living cells. The vital principle men of my class do not understand, but it is there within the womb of the kernel, ready when healthy to burst forth into a beautiful, sturdy plant and bring forth an ear of corn within whose yellow heart there is health and strength for all the nations. We do not KNOW that in this kernel lurks also grim Death. There is reason to believe that this is the case. We do know that " 'Tis safer to avoid what's grown than question how it was born." We know that pellagra exists in this State and is causing deaths among our people.

"Judgment and reason have been grand jurymen since before Noah was a sailor," and this grand jury has upon the testimony of many scientific witnesses rendered a true bill against King Corn. You are here assembled today to try the case as petit jurors and to render the verdict. If it be "guilty" then there is all the more reason for me to be here. When a serious charge—in this case the charge of murder—is written on the indictment, the subject of the charge must be held under grave suspicion, and such proper precautions as are possible to prevent further crime should be taken. . . .

Our chief in our sphere of endeavor, that distinguished official Secretary Wilson, who has done so much for the people of this Commonwealth, tells me, "I recognize fully the necessity of giving every attention to the pellagra disease," and "am naturally interested in the question of the relation of Indian corn to the disease."

Corn stands indicted! When such danger threatens, I for one believe in hoisting the red flag and taking such precautions as our limited knowledge will permit. The corn crop of the country is the principal crop of the country. Last year it was worth nearly as much as the great crops of cotton, hay and wheat combined. It amounts to over two and a half billions of bushels, out of the three and a quarter billions in the whole world, and represents wealth—"wealth," as Mr. Wilson says, "taken out of the soil in four months"—of over a billion and a half dollars, enough "to cancel the interest bearing debts of the United States and to pay for the Panama Canal and fifty battleships." There has been an increase in value of $600,000,000 since 1902, a sum "equal to the gold in the treasury of a rich nation." In this little State the corn crop last year had jumped to nearly 30,000,000 bushels, worth over 26½ millions of dollars, a phenomenal increase in two years of practically ten millions of dollars. . . . In the South corn-growing is just beginning to reach for its flood tide, and we are hourly bringing every influence to bear to reach the goal. . . . No wonder we are searching for evidence to show whether death dealing qualities charged against King Corn are developed in the home-raised goods or in the product brought in from other States.[13]

Watson was imbued not so much with a desire to exonerate corn as the cause of pellagra as to blame a product grown outside the confines of South Carolina. He continued: "The Federal government, under the new Pure Food Law, doubtless finds itself unable at this time to afford adequate protection. In the meantime, if it is true that bad corn and bad corn products produce pellagra —or even if it isn't true—and we must go on the doctrine or an ounce of prevention, then the hour has arrived for the States to act speedily and decisively and at least provide measures of protection against the making of such States as South Carolina the dumping ground for the damaged and dangerous products of the country."

It is easy to ridicule Watson's chauvinistic attitude, but his opinions were shared by many at the congress. A planter, J. Swinton Whaley of Edisto Island, South Carolina, drew a close analogy between "blind staggers" in horses and pellagra in man, both of which he attributed to the consumption of bad corn from the West.[14] A physician, J. D. Jones of Sweet Water, Alabama, remarked: "The idea has been advanced here that corn is doing the damage. Corn is one of the chief merchantable commodities of the United States, but I tell you gentlemen, it is not corn according to my idea. It may be damaged corn, but pure, fully developed, hardened corn—hardened by the rays of the noonday sun—will never produce pellagra." [15]

Various opinions were expressed concerning the etiology of pellagra. Although most emphasis was placed on the role of spoiled corn, some speakers emphatically contended that the disease was caused by a microorganism, probably a protozoan, since it appeared that pellagra responded to antiprotozoa treatment. After many speakers had stated their theories and had been unwilling to listen to criticism, Dr. Hiram Byrd of Jacksonville, Florida, spoke up like the little child in "The Emperor's New Clothes:" "Let us not put ourselves on record prematurely. . . . If there is one thing that this conference has forced upon me it is the belief that we do not know the cause of pellagra, that we are today in the dark." [16]

10 | Transmission of the Disease

Flies, Parasites, and Swamps

Although it was unequivocally shown by Roussel and others that endemic pellagra occurs in populations subsisting on maize diets, the zeist theory was not generally accepted. Indeed, as late as the second decade of the twentieth century suggestions that pellagra was an infectious disease were seriously entertained.

Louis Sambon, a British physician and biologist noted for his work on the role of the tsetse fly in trypanosomiasis, firmly believed that pellagra was spread by an insect vector.[1] He visited the pellagra-affected districts of northern Italy in 1900 and again in 1903. He became acquainted with district health officers, had discussions with Italian physicians who had devoted special attention to pellagra, and met Dr. Claude Lavinder and Dr. Joseph Siler who were visiting Italy from the United States.

Before he left London for Italy, he formulated a theory that pellagra was a parasitic, insect-borne disease carried by a blood-sucking fly of the genus *Simulium*. His reasons for this belief were mainly connected with the periodicity of symptoms. For Sambon, the cyclical waxing and waning of pellagra with the seasons could be explained by periods of latency and activity of an insect. It appeared to him that pellagra must be an insect-borne disease, not only because of seasonal variations in its prevalence, but also because it was not directly contagious, because neither food nor drink could account for its peculiar epidemiology, and because it was almost entirely restricted to field laborers and their families,

84

who were overexposed to the flies. The idea that the contagion was spread by a *Simulium* occurred to him because there was a correlation between the pellagrous areas of Italy and the areas of distribution of the *Simulium* flies. He also noted that the imago stage of the fly presents the same seasonal incidence as pellagra itself.

We can imagine that Sambon's observations of pellagra were biased by his preconceived ideas. Wherever he traveled in Italy, he would ask the local health officer whether pellagra was equally distributed throughout the district. Since the answer was invariably No, he would obtain an enumeration of the localities affected. Both in northern and central Italy, he found that there were pellagrous districts in narrow valleys through which ran streams infested with *Simulium*. He noted that the disease also spread into the plains along the streams as far as the reach of *Simulium* life. Much was made of the epidemiology of pellagra, which Sambon compared to that of malaria, trypanosomiasis, Rocky Mountain fever, and other diseases known to be transmitted by insect carriers. While in nonendemic areas he found only one or two pellagrins per household, all of whom were adults who had at some time worked away from the area, in endemic areas he found that pellagra attacked all age groups and whole families were affected (clear proof of the insect-vector theory).

Sambon discovered that official opinion in Italy opposed the theory that pellagra was infectious. He was told again and again that pellagra was caused by the consumption of unsound, infested maize. This he would not believe; if it was true, he surmised, the distribution of pellagra would shift with that of the diseased grain, which was clearly not the case. Argument would not convince him. Pellagra in 1903 existed in exactly the same places it had in 1776, when Odoardi made his original report.

How could the peculiarly restricted pellagra be due to poverty, insufficient nourishment, damaged maize, and grinding labor, when not all field laborers succumbed, though all lived under similar conditions? For Sambon, the limitation of the disease to the field laborers of pellagrous districts could easily be explained by the *Simulium* theory, while none of the several other hypotheses on the etiology of pellagra could account for it satisfactorily.

In 1905, at the Leicester meeting of the British Medical Association, the first report was received from Sambon that pellagra was an insect-borne disease.[2] Two years later, he was asked to deliver lectures before the London School of Tropical Medicine; using the general title "Progress Report on the Investigation of Pellagra," he described his studies in Italy and promulgated the *Simulium* theory. In the last part of his report, he admits that all his endeavors failed to demonstrate a parasitic agent in pellagra, but he clings to the idea that the ultramicroscopic dimensions of the infective agent may have precluded optical resolution. By making an analogy between pellagra and yellow fever, he concludes that establishment of the vector alone had made possible the stamping out of one scourge and by inference could do so again. (In his text Sambon mentions that he first suggested that a *Simulium* might be the transmitting agent of pellagra on January 21, 1910, at a meeting of the Pellagra Investigation Committee at Dr. James Cantlie's house in London.) [3]

Sambon's theory was not considered as illogical in his time as it is today. Indeed, in the United States it stimulated a biological survey in pellagrous districts. Harrison Garman, a competent entomologist and botanist, made a study of localities in Kentucky throughout which pellagra was prevalent, referring to the condition of the corn crop and to the possible presence of an insect or other agent by which the disease was spread. His investigations were published in 1912. From his discussion it is apparent that although the author was painstaking in his work and well versed in the minutiae of insect life in the area, he knew nothing about pellagra. After examining a few patients and noting the localization of skin lesions on light-exposed areas, he decided that some agent in the air was involved in the spread of the disease. He was attracted to Sambon's theory because he realized that the disease does indeed become active in the spring, just when the local gnats or flies of the *Simulium* genus come from the water in the greatest numbers as adults. On the other hand, though in some streams near the dwellings of pellagrins Garman found larvae and pupae of *Simulium* species, these were sometimes difficult to find, and they did not outnumber the rest of the insect population. Although he sometimes saw patients with pellagra living close to insect-breeding areas by the river and streams, he discovered that in certain instances the disease had been contracted before the people had come to live in the area. Garman's uneasiness about Sambon's theory can best be summarized in his own words, appended in a footnote: "The writer has not at any time committed himself to the 'insect theory' of the spread of pellagra. He is not satisfied with the evidence, and intends in this bulletin simply to present facts which may bear upon the problem." [4]

Lavinder, who had spent time with Sambon in Italy, followed up the suggestion that pellagra was caused by an ultramicroscopic organism. He examined the blood of pellagrous patients for intracellular parasites. Reporting on his investigation in 1909, he stated that while pellagrins have a fairly constant secondary anemia, nothing resembling a protozoal parasite could be found in the blood and all blood cultures were negative.[5]

Dr. Henry Nichols, who worked with Joseph Siler at the Peoria State Hospital in Illinois, produced some evidence to support the causal role of protozoa in pellagra. He examined the stools of 88 pellagrous inmates of the hospital. In addition, he examined the stools of 101 nonpellagrous inmates and of 453 nonpellagrous soldiers. This study revealed that 85.3 per cent of the pellagrins had protozoa in their stools, whereas the percentage of the nonpellagrous inmates of the asylum was 48.6, and of the soldiers 51.2. Amebae and flagellates were found in the drinking water of the hospital. Nichols assumed that in the majority of cases of pellagra in Peoria, protozoal infections of the colon were the exciting cause, but he found it difficult to account for all the symptoms on the basis of a parasitic infestation, particularly since blood cultures and organ cultures at autopsy were negative. Could the role of the protozoa in the development of pellagra be better explained? Nichols could soon answer in the affirmative. After one brief trip to the Department of Botany at the University of Illinois, where he discussed corn parasites and molds with the faculty, he came to the conclusion that pellagra was caused by the adverse effects of corn toxins on an intestine damaged by protozoal infection.[6]

Findings of a Federal Commission

When the first National Conference on Pellagra was in progress, a number of physicians supported Nichols' contention that protozoa might play a predisposing role in the induction of pellagra.[7] The delegates could not settle the argument as to whether the disease was due to infection or to the consumption of moldy corn, and Nichols' ideas were therefore attractive. After the conference ended, commissions were set up to investigate the epidemiology of pellagra.

The Illinois Pellagra Commission studied the course of the disease in patients admitted to the Peoria State Hospital and in those treated or seen by physicians in the state. The commissioners recorded 408 cases between 1909 and 1911; of these, 189 died. They deliberately fed some of the patients at the Peoria State Hospital a high-corn diet, while others were given a corn-free menu. Finding that these dietary manipulations had no effect on the course of the disease, they discredited any assumption that pellagra was related to corn eating.[8]

In 1912, Dr. George N. Miller, then president of the New York Post-Graduate Medical School, obtained funds to support research expenditures for the investigation of pellagra in the United States. Financial support was given by Colonel Robert M. Thompson of New York City and J. H. McFadden of Philadelphia. It was decided that a commission of three should be formed, one member to be designated by the Surgeon-General of the Army, one by the Surgeon-General of the Navy, and one by the authorities of the

New York Post-Graduate Medical School. The commission was constituted as follows: Captain Joseph F. Siler, Medical Corps, U.S. Army; Passed-Assistant Surgeon Philip E. Garrison, U.S. Navy; and Dr. Ward J. MacNeal, professor of bacteriology and pathology and assistant director of laboratories, New York Post-Graduate Medical School.

The federal investigation was conducted by a group that became known as the Thompson-McFadden Pellagra Commission.[9] This commission was first given the problem of studying the occurrence of the disease and its relationship to various socioeconomic factors. From the reports of this body, it is apparent that those who guided the investigation had fixed ideas about the probable causes of the epidemic. They studied the diets of the families where pellagra was prevalent, particularly in Spartanburg, South Carolina, and in certain cotton-mill villages of Spartanburg County. Their methods of obtaining diet histories were primitive, and the sort of questions asked of the victims did not draw out much valuable information. They only attempted to establish whether certain foods were eaten regularly, occasionally, or not at all. The answers they obtained from the afflicted families were probably inaccurate and were certainly poorly evaluated. Indeed, in the first report the only significant finding was that pellagrins appeared to eat very little meat or other animal protein. The investigators, however, were unable to associate pellagra with poor nutrition, with the consumption of corn or corn products, or with a history of inadequate food intake.[10]

Not finding definitive evidence that pellagra was associated with a faulty diet, the physicians in charge turned to a more formal epidemiological study. They showed that pellagra was more prevalent in certain villages than in others, that there was a familial grouping of cases, and that in the cotton-mill communities the wives of the factory workers were more frequently affected than the men. No attempt was made to look into the precise economic variables which determined the peculiar incidence of the disease. The doctors did not hunt for the forms of social deprivation that might be responsible for the spread of the disease in these communities. Looking back at the work these men performed, we are perhaps amazed and shocked at their type of approach to the pellagra problem. Why, we may ask, did they not observe that pellagra was not only associated with poverty, but occurred in people who were dependent on others for the very food they put into their mouths? Lest we be too critical of their approach, it is useful to remember that in more recent times when the problem of hunger in the United States was reinvestigated and the book *Hunger, U.S.A.* was published,[11] people did not believe the findings.

Reports of the Thompson-McFadden Commission were published from 1913 to 1916. They had studied factors that might account for the inequalities in the geographical distribution of pellagra, and they showed that unsatisfactory methods of sewage disposal might be determining elements. In the city of Spartanburg they found a distinct tendency for the endemic foci of the disease to occur in sections of the city where there were unscreened surface privies, whereas in cotton-mill villages equipped with a water-carriage system of sewage disposal they could not find cases of pellagra that had originated in the vicinity.[12]

Under their direction, entomologists from the United States Department of Agriculture made an intensive study of insects as pellagra carriers. They were unable to find any association between the occurrence of buffalo gnats (*Simulium*) and the incidence of the disease, nor could they find a correlation between endemic areas of pellagra and such infesting insects as ticks, lice, bedbugs, mosquitoes, fleas, and houseflies. They believed, however, that the common stable fly (*Stomoxys calcitrans*) qualified as a transmitter of the disease, because it had a seasonal activity which corresponded with that of pellagra, was an abundant inhabitant of the rural pellagrous areas, and traveled long distances which could account for sporadic cases.[13]

Bacteriologic studies were directed by Dr. MacNeal. The possible role of the intestinal bacteria in pellagra was investigated, and a large number of agglutination tests were carried out with various bacterial strains. Quantitative changes in the bacterial flora of the feces in pellagrins were such as might be expected from irritation of the digestive tract; the agglutination tests failed to demonstrate the specific relationship of any organism to the disease. Numerous attempts to produce pellagra in monkeys (*Macacus rhesus*) by the injection of blood from pellagrous patients failed to reproduce the disease.[14]

In spite of these results, the commissioners stated in the summary of their first report: "In our opinion the view that pellagra is an intestinal infection, transmitted by contaminated food, to which the individual is rendered more susceptible by malnutrition, poorly selected or poorly prepared food and by the common gastro-intestinal disturbances resulting from errors in diet, is a conception worthy of further study."

At the conclusion of their studies, they came up with largely negative findings. They could not associate any dietary element with the disease. They found no evidence that pellagra was inherited. Their work on transmissibility yielded equivocal results. Lacking new and definitive information on the etiology of pellagra, they were nevertheless willing to state that in some way it was transmitted from a pre-existing case to nonpellagrous persons and that one of the factors in this transmission was residence in the immediate neighborhood of a pellagrin.[15]

Further evidence to support the infectiousness of pellagra was presented by Charles Davenport, who also believed in the constitutional similarity of pellagrins. In a paper published under the auspices of the Thompson-McFadden Pellagra Commission, he mentions that a woman from Spartanburg County who died of pellagra in 1894 contracted the disease after working with Italian immigrants—the inference being that the infection was brought into the United States from Italy.[16] Davenport's idea was a variant of the popular rumor blaming Italian immigrants for the pellagra epidemic. It was held by some that Italians brought in foods contaminated with a pellagra-causing fungus. Thus, it was recommended that the United States government have the food of all immigrants examined immediately on arrival from pellagrous countries.[17] That the commissioners subscribed to this viewpoint appears improbable, since it is nowhere mentioned in their reports.

Siler and his co-workers were criticized in their own time. Carl Voegtlin, a professor of pharmacology associated with the United States Public Health Service, believed that a dietary deficiency could play a role in the production of pellagra. He answered Siler in 1914:

The Thompson-McFadden Pellagra Commission asserts that pellagra is an infectious disease. The proofs advanced so far are only indirect and, therefore, not conclusive. The methods used by the Commissioner for the study of the relation of food to pellagra are defective inasmuch as they do not take into full consideration the quantity and quality of each food in the diet. It is a great mistake to make such superficial dietary studies, which often lead to false conclusions. . . . I can say that just as much weight of argument is on the side of the nutrition theory as on the side of the infection theory.[18]

Pellagra Remedies

When opinion was divided as to whether pellagra was an infection or an intoxication from moldy corn, physicians had some justification for using anti-infective drugs or treatment which might counteract the corn poison. A traditional drug used in the treatment of infections was arsenic. The widespread therapeutic use of inorganic arsenic began after Dr. Thomas Fowler's report on the cure of fevers appeared in 1786.[19] He used an alkaline solution of potassium arsenite, still called Fowler's solution. This form of arsenic was employed in the treatment of pellagra during the first two decades of the twentieth century. It was not only thought to combat the hypothetical infection, but it was also used because Lombroso considered it a valuable antidote to toxins of spoiled corn.[20] Whether its continued use was mainly the result of his teaching is open to question, because at the time it was most popular as a pellagra remedy, it was also used as the treatment of choice in other chronic diseases. Fowler's solution and arsenic bromide were used as anti-infective drugs to clear recurrent boils. Inorganic arsenic was also used to treat rheumatoid arthritis, chorea (St. Vitus' dance), and psoriasis, not only because there were advocates of an infective or toxic causation for these diseases, but also because a cure could easily be claimed.[21] Like pellagra, these diseases show periodic or seasonal remissions in their natural course, and if the arsenic was given just before the spontaneous improvement, the physician could claim he had achieved his objective.

Physicians such as Claude Lavinder and Joseph Watson, who observed pellagrins year after year, realized that arsenic did not cure the disease and were critical of its use even as a palliative.[22] Nevertheless, as new arsenic preparations became available, each was tried with initial enthusiasm. About the time pellagra was recognized in the southern states, organic arsenical compounds were being used with success in the treatment of chronic infections such as sleeping sickness and syphilis. Atoxyl (sodium amino phenyl arsenate) was used to treat patients with sleeping sickness after it had been demonstrated that the drug had a lethal effect on the isolated trypanosomes which cause this disease. Paul Ehrlich found that Atoxyl would also kill the spirochetes of syphilis in a test tube, but when he tried this drug in syphilitic patients, it was ineffective. After experimenting with a large variety of other organic arsenicals for the cure of syphilis, in 1907 he discovered that an arsenobenzene compound, No. 606, subsequently called Salvarsan, was effective as a cure for early syphilis.[23]

Atoxyl had a brief popularity in the treatment of pellagra; it is not surprising that it soon fell into disrepute because blindness was recognized as a frequent side effect.[24] Joseph Siler, who had much experience in using this drug to treat pellagrins in the Peoria State Hospital, reported, "In only one or two cases could improvement be attributed to medication." [25]

Those who thought that pellagra had an infective origin also gave courses of injections of Salvarsan, or 606, because they reasoned that if this compound could cure syphilis even when the brain was affected, it could also reverse the nervous symptoms of pellagra, which must be caused by invasive germs. In the spring of 1911, two physicians, Charles Walker and John Yarbrough of the Georgia State Sanitarium, cast doubt on the efficacy of 606 injections when they found that two of their three patients thus treated had a recurrence of symptoms during the following pellagra season. This clinical observation prompted a trial of 606 in eight other cases of pellagra in the same institution. Dr. William J. Cranston, who had followed the progress and fate of all eleven inmates, described the outcome: "Of the 11 patients given Salvarsan in 1911, two went out on furlough clinically cured, and we have not heard from them since the opening of the pellagra season. One was supposed to have been well until the nausea developed a few days ago (April 1912). As stated, this is constituted as a return of pellagra; three have relapsed and have been treated the second time; one is unimproved; four are dead. Not a very encouraging showing." [26]

Since pellagra victims were not in the habit of reading medical journals but were influenced by newspaper articles that told of miraculous cures resulting from the drug, they continued to seek one-shot or ten-shot treatments of 606 for their disease, and doctors complied with their wishes. Lavinder, much disturbed by the indiscriminate use of the drug, pointed out publicly that the treatment was not only valueless but that it was also very dangerous, producing serious side effects.[27] This warning, given in 1913, may have alerted doctors to the risks they were taking in giving organic arsenic to debilitated pellagrins, but undoubtedly the drug fell into disrepute as the cure for all pellagra because its alleged success was short-lived and because, despite the "magic bullet," the death toll rose ominously.[28]

In the years 1906–1916, there was general reliance on drugs for the treatment of pellagra; prevailing opinion was summarized by Dr. Isadore Dyer: "We are emphatic in the belief that most cases of pellagra will get well under medication, irrespective of diet." [29] Physicians purged their pellagrous patients; they injected antiseptics into their appendixes; they gave them tonics of iron, strychnine, and quinine; and they recommended transfusions of blood from recovered pellagrins as a source of antitoxin.[30] One, a Dr. David H. Yates of Madison, Florida, claimed spectacular results from a technique involving the use of static electricity. Very few questions were raised about the justification for such methods; indeed, they were acceptable and respectable because they usually had the blessings of the local medical associations or state officials. With his electrical treatments Dr. Yates claimed a curative record of 95 per cent. His renown reached Washington, where his congressman told health officials that Dr. Yates's treatment for pellagra was "simply marvellous." [31]

For thousands of impoverished pellagrins, a visit to a doctor's office was the last resort. For many, contact with the medical profession was limited to the time shortly before their demise when they were admitted to mental hospitals. Rather, they sought help from vendors of patent medicines, whose wares seemed a greater bargain than a doctor's fee. Quacks grew rich on the misfortuncs of the afflicted. Sensational pellagra remedies were sold that purported either to have been divinely inspired or guaranteed by a recognized authority in Washington. In 1911 a millworker in Belton, South Carolina, named Ezxba Dedmond began to manufacture "Ez-X-Ba River, The Stream of Life," a product said to cure pellagra in a matter of weeks. It sold for five dollars a bottle. Financed by South Carolina businessmen and with a capital stock of $100,000, the Dedmond Remedy Company flourished; within a few months, Dedmond claimed six hundred cures.

According to Elizabeth Etheridge, who found a number of newspaper clippings pertaining to Dedmond and his background, this man was a religious crank who believed he was in partnership with God. Certainly he had no hesitation about proclaiming that his cure for pellagra was formulated through personal revelation. Such was his self-confidence that he not only advertised his medicine in the South Carolina newspapers and in personally distributed pamphlets, but he actually asked Dr. Babcock to try it at the State Hospital for the Insane. This was an unwise move on his part, for shortly afterward an investigation of Dedmond's claims was undertaken, and it was found that some of his claims of so-called cures could not be substantiated. Dr. Lavinder took charge of the matter and sent samples of Ez-X-Ba to the Public Health Service's Hygienic Laboratory in Washington for analysis.

In the March 2, 1912, issue of the *Journal of the American Medical Association,* an editorial appeared entitled "Pellagracide and Ez-X-Ba: Fraudulent Nostrums Sold as Cures for Pellagra." The analysis of Dedmond's remedy, in liquid and tablet forms, was set forth. The liquid consisted essentially of a watery, slightly acid solution of iron, aluminum, magnesium, and calcium salts contaminated with a mold growth. The tablet contained similar mineral salts mixed with sugar and starch. Pellagracide, a product of the National Pellagra Remedy Company of Spartanburg, South Carolina, was like Ez-X-Ba in formulation and composition. The editors of the journal expressed their disapproval of these products and of the unethical labelling that had been used in the following comments: "How long will the United States government not only permit its afflicted citizens to be imposed on in this manner but actually aid the nostrum manufacturers by permitting the use of the 'Guaranteed under the Food and Drugs Act' in a manner to lead even the intelligent to believe that the government has some control over such 'remedies' and to afford such opportunities for the exploiters of nostrums to deceive the public?"

Dedmond did not disappear, though much less was heard of the man and his medicine until 1921, when together with other patent remedies, Ez-X-Ba enjoyed a brief second wave of popularity.[32]

Dedmond was undoubtedly the most colorful character among the quacks who sold patent medicines for pellagra. "Dr." Baughn also realized that a profit could be made from pellagra remedies. Sponsored by the banks of Jasper, Alabama, he founded the

American Compounding Company Incorporated to sell his pellagra "cure." In 1913, the Jasper newspaper carried a full-page advertisement of Baughn's Pellagra Remedy with the eye-catching headline "Spread the Glorious News! Pellagra Can Be Cured." He sold a powder for external use and capsules for internal use at ten dollars a bottle. His activities were brought to the notice of the American Medical Association by Dr. William H. Sanders, State Health Officer of Alabama, who reported that the sale of the cure in pellagra-ridden districts "was hindering the efforts of the medical profession in its campaign of sanitary enlightenment." He found that Baughn had no license to practice medicine in the state of Alabama and asked that the Association's laboratory have the "cure" analyzed. The capsules were found to contain dirt, straw particles, charcoal, iron, and quinine; the powder contained salt, iron, and sulfates also compounded with some dirt. An editorial entitled "Baughn's Pellagra Remedy: A Worthless Nostrum Sold under Fraudulent Claims," which was published in the November 15, 1913, issue of the *Journal of the American Medical Association,* asserts that the "nostrum fakers are damned. It is they who feed carrion-like, on the fears of suffering humanity. To those stricken with a well-nigh incurable disease, they hold out the hope of a sure cure." [33]

In the dirt of Baughn's remedy there was quinine, and in Dedmond's solution there was some iron, and in Yates's electrical treatment there was the stamp of authority. Contemporary medical opinion held that quinine, iron, and electrical excitation should be used in the treatment of pellagra. In 1912, George M. Niles, professor of gastroenterology and therapeutics at the Atlanta School of Medicine, suggested that iron preparations should be given for the associated anemia, quinine for the malarial complication, which he thought was often present, and iron arsenite as a "constitutional treatment." [34] While admitting that a specific treatment for pellagra had not been found, he recommended medications that in his time were appropriate for the treatment of infections. Possibly the purveyors of quack remedies had a vague idea that quinine and iron were considered good for those with pellagra. They certainly were aware that quinine and iron salts gave a bitter taste to their mixtures, which would suggest to the pellagrin that they were good medicine. As for Yates's electrical treatments, he may have taken the idea from Dr. Botho Scheube's famous book on tropical diseases published in 1900, which states dogmatically that the nervous symptoms of pellagra can be controlled by salt-water baths, massage, and electrical stimulation.[35] Electrotherapy was in vogue long after the publication of Scheube's treatise; in 1915, when Yates initiated his electrostatic treatment of pellagra, similar methods were employed by well-known physicians for the therapy of various disorders of the skin, nervous system, and intestine, whether these were believed to be infective or not.[36] Yates, then, was not guilty of malpractice. He, like his peers, was aware that pellagra was a disease of unknown origin; his treatment and theirs were directed toward the alleviation of symptoms or to making the pellagrin think he felt better.

11 | Goldberger Goes South

Two months after the publication of the second report of the Thompson-McFadden Pellagra Commission, the Surgeon-General, Rupert Blue, wrote to Joseph Goldberger, an experienced but little-known officer of the United States Public Health Service, asking him to take on the task of re-evaluating the pellagra problem. The Surgeon General's letter emphasized the fact that Goldberger was being assigned a problem which had defeated all his contemporaries. It began: "Within the past several weeks, the importance of pellagra has been urged on me by members of Congress and other prominent people from sections in which the disease prevails. It is undoubtedly one of the knottiest and most urgent problems facing the Service at the present time." [1]

Joseph Goldberger grew up in New York City's lower East Side, studied engineering for two years at the City College of New York, and then entered Bellevue Hospital Medical College. He graduated with honors in 1895, interned in Bellevue Hospital, practiced in New York City and then in Wilkes-Barre, Pennsylvania, and joined the United States Public Health Service in 1899. During the following years he performed important epidemiological studies, investigating the transmission of yellow fever by mosquitoes; of a typhus-like disease, *tabardillo,* by lice; and of an eruptive skin disease occurring in the crews of boats on the Delaware River, which he found to be caused by a mite. In each instance, his work was a synthesis of direct observation and experimentation. He not only succeeded in identifying the disease vector but also promoted the introduction of insect control, which largely eliminated these infectious diseases from the endemic areas.[2] Goldberger's studies of insect-borne disease were carried out in many different environments, so he became familiar with the problems of field research in rural as well as urban areas and knew how best to enlist the assistance of local health authorities and fight local bureaucracies.

His first report on pellagra was made in June 1914, about two and a half months after he started on the assignment. It is clear that from the outset he had the capacity to view afresh the causative factors which produced the spread of pellagra in the southern states. After he had read the documents pertaining to the incidence of the disease in mental asylums and made personal inquiries of the superintendents of these hospitals, he discovered that although pellagra was a cause for admission and also occurred in short- and long-term inmates, attendants and nurses were exempt. This seemed to him curious, since the ward personnel spent fourteen hours a day on duty, in close association with the patients, and often lived in the buildings with their charges. If pellagra was infectious, the chances that the attendants would contract the disease would have been very high. For Goldberger, this peculiar immunity of the nursing staff was inexplicable if the disease was communicable unless it was assumed that the incubation period was extremely long, perhaps ten to twenty years. That was clearly not the case, because patients would succumb a few months after admission. Looking for environmental factors which might distinguish the nurses from the patients, he found that the former had the privilege of selecting the best food in the institution and also that they could supplement their diets by buying food when they were off duty.

From a study of certain institutional dietaries, he discovered that vegetables and cereals comprised much more of the diet of patients than they did of most well-to-do people, who were not subject to pellagra. He did not believe that corn or corn products as such were essential to the production of pellagra, but rather that a preponderance of corn together with other cereals in the diet might be injurious. Hence, he urged that the hospital diets should reduce the amount of these items and increase the amount of fresh animal foods, including meats, eggs, and milk.[3]

Prevention of Pellagra in Institutions

During the summer of 1914, field studies were planned to test his hypothesis that pellagra was endemic in institutions because of the poor quality of the diet. The program was designed to show whether the incidence of the disease in these places could be reduced by dietary manipulation and supplementation. Permission was obtained to study these modalities in two orphanages in Jackson, Mississippi, and in the Georgia State Sanitarium. In one orphanage, 79 cases of pellagra had been observed in children during the spring and summer of 1914; some of these children had had pellagra on admission, and others had developed the disease after a long period of residence in the institution. In the other orphanage, located a mile away, the superintendent had records of pellagra in the children for the preceding thirteen years. In that summer of 1914, 130 cases had been observed. Hygiene and sanitary conditions in both institutions were very poor, but Goldberger requested that no attempt be made to change this state of affairs, because he wished to study the effect of diet alone on pellagra prevention.

He arranged for the diet in both orphanages to be supplemented by the United States Public Health Service. In particular, the milk supply was increased so that each child under twelve had seven ounces of milk twice a day; those under three had milk three times a day. Buttermilk was also supplied to the children, and they received an egg a day, and beans and peas at the midday meal. The breakfast cereal was changed from grits to oatmeal, and meat, instead of being served once a week, was served three or four times a week. After one year, only one case of pellagra occurred within these two institutions.[4]

In the Georgia State Sanitarium, one hundred beds were put at Goldberger's disposal. These were located in two female wards, one for black and one for white patients, to each of which approximately 40 adult pellagrins were admitted during 1914. During the experimental period, prescribed diets included seven ounces of milk per day and two cups of buttermilk. Half a pound of fresh beef and two and a half ounces of field peas or beans entered into the daily ration. Grits were replaced by oatmeal, but corn products were not entirely excluded from the diet. Patients remaining on the study were evaluated on the anniversary date after their last attack of pellagra; in a group of 36 black and 36 white patients none presented recognizable evidence of a recurrence. On the other hand, in a control group of 32 female pellagrins fed the standard hospital diet, 15 presented recurrences about a year after their last preceding attacks.

Goldberger realized the shortcomings of these experiments, particularly the small size of the control group. Knowing the tendency of pellagra to recur annually, he believed, however, that dietary measures could prevent the development of pellagra and its recurrences.[5]

Transmissibility of Pellagra

His next task was to re-examine the theory of transmissibility— a concept that in 1916 was still widely held. It was fostered by the supposed similarity between the epidemiology of pellagra and that of certain infectious diseases. In the United States, moreover, it was a fashionable idea held not only by the uninformed but also by eminent physicians who had investigated the prevalence of the disease. Thus when Goldberger sought to find the truth, he stood like David against Goliath.

He knew that the ultimate test of contagion must consist of a deliberate attempt to pass on the disease by administering secretions or excreta of pellagrins to normal human subjects. Twenty persons volunteered for the study, but for various reasons it was found practicable to utilize only sixteen, among them Goldberger and his wife. Thirteen of the subjects were physicians residing in several different localities, including Washington, D.C.; Columbia and Spartanburg, South Carolina; Milledgeville, Georgia; and New

Orleans, Louisiana. The volunteers were advised to continue their normal habits and diet and were permitted to travel freely and to attend to personal or official business. Nasopharyngeal secretions, blood, urine, and feces from seventeen cases of pellagra were given to the subjects. The secretions were applied to the lining mucosa of the nose; the scales, urine, and feces by mouth; and the blood by intramuscular injection. Excreta were mixed with flour and administered in the form of pills. Immediate side effects included diarrhea after eating the "pills" and transient pain at the site of the blood injections, but during a period of close observation lasting for a period of seven months, none of the volunteers developed pellagra. It was therefore assumed by Goldberger and his colleagues that the disease could no longer be considered infectious.[6] Proponents of the contagion theory gradually lapsed into silence. More and more people came to agree with Goldberger that pellagra was due to a dietary deficiency, though some who witnessed the acute forms of the disease in endemic areas of the South were still unconvinced.

The Rankin Farm Experiment

During 1914, while the other studies were in progress, plans were made to test the dietary association of pellagra further, to investigate whether the disease could be produced experimentally by feeding the pellagrins' diet to previously healthy people. Goldberger made arrangements with the authorities in charge of the Mississippi State Penitentiary to study this problem using as subjects convicts who were under detention at the Rankin Farm colony. Permission was given for him to obtain volunteers from the "farm" population and to feed them experimental diets for a period not exceeding six months, with the understanding that at the end of that time the men would be given pardons and freed. Twelve men, who became known as the Pellagra Squad, were segregated and placed under special guard in order that they might be kept under close scrutiny. None of these men had ever had pellagra. They were on a special diet from April 19, 1915, until October 31, 1915. The ingredients were white wheat flour, corn meal, hominy grits, cornstarch, white rice, granulated cane sugar, cane sirup, sweet potatoes, pork fat, cabbage, collard greens, turnips, turnip greens, and coffee. During the period of the study, thirty-five convicts at the same institution were kept under observation but were fed their accustomed diet supplied by the "farm" kitchen.

Eleven members of the Pellagra Squad remained on the special diet for the complete study period; of these, seven developed distinctive skin lesions. Actually, the observed skin changes, beginning on the scrotum, suggest that, at least in some of the subjects, the diet-induced nutritional deficiency was primarily in riboflavin, the lack of which is now known to cause such lesions. Goldberger was, however, convinced that the early skin changes that occurred in these seven men, as well as the symptoms of ill-health—including weight loss, weakness, abdominal discomfort, and headache—that were described in all the volunteers were symptoms of pellagra. In retrospect, it appears that the experimentally induced pellagra in the group must have been limited to those men who late in the study developed a more characteristic pellagrous dermatosis with symmetrical redness, peeling, and pigmentation of light-exposed areas of skin. The control group showed no evidence of pellagra.

Goldberger thought that the test diet lacked some essential protein component, probably an amino acid, and that it might also be deficient in a vitamin—concepts that could not then be proved but that were later found to be close to the truth. He was cautious in making claims that the experiment conducted in the penal colony reproduced the situation occurring in endemic pellagra, both because the diets of pellagrins and the prisoners were somewhat different, and because environmental variables in the naturally occurring and induced diseases were obviously present.[7]

Community Studies

In the succeeding years, Goldberger sought to define the social and economic problems which induced the spread of pellagra. He selected seven cotton-mill villages grouped near the city of Spartan-burg, and through observations made in the homes of the mill operatives, he was able to study several separate but interdependent variables. He wanted to know whether pellagra was in any way related to the type of house in which the pellagrins lived, whether the people were infested, whether adequate hygiene or toilet arrangements really had any effect on pellagra incidence. He compared the incomes of pellagrins and nonpellagrous working people. It was soon evident that pellagra could not be associated with the hygiene of the home or with sewage disposal, nor was it related to the presence or absence of infestation. There was, how-ever, an inverse relationship between the incidence of pellagra and the income of those with the disease.

Looking at the different cotton-mill villages, Goldberger noted that in some there was a very low incidence of the disease, while in others the incidence was much higher. He therefore made an intensive study of the two villages that showed the greatest differ-ence in morbidity. In these two, he looked at various economic and social factors which might condition the problem. Insight and a knowledge of previous occurrences of pellagra in Italy, France, and Egypt led him to look first at the availability of foods to the cotton-mill operatives and their dependents. In the village where pellagra was least frequent, he found that although the villagers who were employed at the mill obtained their basic supplies from a commissary operated by the factory owner, they also had access to certain fresh foods which were sold at an independent grocery on the edge of town. They bought corn meal, soap, and coffee from the mill, but in addition, a little fresh meat and occasionally milk and a few eggs from this store. Fresh vegetables and fruit were purchased from an itinerant vendor who came to the village about once a week.

This situation was in contrast to that in another village, where pellagra was very prevalent. In the latter, the workers and their families were entirely dependent upon the company-owned store at the mill for their food supplies. The village market, which had sold fresh meat to mill operatives either for cash or on credit until January 1, 1916, had fallen on hard times, probably through poor management. Therefore, during January and February of 1916 it was open for trade only one or two days a week, and credit was extended only to households that had been prompt in making payments. In the latter part of February the market closed; the only way for the villagers to obtain fresh meat was to go to a small town at least a mile away where meat was sold for cash only, so that only a very few people could afford it. During the spring of 1916 there were no regular sellers of farm produce, and hucksters rarely appeared bringing milk, eggs, butter, or vegetables, because it was more profitable for them to sell their wares in the local town.

Differences in the supplies of home-grown vegetables in the two villages were found to be due to differences in the relative availability of plots of land suitable for cultivation. In the village where pellagra was common, very little space was to be found for raising produce, and indeed many dwellings had no room at all for a garden, whereas the other village had good-sized plots. Although neither community produced many good garden crops, because the households were employed for very long hours at the mills, the consumption of peas, green onions, and "greens" was somewhat higher in the village where pellagra was rare.

Goldberger and his colleagues concluded that differences in the incidence of pellagra among households of the same income were attributable to differences in the proportion of family income spent on food, and especially to differences in the availability of food supplies from such sources as markets and traveling vendors.[8] The economist Edgar Sydenstricker played a major role in developing these field studies. As a result of that experience he maintained a lasting interest in community health. In his book *Health and Environment,* published in 1933, he recalled those days of 1916 when he saw the wretched conditions in the cotton-mill villages:

The inverse correlation between income and pellagra incidence was unmistakable. Family income was an important factor, since it determined the extent to which the foods containing the pellagra-preventing essential could be purchased, especially in industrial communities where the entire population were on the margin of subsistence. But income was not the only economic factor involved in pellagra. The availability of food supplies, and the various conditions determining the nature, variety and amount of food supplies were equally important factors.[9]

At last the crucial social problem of pellagra had been delineated: this was not only a disease of the poor and of those who lived on corn, but it was a deficiency disease which developed because certain groups of people were unable to raise or purchase those items of diet which would maintain them in health.

12 | Blacktongue

In the quest for the cause of pellagra, Goldberger as well as others of his generation, realized the limitations imposed by the utilization of man as the experimental subject. Should one deliberately induce pellagra? Should one withhold treatment in order to carry out a particular experiment? While these ethical considerations probably influenced Goldberger's determination to return to the laboratory after 1916, there were other reasons for his decision to use experimental animals in his pellagra research. Some of his human studies were not accepted by his contemporaries. His wife, Mary Farrar Goldberger, recalled that after the now classical prison experiment, her husband "was badgered with verbal brickbats and harangued by the doctors." A noted Atlanta physician spoke of "Goldberger's half-baked experiments." She recalled that "Dr. McNeal, a professor of medicine at Columbia University," accused him at a meeting of the alumni at Bellevue, which he had been asked to address, of "faking the prison experiment." There, among his colleagues and as a graduate of Bellevue Medical School, he answered: "I do not wish to get in a controversy with Dr. McNeal. I shall rest on my published works on pellagra." Again, he wrote on November 25, 1915: "The blind, selfish, jealous, prejudiced asses will write themselves down in more conspicuous letters by braying forth their so-called criticisms." [1]

In her reminiscences, Goldberger's wife was not entirely accurate about her husband's most vigorous opponent. The "Dr. McNeal, a professor of medicine at Columbia University," was none other than Ward MacNeal, director of laboratories at the New York Post-Graduate Medical School, who had long been associated with the Thompson-McFadden Pellagra Commission. He attacked Goldberger, not only at a meeting of the alumni at Bellevue, but also in print. In a brief communication to the *Journal of the American Medical Association* for March 25, 1916, he expressed his doubts about the production of pellagra in the Rankin Farm volunteers: "The claim that pellagra has been produced by a restricted diet should be regarded with suspicion and it would be well for those who have not yet acquired a knowledge of this disease by personal observation or by a somewhat comprehensive study of the literature to retain an open mind concerning the essential factors in its causation." He thought it very doubtful that any of the convicts acquired pellagra from being fed the "unbalanced" diet, and he questioned Goldberger's motives for not demonstrating these cases at the 1915 meeting of the National Association for the Study of Pellagra, held in Columbia, South Carolina.[2]

We know that Goldberger was not daunted by disbelief; on the contrary, he thrived on it. In order to explain his need for experimental animal models for the disease, we have to turn to scientific rationale. Knowing that maize diets caused pellagra and that certain foods prevented it, he wanted to find out what the pellagra-preventing factor is in these foods.

Luckily, Goldberger, with his penchant for detailed justification of his work, has furnished us with the background of his search for pellagra in animals. He was interested in obtaining an experimental animal from the very start of his research on pellagra. Let us read his account of the preliminary animal work:

With the beginning of our investigations of pellagra, early in 1914, thought was given to the need for an experimental animal. Accordingly, at our suggestion, Surgeon Edward Francis, United States Public Health Service, beginning December 1, 1914, carried out a feeding experiment in six rhesus monkeys at the United States Marine Hospital, Savannah, Georgia. The diet fed those monkeys consisted of hominy grits, 900 grams; rutabaga turnips, dressed 3.6 kilograms;

sodium chloride, 11 grams; sirup (a commerical can and corn compound), 565 grams. The feeding was carried on for eight months—that
is to July 31, 1915. Doctor Francis reported that the animals remained
healthy, showing no change other than some loss of weight.

The possibility that the dog might serve our purpose first struck us
in 1915, on reading in Chittenden's "The Nutrition of Man" among
other things the following, ". . . A dog transferred suddenly from a
daily ration in which meat and milk are conspicuous elements to a
diet in which these are wholly wanting is very liable to show disturbing
symptoms almost immediately." [3]

Goldberger then quoted Russell Chittenden's account of how he
watched malnutrition develop in a dog when it was fed bread and
lard alone instead of a mixture with meat and milk and of how
it recovered when meat and milk were again supplied in the ration. The poor diet made the animal's mouth sore and the dog developed bloody diarrhea. Chittenden went on: "This is by no
means an exceptional case, but we can cite many other examples
of like results where the animal when restricted to a purely vegetable diet, such as bread, pea soup, bean soup etc., reinforced with
an animal fat, quickly passed from a condition of health into a
state of utter wretchedness, with serious gastrointestinal disturbance." [4]

Goldberger thought that the inflammation of the dog's mouth
and the accompanying gastrointestinal disturbance were reminiscent
of pellagra and that the resemblance was enhanced by the curative
effects of animal protein foods. At the first opportunity, which
came late in the summer of 1916, Goldberger, in association with
Dr. Atherton Seidell, tried to repeat Chittenden's experiment on
dogs with a bread and lard diet but without significant results. He
had no time to pursue the matter further until the summer of 1918,
because he was fully occupied with the field work. Then, during a
period when he had a little respite from his community studies, he
familiarized himself with all the literature pertaining to deficiency
diseases in dogs.[5]

A pellagra-like condition had already been produced in dogs

by Dr. Chittenden and Dr. Frank Underhill of the Sheffield Laboratory of Physiological Chemistry at Yale University. In a paper
published in August 1917, they described how they fed dogs a diet
of boiled dried peas, cracker meal, and cottonseed oil, thus causing
the rapid development of a state of malnutrition. The condition
was described as follows:

The onset of the pathological symptoms is generally very sudden.
Usually the first abnormal manifestation is a refusal to eat, and
examination will reveal nothing to account for the loss of appetite.
The animal lies quietly in its pen and is apathetic. After continued
refusal to eat for a day or two, the mouth of the dog will present a
peculiar and characteristic appearance. The inner surface of the cheeks
and lips and the edges of the tongue are so covered with pustules as to
give the impression of rotten flesh. The odor from these tissues is foul
and almost unbearable. When stroked with absorbent cotton the
mucous lining of the mouth comes away in shreds. Intense salivation is
present. The teeth appear to be solid and normal. A bloody diarrhea
is present, attempts at defecation being very frequent and resulting
in the passage of little more than a bloody fluid or foul odor. In some
cases, the thorax and the upper part of the abdomen may contain
many pustules half an inch in diameter which are filled with pus
organisms. No other skin lesions are prominent. Death usually results
without any particularly striking features.
    . . . At autopsy two types of conditions are recognizable: In the
animals presenting foul mouth and bloody diarrhea the chief interest
centers in the lower bowel and rectum, which exhibit an intense
hemorrhagic appearance. With those animals dying rapidly from convulsions the only visible abnormality of the alimentary tract is the
presence in the duodenum of one or more large ulcers.[6]

Goldberger was much interested in this report. He soon realized
that there was a striking similarity between Chittenden and Underhill's pellagra-like syndrome in dogs and the condition known to
American veterinarians as blacktongue. Blacktongue was first described by Hofer of Munich as *Typhus der Hunde* ("typhoid of
dogs"). He mentioned among the symptoms an abrupt onset,

vomiting, retching, and loss of appetite. The mucous membrane lining the mouth was described as either dirty red or yellow, and an evil-smelling saliva drooled from the corners of the mouth. In pernicious cases there was a bloody rectal discharge. Post mortem, Hofer found congestion of the gastric and intestinal mucosa, with ulceration scattered throughout the digestive tract.[7]

In 1899, Klett, knowing of Hofer's observation, made an extensive study of the condition during an outbreak in Stuttgart. Klett's clinical observations can be summarized as follows: The onset is very abrupt, with vomiting, followed by loss of appetite and thirst. The dog is indifferent to his surroundings, and his strength is diminished. The lining of the dog's mouth and throat is brownish or dark red, with erosions and pustules. The mucosa of the tongue is similarly altered. In advanced cases, the mucosa of the mouth, throat, and tongue is covered with a thick chocolate-colored coating. The mouth invariably gives off an extremely foul odor. Constipation and constipated stools are the rule, but in some cases there is uncontrollable diarrhea of a bloody character. The conjunctiva of the eye is invariably red. The temperature is normal. In some cases convulsions may occur.[8]

American writers confirmed these observations. They reported certain variations in the disease, especially cases in which the dogs' tongues showed a purplish discoloration and other instances in which vomiting, persistent diarrhea, and an elevated temperature were manifested. In 1921, George A. Wheeler and Goldberger conducted autopsies on two dogs with blacktongue that died in Spartanburg, South Carolina. In the paper describing these animals, they commented that the disease had generally been considered infectious, even though "the results of the recorded experimental attempts at transmission from sick to well dogs had not lent much support to the conception that the disease is an infection." Although at this time Goldberger and his colleague were very cautious about asserting that blacktongue in dogs is analogous to human pellagra, their report includes references to veterinarians and physicians who had previously noted the similarity of the two conditions.[9] The first of these was a man called Spencer, of Concord, North Carolina, who in 1916, after studying both these maladies, stated that he was "forced to the conclusion that the so-called blacktongue is canine pellagra." [10]

Four years later, C. A. Cary of Auburn, Alabama, recognizing the resemblance of blacktongue to the experimental condition reported by Chittenden and Underhill, classed blacktongue among the deficiency diseases and again referred to the similarity of the manifestations of "sore mouth" in dogs to those of pellagra in man.[11] The same year, Dr. Marshall B. Saunders of Waco, Texas, suggested that there might be a causative relationship between "sore mouths of dogs" and the human disease. Goldberger was particularly interested in Saunders' reminiscences, which read like a pocket diary:

Some five years ago I bought a very fine dog in New Jersey and brought him to Texas. The second year in Texas he died with what the veterinarian pronounced "sore mouth." Now, a dog dying with sore mouth was as novel to me as was a man dying from pellagra. I noticed that my dog was losing hair from his front legs (paws). In commenting on the cause of my dog's death with my friends I find that it is a relatively common disease, and that there is a large strip of country east of town on a branch called the Tehuacana, where they cannot have dogs, as they all die of sore mouth. Now this strip of country has furnished some 40 or 50 pellagrins to the nearby doctors for treatment. The question is, how much the dog plays in the etiology, or are they both, man and dog, infected from the same source, or is sore mouth a different disease and is it a coincidence that they are found here side by side? [12]

Apparently, Goldberger must also have discussed the problem of "sore mouth" with southern veterinarians, because in his publication of 1922 on the autopsy findings in the two cases of blacktongue he remarks: "Blacktongue seems to have a geographical distribution in the United States singularly like pellagra. Seemingly it occurs principally, if not exclusively, in the South. Seasonally it is reported to occur most frequently in summer and autumn and to affect cur dogs less than those of higher grade. There is some evidence that it may occur more than once in the same animal." [13]

In the following year, Goldberger had an unusual opportunity to see a case of blacktongue and to find out how pedigreed dogs in the South succumbed to this disease. On Friday, September 7, 1923, a black and tan foxhound belonging to a Mr. A. J. Collins, who lived near the Georgia State Sanitarium, fell sick about noon. With fourteen other hunting dogs, this animal had that morning participated in a fox hunt. After the fox had been dispatched, the fifteen dogs were carried home in a motor truck. Collins told Goldberger that on reaching home, he offered his dog some food and that its attempts to take this were so bizarre as to suggest that there was something the matter with its mouth. On examination, he found its mouth to be "sore." The next day he cleansed the dog's mouth with hydrogen peroxide, and again on the following day. On the morning of the fourth day (September 10), he administered a dose of about four ounces of castor oil, and in the afternoon he gave the animal some eggs. The dog had been without food since the day on which the soreness of the mouth was discovered. At about 7:00 P.M. on Tuesday, September 11, the fifth day of the dog's illness, Collins asked Goldberger and his colleague, Dr. William F. Tanner of the United States Public Health Service, as well as Dr. Ernest B. Saye, the pathologist at the Georgia State Sanitarium, to come and see the sick animal. Goldberger records, "At that time the animal was lying down in the yard of the Collins home, evidently very sick, for she made no attempt to rise at our approach—just wagged the tail very feebly." That the dog had all the clinical signs of blacktongue was obvious. The next day, when they saw the dog again, it was unconscious, evidently dying; it died at about 11:30 A.M. Necropsy, which was performed on the afternoon of September 12 showed that, as anticipated, the dog had every sign of advanced blacktongue.

Of interest is the story of the dog's diet as told to Goldberger by its owner. The usual food of this animal had consisted of table

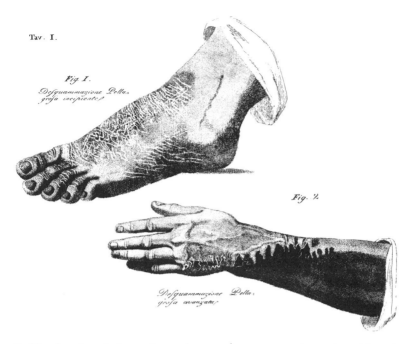

I. The hand and foot of a polenta eater. From Vincenzio Chiarugi, *Saggio di ricerche sulla pellagra* (Florence: Allegrini, 1814).

II. Roussel's moldy corn. From Kentucky Agricultural Experiment Station Bulletin 159 (Lexington, 1912).

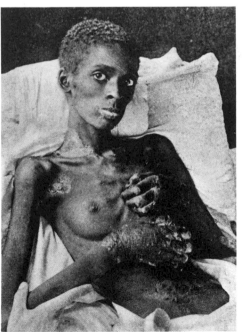

III. A Kentucky family with three pellagrins observed by the entomologist Harrison Garman. The second, third, and fifth persons from the left were shown to him as cases of pellagra contracted from bites of the buffalo gnat. From Kentucky Agricultural Experiment Station Bulletin 159 (Lexington, 1912).

IV. A pellagrin from South Carolina. From A. Marie, *Pellagra* (Columbia, S.C., State Co., 1910).

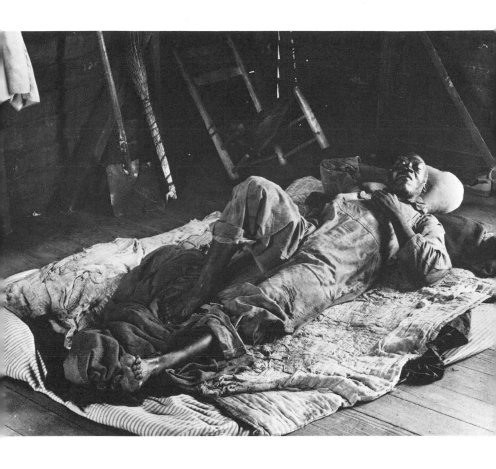

V. A dying pellagrin. From a photograph entitled "Mathews, Georgia," in Erskine Caldwell and Margaret Bourke-White, *You Have Seen Their Faces* (New York: Viking Press, 1937). Courtesy of Time-Life Syndication Service.

VI. The sharecropper's lot: a wretched cottage, a few corn plants, and a luxurious growth of cotton, a plant that cannot be eaten. From a photograph entitled "Marion Junction, Alabama," in Erskine Caldwell and Margaret Bourke-White, *You Have Seen Their Faces* (New York: Viking Press, 1937). Courtesy of Time-Life Syndication Service.

VII. A case of acute pellagra, Mwanza, Tanganyika (Tanzania), 1965. Courtesy of Michael C. Latham.

scraps, including a little meat two or three times a week. Late in July 1923, in order to prepare the animal for the hunt, he reduced the allowance of the ordinary diet by about half, making up for the difference with corn bread. In this way, he hoped to reduce the animal's weight and so enable her to run better in the chase. This, he explained to Goldberger, was in accordance with the current practice of hunting men in that region. Collins also volunteered the information that a year before he had done the same thing to the diet of this animal and that she had become sick in the same way, but the attack was milder and she recovered. Furthermore, at the time the dog sickened a year before, he had been keeping another dog in the same yard, but fearing infection, he separated the two. After keeping the other dog in isolation for about a month, and finding it quite well, he took it a few miles away to a trainer, where after about four weeks the animal fell sick with what was believed to be blacktongue and died. Collins was of the opinion that the trainer had fed this dog principally, if not exclusively, on corn bread. For Goldberger, the story that the dying dogs had been fed corn bread was the vital link between blacktongue and endemic pellagra.[14]

This was not the first time that an experimental animal model for a human disease was discovered through the realization that animals and human beings had eaten the same food and that similar illnesses had followed. In 1897, Christiaan Eijkman published observations on "an illness in fowls similar to beriberi." Eijkman, who was then the physician of a Netherlands East Indies prison, saw these hens pecking away at the leftovers from the inmates' diet and developing stiffness and weakness in their legs similar to what he saw in his beriberi patients. At that time he postulated that the disease was caused by a toxin in polished rice, which was the principal constituent of the prisoners' diet.[15] In 1901, his associate, Dr. Gerrit Grijns, suggested after working with the birds, that the disorder resulted from a lack of something in polished rice. From this idea the concept that beriberi was a deficiency disease began to develop. Subsequently, these two men working together found that it was possible to cure the disease in birds by adding discarded rice polishings to their diet.[16]

In a similar manner, Goldberger and his colleagues came to realize, not only that canine blacktongue was the counterpart of pellagra, but also that the disease in dogs could be used in the intensive study of the food factor which might prevent and cure both maladies. Their experimental feeding of dogs was resumed about the middle of January 1923 and was continued until 1928, when they published their findings in a series of papers which appeared, as did most of their other writings, in Treasury Department public health reports issued weekly by the United States Public Health Service. The first important series of investigations made it clear that a pathological condition could be induced in a dog by feeding either a type of diet that had been observed in association with endemic pellagra or one that had been previously found by experimental tests on human volunteers to be pellagra-producing. The diet-induced disease was indistinguishable from blacktongue. The investigators thought it highly probable that it was also identical with the Chittenden-Underhill pellagra-like syndrome. They were especially interested to find that in the male dogs in which blacktongue was produced a dermatitis of the external genitalia appeared which they believed was very like the skin lesions of pellagra.[17]

Before Goldberger and his co-workers succeeded in producing blacktongue by dietary means, they failed in more than one attempt. The different outcome of the last experiment, they suspected, was due to apparently small changes made in the animal diets. The pellagra-producing diet contained no milk and no yeast, whereas the earlier unsuccessful diet included small amounts of both. From their human studies and also from their experience of blacktongue, the Goldberger group already had reason to believe that milk possessed pellagra-preventive properties, but as the amount of milk in the previous test diets was very small, it seemed to them improbable that their failure to produce pellagra was attributable to the milk. Although they had no real suspicion that some element in yeast could be the pellagra-preventing factor, they thought that yeast rather than milk had probably prevented the induction of blacktongue in their unsuccessful studies. Reasoning in this way, they decided to test their hypothesis. In the investigations that followed, they compared the effects of their basic black-tongue-producing diet, containing mainly corn meal, to which were added cowpeas, milk protein, sugar, cottonseed oil, cod-liver oil, and a salt mixture, with a similar diet supplemented with yeast. They also compared various modifications of these two diets. Soon it became clear that yeast, ordinary dried brewers' yeast, could prevent blacktongue. Further experiments showed that the component of the yeast that prevented blacktongue was inactivated by heat sufficient to char the yeast, but was still active after autoclaving. It could not be identified with any of the older well-recognized dietary essentials but was believed to be identical with a heat-stable factor that had previously been described by two other writers.[18]

The finding that yeast, or rather an isolate of yeast, could prevent blacktongue, as it was soon found to prevent pellagra, stimulated Goldberger to evaluate the preventive properties of a wide variety of foods. Sixteen foodstuffs were studied for their black-tongue-preventive action, and the results were correlated with the pellagra-preventive action of the same foods. The concluding sentences of Goldberger's report on these studies convey the message derived from this research:

So far as they have been studied, the foodstuffs that appeared to be good sources of the blacktongue preventive also appear to be good sources of the pellagra preventive; those that appear to be poor sources of or lacking in, the blacktongue preventive likewise appear to be poor sources of, or lacking in the pellagra preventive.

Considering the available evidence as a whole, it would seem highly probable, if not certain, that experimental blacktongue and pellagra are essentially identical conditions and thus that the preventive of blacktongue is identical with the pellagra preventive, or factor P-P.

On the basis of the indications afforded by the test in the dog, liver, salmon and egg yolk are recommended for use in the treatment and prevention of pellagra in the human.[19]

The finding that liver contained the blacktongue-preventive factor soon prompted Goldberger to get in touch with Dr. George R. Minot of the Harvard Medical School who had recently discovered that the feeding of large amounts of raw liver had a very beneficial effect in pernicious anemia.[20] Minot and his colleagues also showed, in 1928, the year in which Goldberger was carrying out his major blacktongue experiments, that extracts of liver could be prepared which had the same effect on pernicious anemia as portions of whole liver.[21] Evidence was, however, presented by Minot's group that the pellagra- or blacktongue-preventive factor present in yeast and in liver was not responsible for the effectiveness of liver against pernicious anemia.[22] Through an introduction from Minot, Goldberger obtained a supply of Minot's liver extract No. 343 from Eli Lilly and Company. This extract had been tested and had proved potent in the prevention and treatment of pernicious anemia. Goldberger found that when given to dogs on a basic blacktongue-producing diet in a daily dose equivalent to a hundred grams of fresh liver, it had a very definite delaying effect on the occurrence of symptoms; when fed to dogs during an attack of blacktongue, it had a curative effect. He assumed that the most reasonable explanation was that the liver extract contained the antiblacktongue vitamin. Furthermore, he believed that Minot's liver extract was a fairly good source of the antipellagra vitamin and that given in a larger amount, it would be of value as a temporary expedient in the treatment of pellagra.[23]

The investigations of Minot's liver extract were the last that were conducted under Goldberger's direction. He died of cancer of the kidney in 1929 before the report on the work was published.[24] His discovery that liver extracts and yeast were both effective in curing blacktongue in dogs was soon applied to the treatment of pellagra. In 1929, the average mortality of pellagra cases in the United States was 33 per cent. According to Virgil Sydenstricker, this figure reflected the extreme deterioration of patients considered ill enough for hospitalization.[25] High-protein diets were the vogue, but loss of appetite, nausea, and psychotic delusions made it impossible to partake of such a diet adequately. Patients would vomit to relieve the burning pain in their throats induced by bulky food or would bring up the meals that were force-fed by stomach tube. Death from dehydration was common. Yeast and liver extracts administered orally reduced the mortality rate to 25 per cent, but it was still very difficult to induce patients to keep these sources of the antipellagra vitamin down. Injectable liver extracts did not prove to be effective as a cure for pellagra in the amounts used. The situation was still bad for the dying pellagrin.

Only the pellagrins who could still retain nourishment benefited from the yeast treatment that was given free to hospital outpatients. The liver extracts were too expensive to be given away, and few had enough money to pay for them. In 1930, there were probably more than 200,000 pellagrins in this country—a sad reflection indeed for the team who had worked with Goldberger and had sought to find a cure, using canine blacktongue as their model. Nevertheless, their contribution to the ultimate conquest of the disease should not be underestimated, because blacktongue continued to be the testing ground for all variants of the pellagra-preventing factor and from the yeast and liver extracts the hidden vitamin was finally isolated.

13 | Niacin Is Discovered

Following the investigations of blacktongue in dogs, it had become apparent that the pellagra-preventing factor was a heat-stable, water- and alcohol-soluble vitamin present in liver and yeast. The identification of this vitamin was the result of investigations carried out in a number of laboratories in Germany and in the United States between 1934 and 1937.

In 1935, two biochemists, Conrad A. Elvehjem and Carl J. Koehn of the Department of Agricultural Chemistry at the University of Wisconsin, reported that during the previous year they had found that diet-induced pellagra in chicks could be cured by giving the young birds a filtrate factor obtained from a liver extract.[1] Realizing that the disorder, produced in the chicks by feeding a heat-treated natural grain ration, was not strictly analogous either to human pellagra or to blacktongue, these workers decided to repeat their experiments, using dogs in which blacktongue had been induced by feeding the Goldberger diet of yellow corn, casein, cottonseed oil, and mineral supplements. They gave the dogs either a liver extract, which was known to contain fluorescent yellow compounds called flavins, or the same filtrate extract they had given the chicks. The latter, which they now designated the vitamin G fraction, after Goldberger, cured the blacktongue, while the flavin moiety, from which the vitamin riboflavin had been isolated, had no effect on the progress of the disease.[2] In the following year Elvehjem and his colleagues worked hard to purify the vitamin G fraction and to isolate and identify the active principle. While they

120

were busy with these experiments, Dr. C. E. Graham of the Wilson Laboratories sent them several liver fractions which were by-products in the manufacture of an anti–pernicious-anemia factor. One of these fractions was extracted with 92 per cent alcohol, and the resultant solution was irradiated with ultraviolet light to destroy the flavins. After this treatment, the fraction was effective in inducing growth in rats on a diet of white corn, casein from skim milk, butterfat, and a malt sugar. The chemical properties of this fraction were similar to those of the pyridine nucleotides, which play an essential role as enzyme catalysts in tissue metabolism.[3] In 1934, Otto Warburg and Walter Christian, working in Germany, had shown that nicotinamide is a part of these nucleotides, which can be obtained from red blood cells.[4] Shortly afterward, others showed that nicotinamide can be isolated from the same nucleotides prepared from yeast.[5]

Elvehjem's group decided to extract their liver preparations by using the method Warburg had used with red cells. In time they were able to identify a pyridine nucleotide in the liver extract, but they were unable to separate nicotinamide—a failure they believed was due to the presence of interfering substances in their concentrates. Undeterred, they proceeded to resume earlier work on nicotinamide and its effects on vitamin-G–deficient rats that had not been successful. They realized that the failure was due to the small doses of nicotinamide given. By increasing the dose, they were able to stimulate growth in rats on a corn-containing, vitamin-G–deficient diet; they could also achieve the same results by giving the related compound nicotinic acid.[6]

The question arose: Was nicotinic acid or nicotinamide the pellagra-preventing factor? This, of course, could not be determined by using laboratory rats, because pellagra cannot be induced in these animals, but it could be investigated in dogs. A dog showing all the symptoms of blacktongue was given a single dose of thirty milligrams of nicotinic acid, obtained by Elvehjem from the Eastman Kodak Company. This simple treatment produced a phenomenal result. The dog's appetite improved in a very short time, the mouth lesions disappeared in less than two days, and the growth response was very similar to that obtained with active liver concentrates. The experiment was repeated in a number of other dogs with blacktongue, and the effects of giving nicotinic acid by the oral and the intramuscular routes were compared. A few dogs with the pellagra-like disease were given nicotinamide. All these modalities were found to be successful in effecting a cure. The results presented by Elvehjem demonstrated conclusively that both nicotinic acid and nicotinamide were active in the cure and prevention of canine blacktongue. He further realized that the activity of liver extracts in curing blacktongue was directly related to their nicotinamide content.[7]

The knowledge that nicotinic acid was as active as nicotinamide in the treatment of blacktongue prompted investigators to look into the literature to learn the history of this compound and how it had been used in the past. A derivative of nicotinic acid, trigonelline, had been isolated as early as 1885 by Jahns in Germany.[8] Nicotinic acid itself had been isolated from naturally occurring materials, including yeast and rice polishings, in 1912.[9] The following year, Casimir Funk extracted nicotinic acid from what he called the "vitamine fraction" of yeast and rice polishings, and about the same time he also isolated from lime juice a compound he thought was a derivative of nicotinic acid.[10] He fed various combinations of yeast, the vitamin fraction from yeast or nicotinic acid, plus other yeast extractives to pigeons in which beriberi had been induced by keeping them on a diet of polished rice; he cured them. From these experiments, he concluded that for the cure of beriberi two substances were required: nicotinic acid and another compound which he isolated from yeast and rice husks. Here he was in error, because as was subsequently found, nicotinic acid is not required in the treatment of beriberi, whereas vitamin B_1, or thiamin, which Funk unknowingly obtained from his yeast and rice sources, is the missing vitamin in this disease. What is more interesting is that, in 1912, Funk suggested that pellagra might be a deficiency disease caused by the lack of a "vitamine" in maize.[11] Unfortunately, he did not know that the "vitamine" deficiency in pellagra was due to a lack of nicotinic acid. Funk nevertheless played a very significant role in the story of pellagra. He first coined the term "vitamine" to designate known or unknown food factors needed in small amounts to prevent the occurrence of nutritional diseases; he found out that vitamins were contained in yeast as well as in other food sources; he isolated nicotinic acid; and he had a profound influence on Goldberger, who came to believe that the P-P (pellagra-preventive) factor might be a vitamin.

Let us return to the 1930's and see how Elvehjem's discovery of the curative role of nicotinic acid and nicotinamide in blacktongue was applied to the treatment of endemic pellagra.

Paul J. Fouts and some co-workers published a brief report on the treatment of four pellagrins with this drug in 1937, very shortly after Elvehjem's work had been completed. The reason they were first was that two of Fouts's colleagues, Samuel Lepkowsky and Thomas H. Jukes, had carried out experiments similar to those of Elvehjem's group, and news came to them rapidly when Elvehjem announced that he had obtained 175 milligrams of nicotinamide from 10 kilograms of fresh liver. Incidentally, Fouts and his co-workers noted that skin lesions in their patients healed more quickly following the giving of nicotinic acid than after the feeding of liver extract.[12] It might be inferred that for a while after the vitamin was discovered, its utilization in the treatment of pellagra was the prerogative of a few physicians in major medical centers in the Middle West: those men who had easy access to supplies.

Another very dramatic cure of pellagra with nicotinic acid was reported in 1937. A white farmer was admitted to the hospital of the Duke University School of Medicine in 1937 with a fifteen-year history of recurrent pellagra. During a preliminary control period, the patient was given a diet deficient in the pellagra-preventing factor—a diet, indeed, similar to the one he had before he came into the hospital. He would not eat, became worse, and developed delusions of persecution. Nicotinic acid was administered, sixty milligrams daily by injection, but the diet was unchanged. The response was amazing. His appetite improved within twenty-four hours, and within forty-eight hours his mental condition improved; the patient became rational within six days. The skin symptoms improved within three days and were cured within twelve days.[13]

Also during 1937, Leslie Harris, reporting to the Birmingham University Biological Society in England, not only described the successful treatment of "monkey pellagra" with nicotinic acid, but also reported that a Dr. A. Hassan had treated five pellagrins in Cairo by this method. Two pellagrins in an asylum and three in a prison were given the vitamin by mouth in doses of up to three hundred milligrams per day. Their diet, exercise, and exposure to sunlight remained as they were before the trial. Three untreated control cases were observed in the prison. In the asylum cases the redness of the exposed skin subsided and the general condition of the patients improved, while in the prison cases the beneficial effect of nicotinic acid was restricted to an improvement in the condition of the skin. Harris and apparently Hassan, too, interpreted the difference to mean that nicotinic-acid deficiency is not the only major deficiency in diet-induced pellagra; they based their conclusions on the theory that the different effect of nicotinic acid on the two patient groups was owing to variations in food intake: the asylum diet contained more meat, greens and wheat bread than the prison diet.[14]

Tom Spies and his group, writing of their experiences in 1938, explained that they used nicotinic acid in the treatment of pellagra because they knew that pellagra in human beings and blacktongue in dogs were closely related diseases and because they realized that all food substances that had been curative and preventive of the one had been for the other also. Spies was cautious: In his first experience with nicotinic acid, he administered small doses to thirteen people, including three staff members in the Department of Internal Medicine at the hospital of the University of Cincinnati College of Medicine. Ten nonpellagrous patients were given a watery solution of nicotinic acid supplied by the Eastman Kodak Company. The dose varied from a few milligrams to two hundred per day. The patients and other subjects noted flushing and tingling of the skin but no serious side effects. No adverse reactions were encountered after single doses of nicotinic acid were given intravenously. After it was established that nicotinic acid was well tolerated by a small group of healthy subjects and by a few nonpellagrous patients, a little group of pellagrins was selected to receive the drug. Among those chosen were two with endemic pellagra, three whose pellagra was believed to be secondary to alcoholism, and six whose pellagra was secondary to organic disease.

The dosage of nicotinic acid and the route of administration were quite variable. Oral doses were supplemented by injections. The highest total dosage was five hundred milligrams per day. No food rich in the pellagra-preventing factor was given. Healing of lesions of the mucuous membranes was accepted as an index of efficacy, because five of the patients had pellagra *sine* pellagra; that is, they originally had no skin involvement. Lesions of the mucous membranes, including the red, raw inflammation of the tongue, mouth, vagina, and anal canal, healed promptly after the onset of treatment. Pellagrous dermatitis, complicated by secondary infection, did not improve. Three pellagrins died in spite of being given nicotinic acid: a male alcoholic aged thirty-eight, a woman aged sixty-five who was dying of endemic pellagra at the time of admission to the hospital, and a woman aged thirty-seven who was suffering from very severe general malnutrition following bowel surgery.[15]

The early trials of nicotinic acid in the treatment of pellagra, important though they were, did not have much news coverage. Indeed, the *New York Times* in 1937 made no mention of them. In 1938, however, this paper had no less than seven articles on pellagra; six referred to the use of nicotinic acid, and one of these described a program for sending nicotinic acid to Loyalist Spain. A very interesting editorial appeared in the "Sunday Review" section of the *Times* on June 19, 1938. The writer, reporting on the meetings of the American Medical Association that summer, commented: "The issue of State Controlled medicine so dominated the proceedings of the AMA that little attention was generally paid to scientific papers. These were of the usual varying merit, ranging as they did from the discussion of effects of politics on the intestinal tract to the relation of hormones to the determination of sex. One paper which must be regarded as a milestone was presented by Drs. Tom D. Spies, William Bennett Bean, and Robert F. Stone.[16] It left no doubt that pellagra has been conquered by means of nicotinic acid and its compounds." To Elvehjem and his associates the columnist gave the credit for identifying the curative factor as nicotinic acid, and referred to its cure of blacktongue. Dr. Spies and his co-workers, he continued, had conducted "the most far-reaching experiments," which indicated "the possibility of tiding the poor population of the south over those seasons of the year when milk, eggs, fresh meat and green vegetables are scarce."

What this success means, the statistics proclaim eloquently enough. So far as the United States Public Health Service can determine 400,000 people succumb to pellagra in this country every year—an underestimate. If the diet is not corrected the death rate is as high as 69 per cent. Worse still the mind is affected. Fully 10 per cent of the inmates of our institutions for the mentally afflicted suffer from pellagra.

To restore the victims to health of body and mind by adding to the proper food doses of a cheap chemical seems miraculous. The work that has been done by Dr. Spies and his associates . . . leaves no doubt that an ailment which has baffled medicine for centuries has at last been relegated to the curable diseases and that American Medicine has to its credit a triumph comparable with the conquest of yellow fever.

The accolade given Elvehjem, Spies, and their fellow workers by the *Times* columnist was justified.[17] Success had crowned their scientific efforts: here was life in a vial for the pellagrin and his vulnerable family. A man could now live as a sharecropper, subsist on corn, retain his cabin, his meal ticket, and all the trappings of the traditional pellagrin, yet perhaps be exempt from the disease.

We have spoken of nicotinic acid. What then is niacin? The

late Leonard Maynard, who participated in the discussions which led to the commercial and scientific use of "niacin" as a synonym for "nicotinic acid," explained to me the derivation of the term. In 1941, during negotiations about the enrichment of bread during the national emergency, members of the Food and Nutrition Board of the United States and representatives of the baking industry discussed the terminology to be used in labeling and in publicity about the bread additives, including vitamins. The bakers voiced some concern that if the term "nicotinic acid" was used, the public would immediately associate the name with nicotine, which might influence them against buying the new enriched product. The executive committee of the Food and Nutrition Board chose Elvehjem and a small subcommittee of the board to propose synonyms for "nicotinic acid," one of which might be selected. They offered "niacin," "niamin," and "niacid." [18] On February 14, 1942, the term "niacin" was adopted by the executive committee as a synonym for "nicotinic acid," and "niacinamide" as a synonym for "nicotinamide." At that time it was suggested that the new names be reserved for use in any circumstances in which the public might be involved and that the original names continue to be used in scientific literature. As it has turned out, the synonyms as well as the old names "nicotinic acid" and "nicotinamide" have been used in the United States, both in labeling and in scientific publications.

14 | The Conquest of Pellagra

United States

In an account of the rise and fall of pellagra in the southern United States, Dr. Jack Davies pointed out the seemingly paradoxical fact that pellagra, the disease classically associated with ignorance, poverty, and malnutrition, declined most dramatically between 1930 and 1933, when economic circumstances were at their worst. In 1930, the United States was in the grip of the most severe economic, industrial, and agricultural depression it had ever known. In the South, however, the Depression had a peculiar and relatively happy effect on the impoverished farmer and farm laborer. The whole economy of the southern states had been based on cotton; ever since the Civil War, the South had been more or less an economically bankrupt area. A sharecropping system was general. Tenant farmers mortgaged their prospective crop yields; if crops failed or prices fell, they could not repay the loans. As we have learned from Goldberger, wages were low and food prices high. Cotton operatives bought their provisions from factory commissaries. These supplies consisted mainly of corn and corn products. Food stores could carry only a narrow range of provisions, because the local population could not afford to buy good food, and the shopkeepers had no wish to stock items they would be unlikely to sell.[1]

In spite of all that Goldberger had done, the pellagra situation deteriorated steadily during the 1920's. The incidence of reported cases was greatest during 1929 and 1930. Between 1932 and 1934,

128

however, the number of cases fell, and mortality also declined. Davies is of the opinion that this improvement in the pellagra situation can be accounted for by the work of the agricultural extension service. Established in 1902 with the aim of improving farming practices, it was first instrumental in transmitting Goldberger's views on the cause of the disease to local people. Then in the Depression, when cotton became virtually unsalable, men from the extension service encouraged the destruction of cotton crops in the fields and the reduction of cotton acreage. They persuaded the southern farmers to use their land to grow produce, instead, which would feed their own families. Since at that time cash crops had no sale, the farmers were willing to listen to the advice of the extension service agents, and the number of small productive farms grew. The cultivation of soybeans, peanuts, field peas, and of citrus and other fruits increased, and these crops as well as garden vegetables were used for home consumption.[2] As Davies says, "This departure from the cash crop monoculture led to the sudden decline in pellagra." The decline of the disease in the South did not, however, continue after the mid-thirties, because as basic economic conditions improved, the traditional sharecropping system was not abandoned.

In 1937, Erskine Caldwell and Margaret Bourke-White, the distinguished photographer, published a book about their visit to the deep South the previous year. *You Have Seen Their Faces* gives documentary evidence of the plight of the poor white sharecroppers and the downtrodden blacks of the area at that time. An extraordinary series of photographs shows starving people and multiple evidences of malnutrition, including goiter due to iodine deficiency and pellagra in young and old alike. Here one can see cotton growing up to the very doors of the cabins, hungry children picking at empty plates, grandma squatting down to prepare the inevitable corn bread, and the dying pellagrin in his filthy hovel. Caldwell comments on the situation in cotton states:

The sharecropping system has in recent years branched out into several forms, none of them more economically sound than the source from which they sprang, and most of them working greater hardships on human lives than the plantation system ever did. Sharecropping has deprived millions of persons of what the rest of America considers the necessities of life . . . , wringing dry the bodies of men, women and children; dragging down to its own level from higher economic planes new numbers to take the place of those crushed and thrown aside; breeding families of eight, ten, twelve, fourteen, sixteen and more, in order to furnish an ever-increasing number of persons necessary to supply the rent—cotten for the landlord.

It is foolish to ask a tenant farmer why he remains where he is. . . . Such a question is usually asked for the purpose of covering up an inability to suggest what the farmer could do to lift himself from the hole he stands in. There is cotton to be raised, and he has trained himself to raise it. That is his specialty. It is his life, and if share-cropping continues as an institution, it will become his death.

How sharecropping operated at that time to the peculiar disadvantage of the laborer is epitomized in Caldwell's description of Sanford, a forty-seven-year-old cotton farmer of Emanuel County, Georgia, who had been sharecropping since the age of twenty. The ten persons living in his home ate corn bread and molasses three times a day. The twenty-acre farm was worked on shares. The landlord furnished a mule, half the fertilizer, and half the seed for corn and cotton. Sanford had been without a cow for six years. He planted cotton, cultivated it, and picked it, working every day during the season from dawn to dusk. The last crop, an average one, produced three bales of cotton on twelve acres. After giving half to the landlord, Sanford had 640 pounds of lint left. Selling the ginned cotton for 10¼ cents a pound, he received in cash $65.60 for his crop. The only other money he acquired during the year was his share of the government's benefit payment, $4.88. "As long as the land was fertile enough to produce a living, Sanford was able to make a living. Now the land is eroded and washed thin, Sanford himself is almost broke in health and spirit and he has become resentfully outspoken. . . . It is the last cry of a man defeated by sharecropping."

The overriding despair of the sharecroppers claimed the first attention of Caldwell, but he also realized that the rigid caste system, which placed the poor whites in an inferior social position, had decreased these people's desire to gain economic freedom.

Most tenant farmers are content to work as field hands and sharecroppers, providing they receive a living wage for their labor, and much prefer not to have the responsibility of land ownership. No provision has been made for these workers. . . . They are the men and women who work for from fifty cents to a dollar a day, from three to six months a year and who are forced to live in a dwelling detrimental to health, to wear insufficient clothing in cold weather and to exist on an insufficient quantity and variety of food. These are the people who develop pellagra, and who use snuff to deaden the desire for food.[3]

Why pellagra persisted and why it continued as a major problem in the southern states after the cause had been discovered in 1937 were explained by Virgil Sydenstricker as the result of long neglect. "With nicotinic acid available and quite cheap," he remarked, "it may seem strange that the elimination of endemic pellagra required about five years more (in the United States)." Yeast was plentiful and cheap; it was furnished free by the American Red Cross and by state and county health and welfare agencies, yet the disease increased during the yeast era, because the problem of prevention could not be solved. The ignorance and inertia of that part of the population which succumbed to pellagra did not provide the whole answer. Poor food habits, economic stress, and the enormous backlog of chronic malnutrition were more important. In 1940, there were still more than two thousand reported deaths, in spite of all the effort, educational and therapeutic, put forth by organizations and agencies.

It is apparent that there were two phases in the decline and eradication of pellagra in the United States, one dependent on the improvement in food habits which ultimately was linked to public concern with the needs of economically deprived people. Sydenstricker, commenting on the final phase of pellagra control, pointed out that the Second World War, however costly in lives, could be thanked for the conquest of pellagra in the United States. The great increase in employment and the mobilization of the armed forces provided almost everyone with an adequate income. Rationing inspired even the most backward to eat high-protein foods to which they had not previously aspired.[4]

The war years, from 1941 to 1945, brought about another desirable change that definitely influenced the final demise of endemic pellagra in this country: the enrichment of bread and other cereals with B vitamins. In other words, the nutrients that are removed from grains by milling were put back. In 1939, the Council on Foods of the American Medical Association began discussions about the possibility of improving the health of the public by addition of nutrients to foods.[5] In 1940, the Food and Nutrition Board of the National Research Council endorsed the concept of the fortification of flour and bread with natural and synthetic nutrients.[6] The following year, the so-called enrichment program was inaugurated as a defense measure.[7] This was done with the object of improving the health of the nation. Since 1873, when steam-driven roller flour mills were introduced,[8] the American people had used a uniform degerminated white flour which was inferior nutritionally to the whole-wheat gristmilled product of earlier times. By May 1941, about 30 per cent of the white bread and flour in the United States was being enriched with yeast voluntarily by bakers and millers. By late 1942, 80 per cent of cereal products were being enriched. Niacin, thiamin, and iron were used in enrichment from 1941 onward, and riboflavin was added as soon as it became available. In some of the southern states, legislation also called for the enrichment of corn meal and grits. In January 1943, the enrichment-of-bread program of the Food and Nutrition Board was aided by a war order making the fortification of bread throughout the nation mandatory.[9] The war years saw niacin brought to every man's table; even the most vulnerable population groups could ward off pellagra with the staff of life. Pellagra was wiped out in the United States, as it had been in France about eighty years before, by government action prompted by the demands of medical men and nutritionists and effected by millers and bakers who had been indifferent to the needs of hungry people.

After the Second World War, very few bakers returned to the old habit of producing bread that was unfortified.[10] Furthermore, the Food and Drug Administration set standards for the minimum and maximum amounts permissible of each of the enriching nutrients.[11] In 1953, the American Institute of Baking estimated that 85 per cent of all the bread sold in the United States was enriched.[12]

Not only was the fortification of bread responsible for the disappearance of pellagra among sharecroppers and factory hands, but there is strong evidence that this measure also contributed largely to the decrease in vitamin deficiencies among alcoholics and derelicts. In a study of alcoholics from Chicago's "skid row" and in the House of Correction of the City of Chicago, carried out between June 1948 and July 1949, William Figueroa and his co-workers screened 16,000 inmates for evidence of classical nutritional-deficiency disease. The same investigators studied 451 newly admitted inmates during the height of the "pellagra season." To their surprise, they found only two men ill with pellagra. Diet histories showed that the whole group had been subsisting on bread, coffee, doughnuts, occasional sandwiches or spaghetti, and a very little stew or hash. By virtue of large alcoholic consumption, the caloric intake of these men was high, but it was calculated that the protein intake was low, averaging thirty grams per day. No difference could be seen between the gross food intake of these down-and-outs and that of other groups of alcoholics studied before the war, among whom pellagra had been rife. A change in nutrient intake had, however, occurred: the Chicago men got B vitamins from the fresh or stale bread they habitually consumed. They had thus escaped pellagra and could live to die of liver failure.[13]

No claim is made that the fortification of bread has brought about a social revolution, but it has had a marked effect on the nutritional status of the economically deprived people in this country.[14] It has been a major factor in making pellagra a rare disease. We may wonder whether the outcry of the "ecology"-minded young who disapprove of synthetic vitamins and extol the virtues of "natural foods" may be serving the best interests of the community at large. Granted that whole-meal bread and other cereals may provide a reasonably good supply of B vitamins, including niacin, it must still be emphasized that in the last thirty years those who cannot afford to live on "health foods" have been made healthier, not because of a major change in dietary habits, but because of a careful program of adding nutrients to the most common and the cheapest articles of diet.

Italy

Twenty years ago, when I was visiting the dermatology clinic at the University of Pavia, Dr. Ferdinando Serri, my guide, asked me if I wanted to see a case of pellagra. He brought in a prematurely old woman, clothed in old-fashioned black garments, who bore the classical traits of the disease on her skin. It was springtime, and the sun was shining brightly, leading the few remaining polenta eaters to seek medical advice for their recurring malady. No longer was pellagra a commonplace disease in the area. Here was a case to show foreign visitors; I was having a demonstration of a condition which persisted only among the people of the backwoods, who through a combination of ignorance and poverty continued to follow their traditional food customs. The wheel had come full circle, and it was as if I were Dr. Thiéry visiting Casal and viewing a rare disease I had seldom seen before.

Fifty years after the enactment of the law to control pellagra, it had virtually disappeared from northern Italy. I was not innocent enough to believe that this change was due to a law. Rather, the mezzadria system had died out, the tenant farmer had gained independence, and the poor could for the most part "inherit the earth."

15 | Pellagra Revisited

Long before pellagra was known to be a vitamin-deficiency disease, an inadequate intake of protein from animal sources was believed to be a contributory cause. Indeed, some of the early writers were of the opinion that continued subsistence on a cereal diet led to pellagra, not because of any specific property of the cereal itself, but because no animal or protein food was consumed. This aspect of the problem was studied intensively by William Hawkins Wilson, a colleague of Sandwith at the medical school and the Kasr el Ainy Hospital in Cairo.[1] Wilson's concentration on the protein factor seems to have stemmed from a more general interest in protein nutrition. He followed in the tradition of Karl Thomas, whose dictum was that the minimum requirement of protein varies according to the variety of protein. Thomas' work, first published in 1909, introduced the concept of the "biological value" of individual proteins, by which he meant the comparative estimates of the ability of a particular protein source to maintain nitrogen balance in man. Comparing other common foodstuffs with milk, Thomas awarded the following biological values: milk 100, beef 104, rice 88, potatoes 79, pulse 55, wheat 39, and maize 29.[2]

Wilson used a similar system for computing the minimum protein intake necessary for an average man, given that the protein came from an animal source, from legumes, from one of the cereal grains. On the basis of such calculations, he came to the conclusion that a man would need more than three times as much maize as meat. Furthermore, he realized that the minimal values given for different protein sources were only tenable if the diet had a high energy value: "It will thus be seen that a subsistence diet in which a certain amount of animal protein is given may be sufficient to maintain health with a low calorie value, while a subsistence diet of the same calorie value, derived entirely or very largely from vegetable sources, might be quite unable to do so." He also understood that the adequacy of a protein ration would depend upon a person's activity and that, for instance, the Egyptian convict at hard labor would require more protein from his maize than one on detention.

Not only did Wilson realize that proteins differed in their nutritional efficacy, but from his reading of contemporary sources, he knew that this was because the proteins varied in composition. In explaining his own work, he said, "There can be little doubt that the cause of the discrepancy in the biological value of proteins from different sources is the well-known difference in the proportion of the various amino-acids which compose the protein molecule, some of which appear to be more essential than others in the maintenance of health and growth." [3] Zein, the chief protein of maize, had been investigated by Thomas Burr Osborne and Lafayette Mendel, who had found that it was impossible to maintain animals in a state of health on a diet in which this was the only protein source.[4] Wilson was definitely impressed by this work, as also by the finding of Frederick Gowland Hopkins and Edith Willcock that when tryptophan, an amino-acid, was added to a zein diet, its value was markedly improved.[5]

A distinguished nutritionist of our own day, William Darby, has suggested that Wilson's views influenced Sandwith to state in 1913:

Proteins are absolutely necessary for the continuance of life. . . . If they are not present in the diet in proper proportions the tissues feed on themselves. . . . Of the protein decomposition products the amino acids are predominantly the important class. Among the products is the necessary tryptophane. . . . Now tryptophane is present in nearly all proteins but has been shown to be entirely absent from zein which is the protein of maize. . . . It has been found by physiologists that tryptophane must be given pure to animals, because the animals have no power of synthesizing the necessary tryptophane.[6]

Wilson's concern with pellagra was stimulated by his experience in World War I. On September 13–14, 1915, there arrived at Port Said from Antioch, in Syria, 4058 debilitated Armenian refugees who had survived forty-five days of fighting with the Turks. By the beginning of the following year there was an outbreak of sore mouth and diarrhea among these refugees, followed by classical pellagrous dermatitis. During 1916, a total of 639 cases of pellagra was recorded. At this time, Wilson intervened. He proposed dietary improvements, notably the provision of milk and fresh protein foods. Fortunately, the authorities followed his recommendations, and in 1917 there were only 14 cases of pellagra in the camp of the Armenian refugees. The analyses of the diets involved in this experience served as one of Wilson's arguments for the validity of his theory that escape from pellagra depended on the protein quality of the diet.[7]

During 1916 and 1917, a large number of cases of pellagra developed among Ottoman prisoners of war interned at Kantara, Egypt. An Egyptian pellagra commission was appointed to investigate. Wilson was among its eight members. These men were particularly concerned with the question of whether the disease was either a bacterial or a protozoal infection. None of their studies, however, supported the concept that pellagra in the prisoners was an infectious process. Rather, they concluded that there was a constant association between the lack of good-quality protein in the diet and the occurrence of pellagra.[8]

These findings induced Wilson to study the composition of pellagra-producing diets more closely, with particular emphasis on their protein and tryptophan content. He studied the effect of diet on pellagra observed among the inmates of the Abbassia Asylum for the Insane in Cairo.[9] In treating these pellagrins, he added 45 grams of meat and 50 grams of milk to a diet which already contained 100 grams of meat, 50 grams of milk, and 300 grams of fresh vegetables. This dietary modification had a markedly beneficial effect, causing a reduction in the incidence of pellagra among the inmates. Reporting on this feeding regimen, Wilson stated that it was difficult for him to suppose that the additions could have made any great contribution to the vitamin or mineral content of the patients' diet. He believed that the original diet might have been insufficient for the pellagrins because they could not assimilate the ordinary food to the normal extent. He reckoned that, owing to the digestive disturbances associated with pellagra, much of the dietary protein was lost in the patients' stools in the form of a breakdown product, indican, which we know is derived from tryptophan.[10]

It is apparent that Wilson was aware of a constant problem of the pellagrin: his limited ability to absorb nutrients, because of the destruction of the lining mucosa of the small intestine. This concept, which was new in 1921 when the report was published, has since influenced thinking about the pathology of endemic pellagra and has also provided a rational explanation of secondary pellagra caused by malabsorption. In fact, we now know that there are children born with a diminished capacity to absorb tryptophan, that these children excrete large amounts of indican in their urine, and that they get a pellagra-like rash whenever they go out in the sun.

Wilson had an active correspondence with Goldberger, and he encouraged Goldberger and his associate, Dr. Tanner, to try the effect of tryptophan in a case of pellagra. Tanner commented on this trial: "The improvement in this patient's condition has surpassed anything I have ever seen in a case of pellagra in an equal period of time." [11] At that time, Goldberger was much intrigued with the idea that an amino-acid deficiency was characteristic of pellagra. He had read a paper by two British nutritionists, Harriette Chick and Eleanor Hume, in which the authors described the production of symptoms resembling pellagra in three monkeys that had been fed for a long time on a low protein diet. Such protein as there was in the monkey's diet was obtained largely from maize.[12] Goldberger was critical of the fact that Chick and her co-worker thought that the monkeys had developed pellagra, because the illustrations of the skin lesions produced in the monkeys did not suggest to him a true pellagrous eruption of the kind seen in man. He was, however, interested in the fact that the monkeys' condition improved when they were given tryptophan. He commented: "That some of the symptoms observed in these monkeys may have been due to an amino acid deficiency in the experimental diet seems not improbable, and the improvement reported as having been observed in two of the three animals treated with tryptophan would suggest that a deficiency in at least this one amino acid was involved in the cause of the malnutrition observed in these animals." [13]

In the course of studies of the prevention of pellagra which Goldberger and Tanner conducted at the Georgia State Sanitarium during 1920, they separately evaluated the effects of mineral and vitamin supplements. The mineral supplement contained calcium, sodium, magnesium, iron, and potassium salts; the vitamin supplement included cod-liver oil, cowpeas, and tomato juice as sources of vitamins A, B, and C. Their patients had all had at least one attack of pellagra. Neither the minerals nor the vitamin sources prevented recurrence. Believing that the diets were adequate in energy value and that with the supplements they contained all the necessary nutrients, Goldberger was led to the conclusion that, of the known dietary essentials, an inadequate protein intake was the most likely cause of their failure to prevent pellagra. In their discussion of this matter, the investigators point out that the quality as well as the quantity of dietary protein must be important in the prevention of pellagra, but they are cautious about asserting that pellagra is due to a specific vitamin deficiency, since they would have had only very meager experimental support for such a thesis.[14]

Subsequently, Goldberger turned from his focus on the protein factor and concentrated his energies on the P-P factor and its effects on dogs and men. The vitamin theory took over, and for many years the influence of protein or amino-acid intake on pellagra was either forgotten or put in abeyance. Grace Goldsmith, in the Joseph Goldberger Lecture in Clinical Nutrition in 1965 at a convention of the American Medical Association, gave an account of the course of events when she described how her own interest in pellagra was stimulated:

Our interest in niacin began in the early 1940's after this vitamin had been shown to be the anti-pellagra factor and when methods were being developed to assay some of the urinary excretion products of niacin metabolism. At this time, it was thought that the problem of the etiology of pellagra had been solved completely. However, further studies uncovered findings that could not be explained satisfactorily. Diets in some parts of the world in which pellagra was not encountered contained less niacin than did corn diets which were associated with pellagra. Furthermore, certain pellagra-preventive foods, such as milk, were low in niacin. Investigations at the University of Wisconsin assisted in solving the problem.[15]

These investigations were initiated by Dr. Willard Krehl and his associates. They observed that when young rats were fed diets consisting 40 per cent of corn, there was a cessation of growth. Administration of either niacin or tryptophan restored growth to normal. Their rationale for giving tryptophan was the same as Wilson's: one of the proteins in corn, zein, is low in this amino acid.[16] Very shortly afterward, another group headed by Fred Rosen found that when they gave tryptophan to rats, the animals excreted a large amount of a breakdown product of niacin in their urine.[17] Grace Goldsmith then administered tryptophan to normal human subjects and discovered that the same niacin metabolite (N-methylnicotinamide) was excreted in quantities exceeding those found in the urine prior to the giving of this amino acid.[18]

In 1949, Richard Vilter and his colleagues, John Mueller and William Bean, of the Department of Internal Medicine of the University of Cincinnati Medical School, reported the effects of tryptophan on the acute and chronic manifestations of pellagra. They found that large amounts of tryptophan were effective in the treatment of pellagra. They had two pellagrous patients. The first, a black woman aged thirty, gave a rather unreliable diet history but admitted that she was addicted to alcohol; she had severe acute pellagra. The second patient was a sixty-two-year-old black laborer who said that his appetite was good and that once or twice a day he ate a stew composed of ham skins, ham fat, potatoes, onions, celery, and cabbage. He also drank at least one quart of "D-rail" (denatured alcohol) per day. Although he showed pellagrous skin lesions, his general condition was fairly good. Both patients were placed on diets low in vitamin B complex and vitamin C, and two grams of tryptophan were given three times per day. The first case showed rapid improvement, with clearing of both skin and mucosal lesions. Similarly, in the second case the pellagrous dermatitis healed. The tryptophan was also found to cause an increased excretion of the niacin metabolite in the urine, but the increase was less than that which had been found previously in normal persons.[19]

This clinical study and the rat experiments that preceded it gave the clue to the interrelationship between tryptophan and niacin: tryptophan could be converted in the animal or human body to niacin. This conversion was proved unequivocally in a series of rat experiments involving the use of radioisotopes.[20] Also, data obtained in human subjects by Grace Goldsmith and by Max K. Horwitt showed an average conversion of about sixty milligrams of tryptophan to one of niacin.[21] The end of the road in pellagra research appeared to be near. As Grace Goldsmith herself wrote: "Two centuries after pellagra first was described by Casal in Spain, this disease was shown to be due to deficiency of a vitamin niacin, and its precursor, the amino acid tryptophan." [22]

16 | "H" Families and Other Conundrums

Hartnup's Disease

The idea that a hereditable trait could predispose people to pellagra gained great popularity during Roussel's lifetime; as we have seen, medical men continued to believe this until Goldberger came on the scene. Since then, it has been definitely established that endemic pellagra is caused by a diet-induced nutritional deficiency, by a lack of niacin and its precursor tryptophan, and that it can be cured by replacement treatment. No evidence has come to light that the common form of the disease is influenced by genetic factors. The stories of the occurrence of pellagra in several members of a family have been easily explained by the fact that affected individuals in such households subsisted on the same inadequate diet featuring corn and corn products.

In 1951, when a child with a pellagra-like disease was seen by a group of doctors in London, the medical fraternity was astonished, not only because pellagra was very rare in England and unknown in its endemic form, but more because there was a family history of the condition. During May 1951, a certain Mrs. Hartnup wrote to request an outpatient appointment for her twelve-year-old son at the Middlesex Hospital. She said that his symptoms were those of pellagra and that she knew the diagnosis because her eldest daughter had been treated for this complaint in 1937. At the interview, Mrs. Hartnup related that the boy had had a rash on the exposed areas of his face, neck, hands, and legs for

142

the past three years, which was worse in the spring and summer. She also said that he had been "tottering like an old man" since the beginning of the year and that his hands were shaky. His gait was unsteady, and he tended to fall over, especially toward the right. He had been somewhat backward in his physical development, had been a slow learner, and exhibited the social behavior of a younger child. When he was examined, it was found that he had a red scaly eruption on the skin areas enumerated by the mother and that in addition he had clinical signs of a disorder of the cerebellum: tremors, a poor sense of balance, and double vision.

He was admitted to the hospital for observation and study. During this time his rash got better, while his nervous signs varied from day to day. After his discharge his illness became worse, with progressive unsteadiness in walking and the development of emotional problems including an uncontrollable temper. He became dull and lost his previous interest in reading. In about a year he lost fifteen pounds. In early June of 1952, he sun-bathed for about an hour and a half one afternoon. Afterward the light-exposed areas of his skin became very red and raw; the condition persisted for two weeks before it cleared. In August, he was re-admitted to the hospital, where he suffered from a peculiar illness characterized by jerking movements of the limbs, loss of appetite, diarrhea, and severe depression. All his symptoms were made worse by an intercurrent infection from which he made a slow recovery. In the succeeding three years, he had several other stays in the hospital, each time with a recrudescence of symptoms, and each time the nervous signs, the rash, and the diarrhea cleared up or at least improved when he was given nicotinamide.

This boy's sister, who at the age of six had been under the care of Dr. Alan Moncrieff, presented similar problems, only in her case progressive mental deterioration had been much more serious. At times she had severe behavioral problems and attacks of fainting, and at times she became stuporous and incontinent. As in the case of her brother, exacerbations of her illness, particularly the intermittent rash which appeared on exposure to sunlight, were relieved by nicotinic acid (niacin) and nicotinamide. Before these became available, she was improved while she took large amounts of yeast extract (Marmite) and a crude liver preparation.

When this girl was first seen, a straightforward diagnosis of pellagra was made, and no laboratory studies were performed which might have cast doubt on this diagnosis. It was not until exhaustive studies were carried out on her brother that the physicians in charge of the boy began to realize they were dealing with an inborn error of metabolism. Dr. Denis Baron and his colleagues who looked after the boy at the Middlesex Hospital were first of all puzzled by the clinical course of his illness, which though it bore certain resemblances to pellagra, had some notable differences. His diet history was not that of a typical pellagrin. His symptoms were atypical in many respects, especially his loss of balance and other features referable to a disturbance of the cerebellum, which had not been reported in true pellagra. When they examined his urine, they found that he excreted a number of abnormal substances, including tryptophan and degradation products of tryptophan, which it was known were formed by the action of intestinal bacteria. The urine also contained large amounts of amino acids, which would not normally escape from the body by this route. These urinary changes were subsequently found in the sister and also in two other siblings who did not present the clinical features of the disease.

In all, there were eight children in the family, four of whom, including the boy and girl already described, had a low I.Q. and a history of progressive mental deterioration. Three of the mentally defective members of the family showed grossly abnormal urinary components. In their extensive report of this family, published in 1956, the authors, who had a clear grasp of the genetic background of what they then called the "H" disease, commented, "Our gropings so far have led us to wonder whether the primary gene action may assert itself as a disorder of tryptophan metabolism whereby a metabolic block exists somewhere along the pathway from tryptophan to nicotinic acid." Later in their discussion, they suggested an alternate hypothesis which, as will be seen, turned out to be closer to the truth: "It must still be borne in mind however that the opposite situation is equally plausible—a primary disorder of amino-acid transport processes leading to the development of an abnormal gut flora which distorts the normal sequence of nicotinic acid utilization." [1]

For several years the genesis of "H," or Hartnup's, disease remained an unsolved riddle. Several other families were described in which one or more children had the combination of a periodic pellagra-like skin rash, unsteadiness, emotional instability, and progressive mental impairment. Diarrhea was an inconstant symptom. One of the most characteristic features of these children, which indeed persisted into adult life, was the periodicity of symptoms.[2] Dr. John Jepson and Dr. Mary Spiro, writing about the Hartnup disease in 1960, remarked that of the precipitating factors most likely to induce acute attacks, the most constant was poor nutrition. They tried to explain this provocation of the disease as a result of factors of diet composition by suggesting that there might be a variation with age or stress in the requirement for some nutrient which is in limited supply in a particular person because of a biochemical abnormality. This limiting nutrient might be niacin.[3]

At this time, Malcolm Milne and the group working with him demonstrated a defect in the intestinal transport of tryptophan in Hartnup's-disease children, by showing that when tryptophan was given by mouth, normal peak blood levels for amino-acid loading were not achieved, and also that tryptophan could be found in the stools.[4] Current views on the cause of Hartnup's disease are based on Milne's findings. In this malady the transport of amino acids into cells is defective. The defect involves the cells of the kidney tubules and of the jejunum, the major absorptive area of the small intestine.

Tryptophan is not the only amino acid that is improperly absorbed in Hartnup's disease, but there is ample evidence that certain of the cardinal features of the syndrome result from a conditioned niacin deficiency, that is, a niacin deficiency caused by the loss of the precursor tryptophan. Several of the symptoms, including the photosensitivity, the diarrhea, and some of the neurological features respond to high-dosage niacin replacement treatment. Other symptoms, including the unsteadiness and the tremors, respond poorly or not at all. Perhaps all is not yet known about the consequences of this transport defect.

Retrospectively, it is interesting to consider whether any of the early cases of pellagra believed to be due to a hereditary trait could have been cases of Hartnup's disease. Most of the descriptions of hereditary pellagra in the literature are too vague for us even to hazard a guess. Furthermore, the number of European claims that pellagrins had inherited the disease far exceeds the probability of the incidence of Hartnup's disease in any one population during the nineteenth century. Of greater importance is the fact that pellagroid syndromes can occur as the result of defects in the absorption and utilization of niacin and its precursor tryptophan.

Drug-induced Pellagra

As we have seen, endemic pellagra is for all intents and purposes a diet-induced disease, but other factors, such as malabsorption and conditions conferring an increased requirement for niacin, can predispose people to pellagra.[5] In recent times, a new factor has entered the picture—that of drug intake, which may interfere with the metabolism of niacin. A case in point is the occurrence of pellagra in tuberculous patients who have been treated with a pharmaceutical agent known as isoniazid (INH). This drug was introduced as an antituberculous agent in the early 1950's.[6] Peripheral neuritis and disorders of the central nervous system resulting from the toxic effects of this drug have been amply described,[7] as have skin lesions developed during its use.[8] A review of reactions to INH, published in 1963, states that when the daily dosage of the drug did not exceed 300 milligrams, side effects occurred in 1 to 2 per cent of the patients, but that when the daily dose exceeded 900 milligrams, adverse reactions occurred in 30 to 40 per cent. These figures, however, refer to all forms of toxicity, of which objective skin changes form only a small proportion.[9] Itching without skin eruptions is rather frequent in people receiving the drug for the treatment of tuberculosis and has also been described as occurring among factory employees, nurses, and hospital aides who prepare or handle the medication.[10] Frank pellagra, or a pellagra-like skin eruption, has been seen in persons with tuberculosis who were also debilitated by the effects of the disease or from the combined effects of the disease and a poor diet.[11] It has been suggested that these people already had a borderline deficiency of niacin. P. A. DiLorenzo attempted to explain the drug-induced pellagra as the result of the competitive inhibition of structurally related compounds; niacin and INH have a similar chemical formula. His alternate thesis is more acceptable: INH interferes with the conversion of tryptophan to niacin because it acts as an antagonist to vitamin B_6 (pyridoxine), which is a necessary coenzyme in this reaction.[12]

An excellent paper by P. S. Shankar, head of the Department of Medicine at the Gulbarga Medical College in India, gives reliable evidence that nowadays INH may play a substantial role in precipitating the development of endemic pellagra in undernourished people. He tells of fifty cases of pellagra seen during a period of one year, of whom 90 per cent described their diet as consisting of thin cakes of jowar (millet) flour with small amounts of dal (bean paste), a chutney of chilies, and occasional vegetables. Of these individuals, 76 per cent did not consume any milk, and 70 per cent did not take any wheat preparations. The condition was prevalent in people from rural areas who earned their livelihood as agricultural laborers. Their financial condition did not permit them to buy protein-rich foods. Ten percent of the patients had a coexisting tuberculosis for which they were receiving INH, so the author assumed that the drug may have been the final straw which caused them to become pellagrins. The paper indicates that two other patients had leprosy, for which INH may also have been prescribed. Fortunately, nicotinamide does not interfere with the antituberculous effects of INH, and it will cure drug-induced or drug-associated pellagra.[13] It would be advisable to give ill-fed tuberculosis cases supplementary nicotinamide as well as a high-protein diet to avoid the risk of pellagra. (In this context, it has been suggested that some people on long-term INH treatment may be more susceptible to niacin deficiency than others because they have a lowered ability to excrete the drug, owing to an inborn metabolic difficulty.)

Pellagra in Millet Eaters

Readers who have become accustomed to the often repeated statement that endemic pellagra is a disease of corn-eating people may have noticed that this disease has been seen in people who live on another type of cereal, namely millet. Sandwith noted this occurrence in Egypt in 1898;[14] it has come to public attention in more recent times through the observations of Dr. Coluthur Gopalan and his co-workers in Hyderabad, as well as in the report of Shankar. Gopalan, writing in 1969, stated that pellagra is often seen in the poorer communities of the Deccan Plateau of India. In Hyderabad, nearly 1 per cent of the admissions to general hospitals and in certain seasons 8 to 10 per cent of admissions to mental hospitals are victims of pellagra. The staple cereal of these patients is not corn but jowar, the same type of millet that Shankar found his people consumed. Indeed, in a large series of cases, 65 per cent ate no corn, and the remaining 35 per cent ate very little corn.[15]

Gopalan has shown that the niacin content of jowar is close to that of rice, and rice eaters never get pellagra. From Gopalan's experiments and calculations it would seem that jowar may contain an adequate amount of tryptophan to meet the daily requirement—assuming that little or none of this amino acid is obtained in the daily diet from other sources. One factor has been found in both jowar and maize: the high content of another amino acid, leucine, which has been shown to retard growth in laboratory rats when they are fed a low-protein diet. The poor inhabitants of Hyderabad who succumb to pellagra certainly have a small protein intake. Most of the protein is derived from jowar and other vegetable sources. Gopalan has therefore advanced the theory that in jowar eaters, pellagra is the result of amino-acid imbalance caused, in turn, by an excessive intake of leucine by people who eat very little protein. He has collected a large body of evidence to support this idea, both from studies of experimental pellagra in monkeys [16] and from his more fragmentary clinical experiments, in which he gave leucine to patients with pellagra and caused the exacerbation of mental symptoms.[17] Although his ideas have not yet gained general acceptance, it is important to realize that even today the cause of pellagra is still in dispute and that men of the stature of Gopalan can shed fresh light on the problem.[18] Those working in the field of nutrition await the results of his further investigations and hope for a unifying concept that will fully explain the occurrence of endemic pellagra in millet eaters, as well as in those who subsist on maize products.

17 | The Spring Equinox

The influence of the sun's rays on the lesions of pellagra has been a subject of debate for more than two hundred years. Casal noted a seasonal variation in the incidence of pellagra, with a peak which corresponded with the spring equinox. In Italy, the peasants often called the disease *mal del sole*. Italian physicians of the eighteenth century were so impressed by the fact that pellagrins came back each year as soon as the sun began to warm the fields that they commonly attributed the disease to "insolation" (sunstroke). A tract on this subject was published in Venice in 1784 by D. M. d'Oleggio. The title may be translated "A Theoretical and Practical Treatise on the Diseases of Vernal Insolation, Commonly Called Pellagra." [1] Indeed, this theory derived from the suffering Italian peasants and formulated by their physicians was accepted for many years and found its way into medical textbooks. Good's *Study of Medicine,* published in 1835, in the section on elephantiasis italica says: "For a knowledge of this species we are almost exclusively indebted to the Italian physicians, who have generally given it the name pellagra or pelagra. . . . It is commonly ascribed . . . to the heat of the sun's rays after the chill of winter." [2]

By the twentieth century, however, the idea that the sun actually caused pellagra was replaced by other theories. The controversy about the relationship between sunlight exposure and the appearance of the classical skin eruption continued. Certain students of pellagra, noting the presence of lesions on unexposed portions of

150

the body, denied the influence of sunlight in the production of dermatitis. While Goldberger recognized that an existing lesion could be accentuated by exposure to the sun,[3] Tom Spies stated that the cutaneous lesions would heal equally well whether the patient was kept in the dark or exposed to direct sunlight. He failed to produce lesions in pellagrins by exposing them to the sun.[4]

In 1931, Dr. David Smith and Dr. Julian Ruffin of Duke University School of Medicine undertook a study to find out which of these conflicting views was correct. It soon became apparent to them that a majority of pellagrous patients, when specifically questioned, recalled a prolonged exposure to sunlight shortly before the appearance of the dermatitis. Also, it was noted that the occurrence of dermatitis was almost invariably followed by constitutional symptoms of varying severity. These findings suggested that the severe general symptoms of pellagra were related in some way to the action of sunlight on the exposed surfaces of the body. Thirty-five of the patients with clinical pellagra were hospitalized and given a diet consisting of corn meal, cane sirup, flour, lard, rice, field peas, hominy grits, and fat salt pork, to which was added a small amount of cheese, cod-liver oil, tomato juice, calcium, and iron in order to fulfill their nutrient requirements other than for the pellagra-preventive factor. After a preliminary period of observation, these pellagrins were exposed to the direct rays of the sun in such a way that specific skin sites were irradiated on three to five consecutive days. In thirteen cases, acute dermatitis developed, both on areas of pellagrous involvement and on apparently normal skin, which had previously been covered. The appearance of this dermatitis was promptly followed by moderate or marked accentuation of the constitutional symptoms, including diarrhea, sore mouth, nausea, and dementia. Two other patients showed similar constitutional reactions but no new skin lesions after sunlight exposure.

According to the investigators, the amount of exposure to the sun was not excessive in these patients; as proof, they stated that members of the staff and patients with other diseases who were exposed similarly and simultaneously to the sun failed to show any evidence of sunburn or other untoward reactions. Furthermore, eleven of the patients who exhibited reactions while receiving the pellagragenic diet showed neither skin changes nor general reactions when they were re-exposed to the sun after nutritional rehabilitation. It was considered that the demonstration of tolerance for sunlight was a sign of cure. Smith and Ruffin had more difficulty explaining the fact that twenty of their patients showed no adverse effects from being out in the sun; they were thought to have had better appetites than the light-affected cases and therefore were more tolerant of sunlight. Interestingly, two of these cases showed excessive reactions to radiant heat from a stove at a time when their disease was active.[5]

Analysis of this study makes obvious gross flaws in the experimental procedure. Granted that all the cases initially showed evidence of malnutrition, from the list of presenting symptoms it seems likely that some may have had diseases other than pellagra, especially a deficiency of riboflavin, which gives rise to clinical features that have rather often been mistaken for pellagra. Also, no attempt was made to standardize the testing method for demonstration of photosensitivity. Did the sunlight actually cause an abnormal reaction in the skin and other tissues, or did this natural light act as a nonspecific stress factor in triggering these reactions? Last but not least: Did the light-intolerant patients show an intensification of the normal sunburn reaction or some more well-defined or characteristic lesion of pellagra.

Nevertheless, one conclusion remains: some pellagrins show a peculiar exacerbation of their symptoms when exposed to sunlight. The reactions encountered in the study are quite analogous to those that occur in domestic animals and in man when drugs or plants are ingested that have phototoxic properties.[6] Indeed, we are now familiar with the fact that certain compounds have the property of causing adverse reactions to light when applied to the skin or when consumed, or both. The reactions that occur when phototoxic substances are eaten by malnourished people may mimic acute pellagra, while phototoxic reactions that occur in well-nourished persons tend to be milder.

In 1948, Dr. M. Grzybowski of Warsaw University published a description of a pellagra-like skin sensitization to light in starving Poles. During the Second World War, when the Germans occupied Poland, the poor people in that country, having very little to eat, were forced to use wild plants in their daily diet. Instead of spinach, they ate a vegetable bearing the scientific name *Chenopodium album* which is commonly called goosefoot or pigweed. This plant was fried, boiled, or eaten raw as a salad. Grzybowski saw a number of women who soon after they had eaten pigweed fell victims to a strange malady, but he recorded in print only four of his cases, because notes pertaining to the others were destroyed during the Warsaw insurrection. His account gives a clear picture of the malady.

R. H.—a peasant woman, aged 43, was in very difficult material circumstances and visibly undernourished; her diet before her illness consisted of potatoes and peelings. She often ate Chenopodium variously prepared although she had heard of its bad effects. Some ten days before her admission to the clinic, after having eaten a great amount of Chenopodium salad, she went to work in the field. Immediately, she felt severe burning; the skin of her hands, feet and face became red and very painful and developed blood blisters. Extremely exhausted and in a very bad state, she was admitted to the clinic on the third day of her illness; two days before, she suffered from severe diarrhea.

He gives a similar description of an older woman, who in addition to her intense skin reaction to light following a meal of the toxic weed, showed mental symptoms:

Mrs. M. P., aged 71; hitherto in good health, a permanent resident of Warsaw, of poor origin . . . was admitted to the dermatological clinic on 26 July 1941. A fortnight before, she had eaten boiled Chenopodium with oatmeal and immediately after had gone out into the sun. . . . Painful swellings, blisters, and ulcers appeared on the exposed parts of her skin the same day. After her admission to the clinic, it was noticed that her general health was good. . . . However, the patient was in a state of marked excitement, demonstrated by her aggressive attitude towards the medical staff of the clinic.

Two other patients whose histories were reported received anti-pellagra therapy, in one instance nicotinic acid, in another nicotinamide. The subsequent course of their illness did not differ from that of the two untreated cases. In all cases the skin lesions healed slowly, with scarring, and the patients gradually recovered on a hospital diet. Perhaps the most interesting comment of the author is his postscript, dated October 11, 1948: "Though Chenopodium salad is still eaten by some people in Poland, we have not observed toxic skin lesions in connection with it during the last two years. Probably this is due to the general improvement of food conditions in this country. It can be regarded as proof that the toxic pellagra-like skin lesions are due to undernourishment." [7]

The pellagra-like skin sensitization to light reported by Grzybowski is similar to that described by Dr. J. J. Matignon many years earlier. In 1898, Matignon wrote an account of the light sensitivity he had observed among Chinese peasants. This was published in the *Chinese Customs Reports* under the title "De l'atriplicisme." The title refers to the origin of the condition, which the writer proved was an intoxication caused by the ingestion of *Atriplex serrata,* of the Family Chenopodiaceae. [8]

In 1935, a Chinese doctor, Kuang-Yuan Yu, reported having seen the same disease in two of his patients. One acquired the condition after picking *Chenopodium album* under a scorching sun; the other, after working in a field for half an hour on a bright, cloudy day soon after eating *Amaranthus mangostanus.* [9] Between 1935 and 1957, Yu encountered fifteen additional cases; these as well as his two original cases were reviewed at the eleventh International Congress of Dermatology, held in Stockholm in 1957. Essentially, the presenting symptoms of this group of patients were all the same: they all had acute light sensitivity after handling or eating plants of the genus *Chenopodium* or *Amaranthus.* When these people went into intense sunshine, they very rapidly experienced extreme discomfort, with redness and swelling of the face and other exposed parts of the skin. Also, they all had headaches, fever, and constipation, while some became unconscious. Their malady was not reminiscent of pellagra but was indistinguishable from light sensitivity caused by other plants such as figs or by plant juices. There was no suggestion that Yu's patients were malnourished; rather, he emphasized that the severity of the symptoms varied with skin coloring; it was worse in light-skinned persons.[10]

The question therefore arises as to whether the dermatitis of pellagra really is a photosensitivity. Do pellagrins have an abnormal reaction to ultraviolet or visible light? In the years since accurate testing methods for light sensitivity have been available, nobody has proved this to be the case. Indeed, when pellagrins were tested for their skin reactivity to isolated wave bands of light over a wide spectrum, no abnormality was found.[11]

This does not mean that pellagrous dermatitis is unrelated to sunlight exposure, for we know that there is a consistent association between the seasonal appearance of the rash and the increased intensity of the solar rays. Rather, we have to conceive that the specific nutritional deficiency that exists in pellagra impairs the healing properties of the skin after injury. The injury may be mechanical, as from clothes that chafe the skin; it may be thermal, as after contact with a cooking stove or exposure to the sun's burning rays. That the last has been and is the most common precipitating cause of the pellagrous rash is owing to the fact that for pellagrins, as for well-nourished people, actinic trauma is more frequent than any other form of injury, especially if one's occupation keeps one out all day in the sun. The defect in the pellagrin is one of reparative function. Niacin or nicotinamide in the coenzyme forms in which it exists in the tissues is intimately connected with the biochemical integrity of cells; when these substances are lacking, cell maintenance and reproduction are disturbed. The tissues first affected in niacin deficiency are those with the highest turnover rate, including the epidermis and the lining of the intestinal tract. Therefore, if the skin is traumatized by light or by any other agent, it does not heal in the normal manner. In 1963, Dr. George H. Findlay and his co-workers at the University of Pretoria found that the epidermis of pellagrins was deficient in niacin containing enzymes. When niacin was given as treatment, these enzymes were readily synthesized.[12] During a further study of reactions to light in normal and pellagrous Bantu subjects, this group showed that in comparison with the unaffected control cases, the outer cellular layer of the skin of those with pellagra exhibited a greater degree of light damage and the complete repair of their skin was delayed.[13]

There is evidence, however, that in certain instances the clinical picture of endemic pellagra may be influenced by diet-induced phototoxicity. In Lesotho (formerly Basutoland), where pellagra is widespread, the maize-eating people also eat large amounts of an indigenous "spinach." This spinach is not the common garden vegetable but may be one of a number of plants, mostly *Amaranthus,* a close relative of the plant implicated by Yu in his cases of light sensitivity in China.[14] While there is as yet no direct evidence that the pellagrous dermatitis of the Lesotho population is exacerbated by the light-sensitizing plants in their diet, this is suggested by the severity of the cutaneous symptoms and merits the investigation being undertaken at the present time. Indeed, it would be interesting to reconsider light sensitivity in the other remaining areas of endemic pellagra and to find out how common it is for malnourished people living on maize to consume weeds like *Chenopodium or Amaranthus,* which even in the absence of pellagra cause adverse reactions to light. Taking into account Grzybowski's documentation of the effects of *Chenopodium* on starving Poles, it is easy to predict that if this plant or other plants with similar properties were eaten by those who have a niacin deficiency, the cutaneous reaction would be more severe, healing of the skin would be slowed, and perhaps the intestinal symptoms associated with the light sensitivity would be worsened.

18 | In the Light of Present Knowledge

Like the paintings of Gérôme and the books of George du Maurier,[1] the subject of pellagra has gone out of fashion. How comforting it would be to believe that the lack of interest has resulted from precise knowledge of its causation and the virtual disappearance of the disease from the face of the earth. Unfortunately neither of these statements is in accordance with fact. As late as 1971, a group of South African and American investigators, reporting some new biochemical findings in pellagrins, prefaced an explanation of their recent theories with a remark that might have been made a hundred years ago: "Pellagra has been known for quite some time as a classical nutritional deficiency disease, the etiology of which is very complex." [2] Saying that causal factors are "complex" strongly suggests that one does not know everything about them. From the metabolic standpoint, there is much yet to be learned about pellagra, but as has been pointed out time and again, it is not lack of information that prevents the eradication of the disease in its endemic form. To understand why pellagra still persists in a number of countries long after it has been vanquished in western Europe and the United States, one need not be a biochemist. Read this quotation from the writings of the brothers Joseph and Theodore Gillman: "The most vicious single causative factor of pellagra arises from the perversions of the man-made environment where poverty and misery imposed by man on man constrain large sections of the population to live in abject poverty." [3] That was written in 1951 and was specifically directed toward the effects of social injustice in South Africa. However, the cycle of poverty in that country and its nutritional consequences have their counterparts elsewhere and now.

In South Africa, pellagra is limited to the have-not Bantu population. Various estimates of the incidence of pellagra have been given for this population group. In 1960, Dr. J. F. Potgieter and his colleages at the National Nutrition Research Institute in Pretoria adopted the method of a questionnaire survey, addressed to practicing physicians, to obtain information on the total occurrence of malnutrition among the Bantu and the "coloured" (people of mixed African and European blood). The questionnaire was sent to all general practitioners in the republic and to specialists in obstetrics, gynecology, and pediatrics. An accompanying letter requested the doctors to keep records for a four-week period in May and June and again in November and December 1960 and to state the number of cases of malnutrition that were seen among their patients during those times. Data for the two periods was requested because the investigators thought there might be seasonal differences in the incidence of malnutrition. Approximately 6100 pairs of questionnaires were sent out, one for each period of observation; 203 were returned for the first period, and 172 for the second. Most of the detailed and complete replies were sent by doctors who frequently encountered malnutrition and who were aware of the extent and seriousness of the problem. Many of these responses were received from the Bantu reserve areas, e.g., the Transkei, Zululand, and the northern Transvaal.

Various comments of the doctors suggest that the answers to the questionnaire contain erroneous figures about the number of malnourished persons. Statements of the following nature were numerous: "I rather fear we have missed some cases but have recorded most we have seen." The general opinion was that the vast majority of nonwhites in the rural as in the urban areas were probably malnourished. A physician from Natal observed that the Bantu diet was often distressingly inadequate. The incidence of nutritional disease was considered to be higher in summer than in winter. The most common types of malnutrition seen were kwashiorkor, a protein deficiency in very young children; marasmus, or infant starvation; and pellagra. Pellagra was not seen in the "coloured" people. The overall incidence of pellagra recorded was 1.6 per cent of the total nonwhite population, but it varied from region to region; it was as high as 3.4 per cent among the Bantu of the rural part of the Transvaal. The investigators concluded that little could be said about the total incidence of nutritional disease in the republic from the results of this survey because of the small numbers of questionnaires returned, but that the figures recorded were, in their own words, "surprisingly high." One question that was asked in this study was, "What are the main food items of your non-White patients?" Answers were based on opinions, and no actual figures were given. The responses showed that maize was the staple diet, and it was more often mentioned alone than in combination with other foods.[4]

There is much evidence that pellagra has recently been and continues to be common among the Bantu, particularly the rural Bantu, the overwhelming majority of whom exist well below the poverty line. In 1959, Dr. P. J. Quin published a study in cultural anthropology about a large group of rural Bantu living in the northern Transvaal. *Foods and Feeding Habits of the Pedi* is free from apartheid polemic and racial prejudice. It deals with the Pedi population living on the Sebediela Estates in Sekukuniland. These people, who are of the Bantu group known as the Sotho, follow a traditional method of agriculture. With the exception of the single furrow plough, mechanization is completely lacking, and they rely on such hand tools as the iron hoe to till the land. Their very small agricultural output has been attributed to a combination of factors including the natural infertility of the soil; soil erosion; ignorance of such farming practices as the use of fertilizers, crop rotation, and seed selection; and their inability to seek new ground for cultivation after their restricted territory is exhausted. The chief crops of the Pedi are Kaffir corn, Kaffir millet, and maize or mealies.

Mealies or mealie products form the dietary staple and are

used in the preparation of gruel, porridge, bread, and beer. Native fruits, vegetables, and herbs are used fairly extensively in food preparation; they are mixed with the maize. Three meals at most are eaten per day. The morning meal consists of tea, maize porridge, and bread; the noon meal of maize porridge with wild spinach, caterpillars, or a little meat; and the evening meal of more porridge, perhaps with bread and tea. According to Quin's survey, however, 58 per cent of the people had no food before the middle of the day. Very little fresh milk is drunk, and only a small amount of condensed milk, in tea. Popular snacks include candy and bubble gum, as well as buns, lemonade, and Coca-Cola. The diet is very high in carbohydrate and low in protein foods, which are used mainly as relishes, and low in fat. Traditional dishes predominate, but as the snack foods indicate, modern dietary items may be eaten if they are cheap enough.

According to Pedi lore, pellagra was unknown in Sekukuniland until about eighty years ago. Quin is obviously somewhat skeptical about this assertion. He had discussed various diseases affecting the Pedi with Dr. J. N. du Plessis, the superintendent of the Groothoek Mission Hospital, which served the local Bantu population. Quin was told that in 1958–1959, 90 per cent of the cases admitted suffered from malnutrition in the form of pellagra.[5]

Reports show that pellagra still takes its toll among the Bantu, whether they live in rural or urban communities. P. J. Pretorius published a disquieting article in 1968 which showed that at least 50 per cent of the patients attending medical clinics in Bantu reserve areas had pellagrous skin lesions. More than half of all the Bantu patients admitted to mental hospitals in Pretoria had pellagra.[6] It is difficult, however, to assess the true incidence of pellagra in the republic as a whole or even in those places that have a predominantly nonwhite population. George Findlay, a noted dermatologist who is acclaimed as a distinguished student of pellagra, does not mention the disease in an analysis of 22,000 cases of common skin problems seen in clinics in the Transvaal. In a survey of skin diseases affecting Bantu patients of the Baragwanath Hospital in Johannesburg, M. Dogliotti found that between December 1968 and November 1969, 2.2 per cent of the outpatients and 2.75 per cent of the inpatients had pellagra.[7] Probably differences in the incidence of the disease reflect socioeconomic variations in the sample populations, but there is also the possibility that pellagra is not classified in hospital records as a skin disease but rather as a nutritional disability.

In 1965, Dr. M. L. Neser, of the National Nutrition Research Institute in Pretoria, gave his views about the conquest of malnutrition in South Africa. In introducing this subject he said, "It can be seen that there is no prospect whatsoever of completely eradicating malnutrition in South Africa or anywhere else, for many of the factors which lead to malnutrition are inherent in our human condition." After discussing the nutritional problems of the white population that seem to result from overindulgence, he described the problems of the Bantu. His remarks about the rural Bantu give insight into the attitude of an educated white man and his explanation of the persistence of deficiency diseases among these people:

The general condition of the rural Bantu is one of extreme poverty with a consequent lack of communal resources. It is one of widespread ignorance of the benefits of Western civilization, of superstition, prejudice and binding traditions, and of dependence on a land which is limited in extent and often extremely unproductive because of low soil fertility and low rainfall. Droughts are common and prolonged in many areas, for example the Northern Transvaal. When droughts occur in these areas, the government has to step in with emergency aid to prevent mass starvation, for these people are not in a position to make provision against lean years. . . . The poverty factor seems to me already far beyond the means of our greatly outnumbered White population to deal with. . . . To me it seems that like the poor, we will have the malnourished always with us.[8]

There is another country in the middle of South Africa, the independent state of Lesotho, where pellagra is still the most common deficiency disease. In their own language, Sesotho, the people call it *lefu-la-pone* (disease of the mealies). There is some evidence that the clinical picture may be influenced by the local consumption of light-sensitizing plants. The effect of these photo-toxic plants may be to exacerbate pre-existing pellagrous derma-toses or to induce a pellagroid picture *de novo*. Too little is known at present for us to be able to make an adequate evalution, but the fact that pellagra in Lesotho, as elsewhere, responds to a high-protein diet and to niacin suggests strongly that endemic pellagra, rather than light sensitivity, is the basic disease.

The extent of pellagra and of other deficiency diseases in Lesotho was first revealed during the years 1956 to 1960, when the World Health Organization of the United Nations carried out a nutrition survey there.[9] Following the publication of their report, the Applied Nutrition Program was initiated in 1962 as a joint project conducted under the auspices of the Lesotho gov-ernment, the Food and Agriculture Organization (FAO), and the United Nations Children's Fund (UNICEF). The objectives were to improve and raise the levels of nutrition by increasing local production of nutritionally valuable foods and to train staff who would do field work and teach nutrition.[10]

The laborers in the field are few, however, and the obstacles formidable. In 1959, 7 per cent of all patients admitted to hospitals had some form of malnutrition. In 1968, the figure was still 7 per cent. Pellagra presently affects people of both sexes and of all ages. It is seasonal, occurring from October to February, with a maximal incidence in December. Elisabeth Linusson, who was an FAO nutrition expert for the Ministry of Agriculture in Lesotho from 1967 to 1970, has informed me that during the season, 15 per cent of the population have pellagra, and that 50 per cent of those who are heavy drinkers are affected. (The drink is *jouala,* or Basuto beer, which is made from sorghum.) Pellagra is also very common in lactating women and in the young herd boys who tend the sheep and goats. As Miss Linusson has said, "The prob-lems of malnutrition in Lesotho are being increasingly realized but have not yet been overcome." A major obstacle is the shortage of agricultural land. Two-thirds of the twelve-thousand-square-mile area of Lesotho consists of rugged mountains ranging in height from seven thousand to eleven thousand feet. About one-third of the country's inhabitants live in these highlands, the other two-thirds on a marginal lowland strip. Overutilization of the lowland region has led to a deterioration of the soil through exhaustion and, together with soil erosion, has increasingly limited the amount of arable land. Linusson reports: "In a normal year, even the staple food, maize, has to be supplemented with imports of well over a quarter of a million bags [of grain], excluding gifts from international aid programs.[11]

Sheep, goats, and some cattle are grazed in the highlands. Meat from these animals is eaten by the local inhabitants, with the result that they fare better and have less pellagra than their lowland brethren. Peas, beans, and wheat are grown in the lowlands, but these are still largely used as cash crops rather than as valuable additives to the daily diet. There has recently been a government policy, encouraged by FAO, to teach the people to eat legumes as well as wheaten bread.

The chief exports of the country are mohair from the sheep, and manpower, both to South Africa. Young men of seventeen and older leave Lesotho on contracts to work in the diamond and gold mines.[12] While they are away, for periods of about nine months, their nutrition improves because the mining camps in South Africa have excellent kitchens and dining facilities. Only family loyalty can induce these men to return to poverty and pellagra, the brunt of which is carried by their womenfolk and by the youngsters who are unable to leave home.

Reports of pellagra from other parts of Africa are scanty and emanate mainly from areas where maize eating and a sadly outmoded economy coexist.[13] Michael Latham has published an interesting account of pellagra in Tanzania, where the disease occurs in the maize and cassava eaters only. In 1963, he saw 176 cases in a period of two months near Kondoa Irangi, where poor rural Tanzanians were living by means of subsistence agriculture. This epidemic followed a crop failure, which resulted in a famine so bad that only a little imported American maize was available to eat.[14] Since that time, florid cases of pellagra have been seen only occasionally in Tanzania, because the more vulnerable segments of the population have received niacin supplements. Provision of these supplements has been a government policy and has been enforced in such institutions as prisons, where pellagra formerly occurred.[15] Although, as in the Tanzanian epidemic, pellagra may occur sporadically in tropical Africa among maize-eating people, it is not a major nutritional problem, because the kind of social milieu that conditions the life of a pellagrin seldom exists.

Where there is a large peasant community living on maize or sometimes on millet, the disease tends to persist unless there has been reallocation of land to the cultivators. Such communities exist in Egypt, where pellagra continues to be a very significant health problem among the rural population. As in the time of Sandwith and of Wilson, there is a difference in prevalence rates between Upper and Lower Egypt. The latter region can be considered truly endemic for pellagra. *The State of Nutrition in the Arab Middle East,* by Dr. Vinayak N. Patwardhan and Dr. William Darby, records that the incidence of pellagra showed an almost threefold increase in Upper Egypt between 1948 and 1953 and that the incidence was even higher in the period 1958 to 1963, reaching 45.7 per 100,000. In the following three years, however, the rate dropped to a low 10.3 per 100,000. Fluctuations in the incidence of the disease have also occurred in Lower Egypt, where a declining trend has also been reported.[16] Among nutritionists in Egypt, there has been some conflict of opinion as to whether the incidence of pellagra is increasing or decreasing. After surveying the various Egyptian provinces in 1965, Ismail A. Abdou estimated that 0.2 per cent of the population suffered from pellagra—a prevalence rate of 200 per 100,000. These figures do not accord with the morbidity statistics given to Patwardhan and Darby by the Egyptian Ministry of Health, where it was recorded that between 1964 and 1966 the prevalence of pellagra in Upper

Egypt, as has been previously stated, was 10.3 per 100,000, and in Lower Egypt, 83.2 per 100,000. The disparity can be accounted for, at least in part, by differences in methodology; the Ministry of Health's estimate was derived, not from an overall survey, but from data on the total average annual attendance at special endemic-disease hospitals.

Emphasis has been placed by public-health physicians on the incidence of pellagra among mental patients in Egypt. Abdou estimated that 0.4 per cent of all new admissions to mental hospitals were pellagra cases and that 2.7 per cent of all inmates of mental hospitals suffered from pellagra.[17] It is disturbing to read in Patwardhan and Darby's discussion of the subject that a certain proportion of the patients in mental hospitals in Egypt acquire the disease in these institutions. It should be stressed that the diagnostic criteria for determining that mental patients have pellagra may not be very stringent; it is possible that some may have other deficiency diseases or light sensitivity associated with the use of photosensitizing drugs.

Several factors contribute to the continued occurrence of pellagra in the Egyptian fellaheen or village laborers. Obviously, their deficient diet causes them to succumb to the disease. In Lower Egypt, they subsist on maize bread supplemented by a few vegetables, occasionally cheese made from buffalo milk, and only rarely eggs, meat, or fish. Millet or sorghum is the staple in Upper Egypt, where although the disease is less common, there is no immunity, because pellagra-preventive foods are eaten infrequently by the poor of the countryside. Indeed, it can be generalized that whether in Lower or Upper Egypt, pellagra occurs in those who have to eat the cheapest foods. It has been suggested that pellagra has become more common in Upper Egypt since more land has been brought under perennial irrigation with the result that agriculture has been limited to the production of such cash crops as sugar cane. This has necessitated the transport of food supplies for the laborers from Lower Egypt; because corn from this area is the least expensive food commodity, it is what the peasants receive. An analogy may be drawn between the current situation in Egypt and that of the cotton-mill workers of South Carolina in Goldberger's time who had no chance to grow their own food but subsisted on corn and corn products from the factory commissary. In Egypt, city and town dwellers, whatever their economic status, rarely get pellagra, because they can obtain government-subsidized wheat bread and therefore do not have to depend on corn or millet to assuage their hunger.

An appraisal of the current situation in India has been provided me in correspondence from Dr. Gopalan, director of the National Institute of Nutrition in Hyderabad. In surveys conducted under his direction, it has been found that endemic pellagra still occurs in the Deccan Plateau region and in some parts of the States of Maharashtra, Gujarat, Rajasthan, and Mysore. He referred to hospital statistics showing that in these states as many as 1 per cent of all general hospital admissions, during particular seasons, have pellagra. It occurs among people belonging to the poorer socioeconomic strata, especially agricultural workers. In some parts of India, as on the Deccan Plateau, pellagra occurs in populations whose diets are based predominantly on millet, while in other areas maize consumption is sufficiently high to account for the endemicity of the disease. Whether millet or maize is the staple, the Indian pellagrins rarely take eggs, meat, or milk. In some cases, it is believed that alcohol consumption is a contributory factor, and as has been mentioned earlier, pellagra is seen in patients under treatment for tuberculosis.[18]

In a monograph published by the World Health Organization, Dr. Wallace R. Aykroyd, former director of the nutrition division of FAO, expressed optimism about the eradication of pellagra. He concluded his history of the disease: "Given modern knowledge and opportunities for economic, agricultural and social development, there is every reason to hope that this once widespread and formidable deficiency disease is on its way to extinction." [19] That pellagra has virtually died out as a result of these advances in France, Italy [20] and the United States [21] has been amply borne out by recent nutrition surveys. In eastern Europe, for example in Yugoslavia and Rumania, where various Communist regimes have replaced the traditional peasant economy, pellagra is on the way out and is seen only in isolated communities, whereas formerly the disease was widespread.[22] It is not, however, the opportunity for social, economic, and agricultural progress that determines the decline of pellagra but rather the extension of the

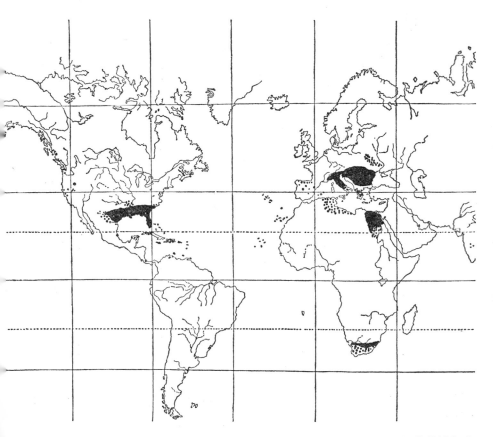

Figure 3. Map showing the worldwide distribution of pellagra, 1906–1912. Solid black ᵉas indicate where pellagra was prevalent. Redrawn from Stewart R. Roberts, *Pellagra* t. Louis: The C. V. Mosby Co., 1913).

benefits of progress to all members of society. The current situation in India, South Africa, and Egypt points up the fact that pellagra will be with us until the dispossessed achieve their right to freedom from want and can choose to eat the foods that prevent the disease.

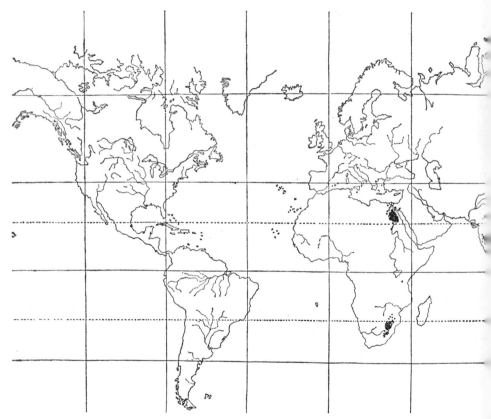

Figure 4. Map showing the worldwide distribution of pellagra, 1966–1972. Solid black areas indicate where pellagra is prevalent.

Résumé

The story of pellagra is about an endemic disease that has appeared in people who subsist mainly on a diet of maize. The account has integrated clinical observations and biochemical studies that ultimately resulted in the definition of pellagra as malnutrition caused by a deficiency of the vitamin niacin. Descriptions of secondary pellagra and pellagra-like syndromes conditioned by food toxins or metabolic defects have been included to emphasize possible causative relationships.

Certain features of pellagra still go unexplained, particularly the intolerance of sunlight that has impressed all observers from the eighteenth century to the present. Complex problems that intrigue the biochemist, unsolved nutritional parameters that may influence the disease, and the preoccupation of medical academicians with rare pellagroid cases remain as sidelights to the total picture of pellagra.

The main purpose of this narrative has been to trace the recurring pattern of social deprivation that has been a constant accompaniment of the disease in its endemic form. We have come to the end of our account of the case of pellagra versus man. Our duty is to consider how the pellagrin has been and is victimized.

Since the time of Casal, the typical pellagrins have been indigent laborers, downtrodden, socially deprived, and ill used. Significantly, they have fared worse than their fellow men when the precursors of famine have appeared: crop failures, soil exhaustion, industrial collapse, inundation, war. The staple cereal diet to which they become inured is one that will not support even the health of domestic animals. The story of the Prodigal Son tells that, "When he had spent all, there arose a mighty famine in that land and he began to be in want. And he went and joined himself to a citizen of that country; and he sent him into his fields to feed swine. And he would fain have filled his belly with the husks that the swine did eat; and no man gave unto him" (Luke 15:14–16). The account applies to the young man turned sharecropper. The

Prodigal Son had the option of escape and return to his Father; the pellagrin does not, except perhaps at his demise.

Granted that pellagra has occurred at one time or another in all maize-growing countries, its spread has been most closely related to the adoption of systems of indentured labor other than apprenticeship. In order to understand why such social systems have denied man his basic right of nourishment and have resulted in outbreaks of pellagra, one has to probe into their evolution.

Let us return to the close of the Middle Ages and look at the attitude of the overlord to the serf. There was a sentimental compassion for the poor, and in an age of waning chivalry, the aristocrat felt it his religious duty to attend to their needs. A ballad of Meschinot composed in the fifteenth century compares the duties of the ruler to those of the shepherd:

> Seigneur, tu es de Dieu bergier;
> Garde ses bestes loyaument.

(Lord, thou art God's shepherd; guard his beasts loyally.)

If the noble ruler thought he could feed and defend the peasant, at best he put his theories into practice and provided bounty for the poor in hard times. At worst, commiseration was expressed in verbal stereotypes, and the poor suffered in spite of it. Meschinot reveals the situation in his poignant verse as he reminds God that the common people are actually neglected:

> O Dieu, voyez du commun l'indigence,
> Pourvoyez-y a toute diligence:
> Las! par faim, froid, paour et misère tremble.

(O God, see the poverty of the common people; provide for them with all speed: Alas! they tremble with hunger, cold, fear, and misery.) [23]

Malnutrition could and can occur in a dying feudal system. Endemic pellagra did not occur in the Middle Ages because corn was unknown in Europe. In later feudalistic systems, as in the

Egypt of Sandwith's day, the disease was rampant. In a peasant society where maize is the staple diet, the laborer and his family can escape pellagra if they receive gifts of food that can prevent the disease from a benevolent landlord or if they have the opportunity to raise and consume their own domestic animals.

The passing of feudal systems basically coincides with the development of commerce. The old order dies when the state demands income from its productivity and new proprietors arise who are more obsessed with the temptations of wealth than with pride in their own domains. These new proprietors, who have experienced living in the preceding peasant society, realize that it is more profitable to hold their laborers under the system of *métayage* rather than to pay them a living wage. As Guy Hunter has pointed out in his book *Modernizing Peasant Societies,* a change to higher productivity within a static economic pattern spells disaster, with more widespread poverty as the end result. The independent farmer makes the métayer as dependent on him as the serf was on his overlord.[24] Similarly, the cotton operative of Goldberger's day was dependent on the factory owner, and the Bantu laborer is dependent on his white boss. To stretch the analogy further, the child in the orphanage is reliant on the supervisors. Indeed, social circumstances and often the imposed will of others deny those destined to pellagra the right to choose what they should do, where they should live, or what they should eat. Pellagra is not the companion of poverty alone, of corn eating alone, but it has been and may still be the destiny of those who are poor because they are landless and are maize eaters because that is all they can get to eat.

The fact that the story of the plague of corn is not yet a completed chapter in the chronicle of medical history should remind us that while anyone can cure pellagra with a handful of pills, social progress is hardly measurable if the disease still makes its appearance in the same conditions of misery that have been its background since the first cases were seen among the Spanish peasants.

Notes

Abbreviations

AIM   *Archives of Internal Medicine*
AJCN *American Journal of Clinical Nutrition*
AJMS *American Journal of the Medical Sciences*
BJD   *British Journal of Dermatology*
JAMA *Journal of the American Medical Association*
JBC   *Journal of Biological Chemistry*
JN   *Journal of Nutrition*
PHR   *Public Health Reports*
SAMJ *South African Medical Journal*
TNCP *Transactions of the National Conference on Pellagra* (Columbia, S.C.: State Co., 1910)

Chapter 1. The Disease Pellagra

1. A. Marie, *La Pellagre* (Paris: Giard et Brière, 1908); trans. C. H. Lavinder and J. W. Babcock, *Pellagra* (Columbia, S.C.: State Co., 1910), pp. 182–183. This book is largely an abridgment of Cesare Lombroso's *Trattato proffilattico e clinico della pellagra* (Turin: Fratelli Socco, 1892).

2. V. Babes and V. Sion, "Die Pellagra," in H. Nothnagel, *Specielle Pathologie und Therapie*, XXIV (Vienna: Hölder, 1901), Part II, pp. 1–87.

3. "Pellagra in Egypt," *Journal of Tropical Medicine*, 1 (1898), 63–70.

4. E. J. Wood, *A Treatise on Pellagra for the General Practitioner* (New York and London: Appleton, 1912), pp. 144–150.

5. V. P. Sydenstricker, "The History of Pellagra, Its Recognition as

173

a Disorder of Nutrition and Its Conquest," *AJCN*, 6 (1958), 409–414.

6. *Diseases of the Skin* (rev. ed.; London: Cassell, 1898), pp. 121–123.

7. *Pellagra*, p. 147.

8. Lombroso, much taken with the concept of a pellagra diathesis, summarized his experience: "Wir haben gesehen dass die Pellagra nicht nur von Bezirk zu Bezirk, sondern such von Individuum zu Individuum variert, je nachdem ein gewisses Organ weniger widerstandsfahig und sonit leichten anzugreifen ist. Deshalb gilt von keinem Leiden in so hohem Masse wie von ihr der Satz, dass es nicht Krankheiten giebt sondern nur Kranke" (Cesare Lombroso, *Die Lehre von der Pellagra* [Berlin: Kurella, 1898], p. 118). ("We have seen that pellagra varies not only from district to district but also from individual to individual; accordingly a specific organ which is more susceptible is more easily involved. On this account no suffering or enormous suffering may be admitted, so giving rise to the saying that there are no diseases [or there is no disease], only sick people.") The origin of the saying is difficult to trace. Salvador de Madariaga refers to it as a proverb; in fact he quotes two related proverbs: "There is no medicine; only medical men"; and "There are no diseases only patients" ("On Medicine," in *Essays with a Purpose* [London: Hollis and Carter, 1954], p. 176).

9. T. Gillman, "Nutritional Influences on the Skin of Man," in *Comparative Physiology and Pathology of the Skin*, ed. A. J. Rook and G. S. Walton (Philadelphia: Davis, 1965), pp. 273–306.

Chapter 2. Pre-Columbian Maize Culture and Its Consequences

1. "The Aztecs and Their Predecessors," *Proceedings of the American Philosophical Society*, 55 (1926), 245–255.

2. "The Origin of Indian Corn and Its Relatives," *Texas Agricultural Experiment Station Bulletin*, No. 574 (1939), 7–315.

3. E. J. Payne, *History of the New World Called America* (New York: Macmillan, 1892), I, 354–364.

4. P. Weatherwax, *Indian Corn in Old America* (New York: Macmillan, 1954), pp. 208–238.

5. P. C. Mangelsdorf, "The Role of Pod Corn in the Origin and

Evolution of Maize," *Annals of the Missouri Botanical Garden,* 35 (1948), 377–406.

6. E. C. Stakman, R. Bradfield, and P. C. Mangelsdorf, eds., *Campaigns against Hunger* (Cambridge: Harvard University Press, 1967), pp. 51–71.

7. P. C. Mangelsdorf, R. S. MacNeish, and W. C. Galinat, *Archaeological Evidence on the Diffusion and Evolution of Maize in Northeastern Mexico,* Harvard Botanical Museum Leaflet No. 17 (1956), pp. 125–150.

8. E. K. Easby and J. F. Scott, *Before Cortes: Sculpture of Middle America* (New York: New York Graphic Society, 1970) (catalogue of the centennial exhibition at the Metropolitan Museum of Art, Sept. 30, 1970–Jan. 3, 1971).

9. *Traité de la pellagre et des pseudo-pellagres* (Paris: Baillière, 1866), pp. 571–573.

10. I. Salas, "Etiologie et prophylaxie de la pellagre," thesis, University of Paris, 1863, p. 51.

11. Easby and Scott, *Before Cortes.*

12. Weatherwax, *Indian Corn.*

13. Easby and Scott, *Before Cortes.*

14. Diego de Landa, *Relación de las cosas de Yucatan,* trans. Alfred M. Tozzer (Cambridge, Mass.: Peabody Museum, 1941).

15. Weatherwax, *Indian Corn.*

16. G. A. Goldsmith, "The B Vitamins: Thiamine, Riboflavin, Niacin," in *Nutrition: A Comprehensive Treatise,* ed. G. H. Beaton and E. W. McHenry (New York: Academic Press, 1964), II, 161–198.

17. E. R. Kodicek, R. Braude, S. K. Kon, and K. G. Mitchell, "The Effect of Alkaline Hydrolysis of Maize on the Availability of Its Nicotinic Acid to the Pig," *British Journal of Nutrition,* 10 (1956), 51–67.

18. G. A. Goldsmith, "Studies on Niacin Requirements in Man; II: Comparative Effects of Diets Containing Lime-treated and Untreated Corn in the Production of Experimental Pellagra," *AJCN,* 4 (1956), 151–160.

19. G. A. Goldsmith, "Niacin: Antipellagra Factor, Hypocholesterolemic Agent," *JAMA,* 194 (1965), 167–173. (Joseph Goldberger Lecture in Clinical Nutrition, read at the 114th annual convention of the American Medical Association, New York, June 23, 1965).

20. "Lime Treated Corn," *Nutrition Reviews,* 18 (1960), 183–185.

21. L. Kaplan, "Archaeological Phaseolus from Tehuacan," in

D. Byers, ed., *The Prehistory of the Tehuacan Valley; I: Environment and Subsistence* (Austin: University of Texas Press, 1967), 201–219.

22. R. S. MacNeish, "A Summary of the Subsistence," in *ibid.*, I, 290–309.

23. *The Problem of Slavery in Western Culture* (Ithaca, N.Y.: Cornell University Press, 1966), pp. 167–173.

24. E. O. Callen, "Analysis of the Tehuacan Coprolites," in D. Byers, ed., *The Prehistory of the Tehuacan Valley*, I, 261–289.

25. G. F. Oviedo y Valdéz, *Historia general y natural de las Indias* (Seville: Cromberger, 1535; Madrid: La Real Academia de la Historia, 1851), Book VII, ch. i, p. 264.

Chapter 3. *Grano Turco*

1. B. de Las Casas, *Historia de las Indias* (Madrid: n.p., 1875; Mexico City: Millares, 1951).

2. P. Weatherwax, *Indian Corn in Old America* (New York: Macmillan, 1954), pp. 8–9.

3. J. B. Thacher, *Christopher Columbus* (New York and London: Putnam, 1903), II, 229, 249.

4. P. Mártir de Angléria, *Decadas del Nuevo Mundo* (Buenos Aires: Bajel, 1944). For a discussion of the various allusions to corn in the early editions of Martyr's work see Weatherwax, *Indian Corn.*

5. *De Orbe Novo: The Eight Decades of Peter Martyr d'Anghera*, trans. F. A. MacNutt (New York and London: Putnam, 1912), I, 64.

6. P. Weatherwax, "Early Contacts of European Science with the Indian Corn Plant," *Proceedings of the Indiana Academy of Science*, 54 (1945), 169–178.

7. "The Coma-Syllacio Document." See Weatherwax, *Indian Corn,* pp. 10–11.

8. After his third voyage, Columbus described maize as "a seed which produces a spike like a cob, which I brought there, and now there is much of it in Castile" (quoted by Salvador de Madariaga, "Vida del muy magnifico señor don Cristobal Colón," *Sudamericana,* 1940, p. 455). See J. J. Finan, "Maize in the Great Herbals," *Annals of the Missouri Botanical Garden,* 35 (1948), 149–191.

9. G. F. Oviedo y Valdéz, *Sumario de la natural historia de las Indias* (Toledo: Petras, 1526); trans. S. A. Stoudemire, *Natural His-*

tory of the West Indies (Chapel Hill: University of North Carolina Press, 1959).

10. J. Bock, *Neuw Kreuterbuch von Underscheid* (Strassburg: Rihel, 1539).

11. L. Fuchsius, *De historia stirpium commentarii insignes* (Basel: Isingrin, 1542).

12. "Maize in the Great Herbals," *Annals of the Missouri Botanical Garden*, 35 (1948), 149–191.

13. P. A. Matthiolus, *Commentarii in libros sex pedacii dioscoridis anazarbei de medica materia* (Venice: Valgrisium, 1565).

14. J. de Acosta, *Historia natural y moral de las Indias* (Seville: Juan de Leon, 1590).

15. J. Gerarde, *The Herball or Generall Historie of Plantes* (1st ed.; London: Norton, 1597).

16. *Ibid.* (2d ed.; London: Islip, Norton, and Whitakers, 1633), pp. 81 ff.

17. Finan, "Maize in the Great Herbals"; Tabernaemontanus, *Neuw Kreuterbuch* (Frankfort on the Main: Bassaeum, 1591).

18. R. Dodonaeus, *Frumentorum, leguminum, palustrium, et aquatilium herbarum ac eorum quae eo pertinent, historia* (Antwerp: Plantini, 1566); M. de l'Obel, *Krudtboeck oft beschryuinghe van allerlye Ghewassen, Kruyderen, Hesteren, ende Gheboomten* (Antwerp: Plantyn, 1581).

19. *Theatrum Botanicum: The Theater of Plants* (London: Cotes, 1640).

20. *Theatri botanici sive historiae plantarum ex veterum et recentiorum placitis proprias: Observatione concinnatae liber primus . . .* (Basel: König, 1658), ch. xxxi, sec. 4, cols. 490–500; quoted from S. Jarcho, *S. J. Caspar Bauhinus on a Disease Associated with Maize*, Bulletin of the New York Academy of Medicine, No. 44 (1968), 504–506.

21. Puritan settlers in New England grew Indian corn from the year 1629 on. When, frequently, other cereals were unavailable, they relied on corn to supply the bulk of their daily diet. The chronicles of those times make no reference to any sickness resembling pellagra, in contrast to their frequent discussion of scurvy, which was the prevalent form of malnutrition among newly arrived immigrants. The absence of pellagra can be explained by the fact that even in times of relative famine, a variety of fish and sea food was caught and distributed to the needy. See Francis Higginson, "New England's Plantation" and "The

Charlestown Records," in *Chronicles of the First Planters of the Colony of Massachusetts Bay from 1623 to 1636*, ed. Alexander Young (Boston: Little, Brown, 1846).

22. *Le vinti giornate dell agricoltera et de piaceri della villa* (1st ed.; Venice: C. Borgominerio, 1593), p. 45; (2d ed.: n.p., 1775), p. 334.

23. P. A. Matthiolus, *Compendium de plantis omnibus* (Venice: Valgrisium, 1571).

24. A. Zanoni, *Dell' agricoltera, Dell' arti e lettere 5: Lette. 15, 1765-1767;* cited by E.-A. Duchesne, *Traité du mais ou blé de Turquie* (Paris: Madame Huzard Libraire, 1833), p. 94.

25. V. Sette, *Memoria storico-naturale sull' arrossimento straordinario di alcune sostanze alimentose osservato nellu provincia di Padova* (Venice: Alvispoli, 1819); cited by Théophile Roussel, *De la pellagre* (Paris: Hennuyer and Turpin, 1845), pp. 351-352.

26. L. Balardini, *Della pellagra, del granturco, quale causa precipua di quella malattia e dei mezzi per arrestaria* (Milan: Societa Degli Editori Delgi Annali Universali Delle Scienze e Dell'Industrie, 1845). See also Roussel, *De la pellagre.*

27. Duchesne, *Traité du mais,* p. 101, n. 7.

Chapter 4. *Mal de la Rosa*

1. Casal held the appointment as city physician of Oviedo for thirty-three years. During that time, he not only came to know the local people but also learned much about the topography and climate of the area. He made notes on the villages of the Asturias, the waters, minerals, trees, food, atmosphere, winds, and diseases. These records were bequeathed to his friend Dr. Juan Joseph Garcia Sevillano, who arranged them for publication after Casal's death (R. H. Major, "Don Gaspar Casal, François Thiéry, and Pellagra," *Bulletin of the History of Medicine,* 16 [1944], 351-361).

2. T. Roussel, *De la pellagre* (Paris: Hennuyer and Turpin, 1845), p. 4. Fiejoo is mentioned in this book as "le père Feijoo, erudit espagnol qui s'était souvent entretenu avec Casal du mal de la rosa" ("Father Feijoo, the learned Spaniard, who often conversed with Casal about *mal de la rosa*"). Benito Jeronimo Feijoo y Montenegro (1676-1764) was a Benedictine monk who became widely known as an essayist and early protagonist of Spanish enlightenment. His voluminous correspondence includes numerous letters to physicians. See

G. Delpy, *Bibliographie des sources françaises de Feijoo* (Paris: Librairie Hachette, 1936).

3. "François Thiéry," *Larousse grand dictionnaire universaire du XIXᵉ siècle* (Paris: n.p., 1876), XV, 125.

4. F. Thiéry, "Description d'une maladie appellée mal de rose aux Austuries: Recueil périodique d'observations de médicine, de chirurgie et de pharmacie," *Journal de Vandermonde* (May 1755).

5. Gaspar Casal, "De affectione quae vulgo in hac regione 'mal de la rosa' nuncupatur," in *Historia natural y medica de el principado de Asturias: Obra posthuma* (Madrid: Martin, 1762), III, 327–360.

6. See the frontispiece of the present volume. Whether the skin lesions around the neck of the pellagrin should be termed "the collar of Casal" or the "necklace of Casal" has been under question. The former name is used in the standard British and American dermatological literature. It should also be pointed out that the late Theodore Gillman, an acknowledged authority on pellagra, used the term "collar" in his writings. Nineteenth-century French writers on the subject used the word *collier,* which can be translated "collar," as in dog collar or necklace. Casal himself described the lesions on the neck as being "quae monilis instar" ("like a collar"—or necklace). The term "collar" therefore has equal rank with necklace.

7. E.-A. Duchesne, *Traité du mais ou blé de Turquie* (Paris: Madame Huzard Libraire, 1833), p. 277.

8. Joseph Townsend, *A Journey through Spain* (London: Dilly, 1792), II, 10.

9. Julius Klein, *The Mesta: A Study in Spanish Economic History* (Cambridge: Harvard University Press, 1920).

10. H. Stokes, *Francisco Goya: A Study of the Work and Personality of the Eighteenth Century Spanish Painter and Satirist* (London: Jenkin, 1914), pp. 225–229.

11. F. Le Play, "Métayer de la Vieille-Castille," in *Les ouvriers européens: Etudes sur les travaux, la vie domestique et la condition morale des populations ouvriers de l'Europe, d'après les faits observés de 1829–1855* (2d ed.; Tours: Mame, 1877), IV.

12.   O let us love our occupations
    Bless the squire and his relations
    Live upon our daily rations
    And always know our proper stations.
    [Charles Dickens, *The Chimes,* in *Christmas Books* (New York: Oxford University Press, 1843), p. 136]

13. F. Le Play, *Les Ouvriers européens.*

14. *De la pellagre.*

15. *Mal del higado* had the literal meaning "disease of the liver," which may have been an allusion to an observed disorder of that organ. However, that does not suggest pellagra. If these peasants of Alcañiz had the same disease Casal described a little more than a century earlier, perhaps the liver was the seat of the condition only in the humoral sense; that is, they suffered a disturbance of the seat of melancholy, which is related to the black gall. For a detailed discussion of this subject, see E. Panofsky, *Albrecht Dürer: Melancholia 1* (Princeton, N.J.: Princeton University Press, 1945), I, 157–159. For a description of the Spanish disease, see E. J. Wood, *A Treatise on Pellagra for the General Practitioner* (New York and London: Appleton, 1912), pp. 10–11.

16. Gimeno's communication was in the form of a letter, dated October 22, 1826, published in the *Diario general de las ciencias médicas* of Barcelona (cited by Wood, *A Treatise on Pellagra,* pp. 10–11).

17. D. F. Mendez-Alvaro, "Noticia sobre la pelagra," *Boletin medico,* Sept. 1847.

18. Roussel knew the report of *mal del monte,* which is discussed in his *Traité de la pellagre et des pseudo-pellagres* (Paris: Baillière, 1866).

19. "La pellagra y mal de la rosa," in *ibid.*

20. *Ibid.,* p. 575.

21. Costallat was determined to find differences between *flema salada* and pellagra. In his observations during 1847 and 1860 of Spanish peasants afflicted with *flema salada,* he made much of their vertigo, which he insisted was rare in pellagrins. It must be understood, however, that Costallat knew that these people lived on a coarse wheaten bread, and he believed pellagra could be caused only by the consumption of moldy corn. In later writings he suggested that *flema salada* was another "cereal disease" induced by the intake of wheat infested with uredo caries, a rust fungus or blight. (*Etiologie et prophylaxie de la pellagre* [2d ed.; Paris: Baillière, 1868], pp. 143–172).

22. "Pellagra and Acrodynia," in Wood, *A Treatise on Pellagra,* p. 17. (See Wood's discussion.) Acrodynia, according to Malcolm Morris' textbook on skin diseases of 1898, "is closely allied to pellagra and ergotism." He stated that the disease had been seen in France, where it had several times occurred epidemically in the army. He commented that the etiology was obscure, that it had been ascribed to

some element in food, but no proof had been forthcoming (*Diseases of the Skin* [London: Cassell], pp. 123–124). This disease is also described in certain modern texts on dermatology, but in O. S. Ormsby and H. Montgomery's standard work the term "acrodynia" is used to designate two separate conditions: the one mentioned by Morris, which these authors say first appeared in Paris in 1828; and "pink disease," a potentially fatal condition of young children which has become virtually extinct in recent years, since it was found to be caused by poisoning from mercury, which used to be present in teething powders (*Diseases of the Skin* [Philadelphia: Lea & Febiger, 1954], pp. 447–480). The epidemic form of acrodynia has not been seen since the mid-nineteenth century, but the symptoms described suggest that it may also have been caused by acute mercurial poisoning.

23. J. Peyri, *Casal Gaspar: Mal de la rosa, su historia, causa casos, curación* (Barcelona: Masnon, 1956).

24. B. Triller, "De la pellagre," thesis, University of Paris.

Chapter 5. The Polenta Eaters

1. F. Frapolli, *Animadversiones in morbum vulgo pelagram* (Milan: Galeatium, 1771). Babcock must have had some difficulty in translating Frapolli's monograph. On the title page, under the typed heading "Observations of Doctor Francis Frapolli, Physician to the Ospedale-Maggiore in Milan upon a Disease Commonly Called Pelagra," he wrote this note to Lavinder: "This is the best I can do. The medicines, doses, etc. need to be worked out. . . . J. W. B."

2. J. Odoardi, "D'una spezie particolare di scorbuto" (Belluno: n.p., 1776); in F. L. Fanzago, *Sulla pellagra* (Padua: Tipographia del Seminario, 1815).

3. H. F. Harris, *Pellagra* (New York; Macmillan: 1919), p. 3.

4. G. M. Albera, *Trattato teorico pratico delle malattie dell'insolato di primavera volgarmente dette della pellagra* (Varese: Motta and Pedemonti, 1784).

5. G. Strambio, Sr., *De pellagra observationes in regio pellagrosorum nosocomio factae a calendis junii anni 1784, usque adfinem anni 1785 in 4°* (3 vols.; Milan: Mediolani, 1785–1789).

6. "On the Pellagra, a Disease Prevailing in Lombardy," *Medico-Chirurgical Transactions*, 8 (1817), 317.

7. From the diary entry for September 14, 1786, describing

Goethe's journey from Brenner to Verona, in J. W. Goethe, *Italian Journey,* trans. W. H. Auden and Elizabeth Mayer (London: Collins, 1962).

8. L. Marchetti, *The Economic Revival of Italy,* trans. M. Sindici (Turin: Unione Tipografico-editrice Torinese, 1918).

9. D. M. Smith, *Italy* (Ann Arbor: University of Michigan Press, 1969), p. 40.

10. *Medical Record,* ed. G. F. Shrady (New York: William Wood, 1881), pp. 413–414.

11. M. F. Neufeld, *Italy, School for Awakening Countries: The Italian Labor Movement in its Political, Social, and Economic Setting from 1800 to 1960* (Ithaca, N.Y.: New York State School of Industrial and Labor Relations, 1961), pp. 135, 190–192.

12. An English translation of this law of July 21, 1902, is in A. Marie, *Pellagra,* trans. C. H. Lavinder and J. W. Babcock (Columbia, S.C.: State Co. 1910), App. I, pp. 383–387. The articles of the law as given by Marie are taken from an unpublished report to the U.S. Department of State, "Pellagra in Italy," by Vice Consul W. Bayard Cutting, Jr., Milan, November 2, 1908.

13. A. Lutrario, "La pellagre qui disparait en Italie," *Bulletin mensuel,* 28 (April 1936).

14. Marie, *Pellagra,* pp. 57–60.

15. W. R. Aykroyd, "Pellagra," *Nutrition Abstracts and Reviews,* 3 (1933), 337–344.

16. V. de Giaxa, "La pellagra: Malattie infettive endemiche dei nostin—clini fasc. 1," *Trattato italiano di igiene,* No. 6 (Turin: Unione Tipografico, 1927).

Chapter 6. Evils of Maize in the French Economy

1. *Maison Rustique or The Countrey Farme . . .* (2d ed.; London: Arnold Hatfield, 1606).

2. A.-A. Parmentier, *Le Mais apprécié sous tout ses rapports* (Paris: n.p., 1812), p. 21; quoted by T. Roussel, *De la pellagre* (Paris: Hennuyer and Turpin, 1845), pp. 353–354. Antoine-Augustin Parmentier was born in Montdidier in 1737. He was trained as an apothecary and for many years operated a pharmacy in Les Invalides. His fame arose from his extraordinary success as an agronomist. From 1769 onward, he revolutionized the French rural economy by demonstrating successfully that potatoes, root crops, chestnuts, and corn could be grown on

land unsuited to the cultivation of traditional cereal crops. While his name survives today as a term for potato soup, in his own time and for years afterward he was recognized in France as the prime innovator of agricultural policy and also lauded as a great philanthropist who established free bakeries and organized the distribution of smallpox vaccine. He died in Paris in 1813, having written a number of popular books, one of which is concerned with the cultivation and uses of corn. His popularization of this cereal caused it to be grown as a cheap source of food and indirectly precipitated the scourge of pellagra among the French peasantry ("Parmentier [Antoine-Augustin]," *La Grande Encyclopédie* [Paris: Société Anonyme de la Grande Encyclopédie, 1886–1902], XXV, 1177–1178).

3. Guyet ("The Steward"), *Le Mémoire sur le Béarn*. Allusions to Guyet's writings are in A. J. Bourde, *Agronomie et agronomes en France au XVIIIᵉ siècle* (Paris: S.E.V.P.E.N., 1967), ch. x. The article "Blé" in the *Dictionnaire oeconomique*, 1709, records that "potages [soups] économiques" containing Turkish wheat were distributed by Mme de Miramion and Mme de l'Ecluse to the poor of their parish in 1693.

4. M. B. B. Edwards, *Arthur Young's Travels in France during the Years 1787, 1788, and 1789* (London: Bell, 1899).

5. E.-A. Duchesne, *Traité du maïs ou blé de Turquie* (Paris: Madame Huzard Libraire, 1833), pp. 87–89.

6. J. Hameau, "Description d'une maladie nouvelle observée sur le littoral de Bassin d'Arcachon," paper delivered at a meeting of Société Royale de Médicine de Bordeaux (May 4, 1829), *Journal de médicine . . . de Bordeaux*, I (1829), 310.

7. Lalesque, Ardusset, Beyris, *et al.*, "Documents pour servir à l'étude de la Pellagre des Landes, *Actes de l'Académie Royale des Sciences, Belles Lettres et Arts de Bordeaux*, 8 (1846), 361–459. Beyris was the public-health doctor of the Gironde who was charged with the investigation.

8. A. Cazenave and H. E. Schedel, *Abrégé pratique des maladies de la peau—d'après les auteurs les plus éstimés et surtout d'après les documents puisés dans les leçons cliniques de M. le Docteur Biett* (3d ed.; Paris: Librairie de la Faculté de Médicine, Béchet Jeune, 1838).

9. E. About, *Handbook of Social Economy, or The Workers' A B C*, trans. W. F. Rae (New York: Appleton, 1873), pp. x–xi.

10. E. About, *Maître Pierre* (2d ed.; Paris: Librairie de l'Hachette, 1858).

11. See n. 7, above.

12. "La Pellagre landaise, sa nature, les Moyens de la prévenir et ceux de la guérir quand elle est développée," *Actes de l'Académie Royale . . . de Bordeaux,* 8 (1846), 420. Lalesque explained the frequency of pellagra by the way of life of the poor people: "The laborers cultivate their wretched inheritance; the sharecroppers [*les colons partiaires*] are in great distress. The unfortunate shepherds, who stay with their flocks at all times, are paid in cereals by their masters. Misery and penury are their lot. The food of the poorer-class Landais is rye bread, corn meal boiled with salt and water known as *cruchade,* soup made with bread, onion, rancid fat, and vinegar, fried ham called *mousset,* and salted sardines. They are badly clothed and housed. Most of their houses are dark, damp, and lit only by the light that comes in through the roof or through the door which is covered by a canvas sheet."

13. J.-M. G. Hameau, *De la pellagre* (Paris: Rignoux, 1853).

14. See n. 12, above.

15. T. Roussel, *De la pellagre,* pp. 160–228.

16. Paris: Baillière, pp. 558–575.

17. A. Marie, *Pellagra,* trans. C. H. Lavinder and J. W. Babcock (Columbia, S.C.: State Co., 1910), p. 337.

18. *Ibid.,* p. 348.

19. *Ibid.,* p. 341.

20. *Ibid.,* p. 342.

Chapter 7. The Zeist Controversy

1. "The Causation of Pellagra," *Nutrition Abstracts and Reviews,* 20 (1951), 523–535.

2. *Memoria sopra pellagra del territorio padovano* (Padua: n.p., 1789).

3. In *Sulla pellagra* (Padua: Tipografia del Seminario, 1815).

4. G. B. Marzari, *Saggio medico politico sulla pellagra o scorbuto italiano* (Venice: Parolari, 1810).

5. V. Chiarugi, *Saggio di ricerche sulla pellagra* (Florence: Allegrini, 1814).

6. P. Guerreschi, "Observazioni sulla pellagra," *Giornale della Societa Medico-Chirurgica di Parma,* 14 (1814), 241–268.

7. L. Balardini, *Della pellagra, del granturco, quale causa precipua di quella malattia e dei mezzi per arrestaria* (Milan: Societa Degli

Editori Degli Annali Universali Delle Scienze e Dell'Industrie, 1845).

8. L. Balardini, "Sulla causa della pellagra," *Gazetta medica Italiana-Lombardia*, 24 (1872), 189; "Contributo alla etiologia della pellagra," *ibid.*, 25 (1873), 125. Balardini, his son, and his assistant experimented upon themselves. They ate moldly corn and observed that it had a nauseating and bitter taste and that, on being swallowed, it produced a sensation of burning in the palate, the throat, and the stomach. The burning sensation was followed by nausea, belching, and a feeling of weakness. So disagreeable were the symptoms induced by the bad corn that the assistant refused to continue as an experimental subject after he had tasted the stuff twice. See H. F. Harris, *Pellagra* (New York: Macmillan, 1919), pp. 68–70.

9. *Encyclopaedia Britannica* (1963), XIV, 345.

10. C. Lombroso, *Studii clinici ed esperimentali sulla natura, causa e terapia della pellagra* (Bologna: Fava e Garagnani, 1869); *Trattato profilattico e clinico della pellagra* (Turin: Fratelli Socca, 1892); "Sull' etiologia e sulla cura della pellagra," *Lavori di Congresso di Medicina Interna, 1892*, 5 (Milan, 1893), 160–186.

11. C. Lombroso et al., "Sulle sostance strichnoidiche e narcotiche del maize guasto," *Rendiconto del Reale Istituto Lombardo*, Ser. 2, No. 9 (1876), 91, 133–147.

12. T. Roussel, *Traité de la pellagre et des pseudo-pellagres* (Paris: Baillière, 1866).

13. A. Marie, *Pellagra*, trans. C. H. Lavinder and J. W. Babcock (Columbia, S.C.: State Co., 1910), ch. iii.

14. P. Typaldos, *Essai sur la pellagre observée à Corfu* (Athens: n.p., 1866); abstract by C. Lombroso, *Rivista clinica di Bologna*, 1875, p. 250.

15. Tilbury Fox, *Skin Diseases, Their Description, Pathology, and Treatment* (London: Renshaw, 1873); H. F. Harris, *Pellagra* (New York: Macmillan, 1919), p. 7.

16. G. F. and G. J. Gaumer, "Pellagra in Yucatan," *American Medical Journal*, 38 (1910), 89–101.

17. *De la pellagre* (Paris: Rignoux, 1853).

18. J. Odoardi, *D'una spezie particolare di scorbuto* (Belluno: n.p., 1776), in F. L. Fanzago, *Sulla pellagra* (Padua: Tipographia del Seminario, 1815); G. M. Albera, *Trattato teorico pratico delle malattie del'insolato di primavera volgarmente dette della pellagra* (Varese: Motta and Pedemonti, 1784).

19. *Due dissertazioni sull'pellagra* (Milan: n.p., 1794), II, 38–39.

20. "Rapporto intorno ai pellagrosi d'ambo i sessi stati assoggettati

nell'ospedale maggiore di Milano alla cura balnearia, . . . nella estate dell'anno 1843," *Annali universali de medicina,* 1844, pp. 47–48.

21. C. G. Calderini, "Notizie medico-statistica, sulla Pellagra," *Annali universali di medicina,* 123 (1847), 372–432.

22. C. Lombroso, *Die Lehre von der Pellagra* (Berlin: Kurella, 1898), p. 116.

23. C. B. Davenport, "The Hereditary Factor in Pellagra," *AIM,* 18 (1916), 4–31; E. B. Muncey, "A Study of the Heredity of Pellagra in Spartanburg County, S.C.," *AIM,* 18 (1916), 32–75.

24. P. Thouvenel, *Traité sur le climat d'Italie considéré sous ses rapports phisiques, météorologiques et médicinaux* (Verona: n.p., 1797).

25. T. Roussel, *De la pellagre* (Paris: Baillière, 1845), pp. 149–150.

26. F. Frapolli, *Animadversiones in morbum vulgo pelagram* (Milan: Galeatium, 1771).

27. This saying of Strambio is quoted by Roussel as learned proof that pellagra is not caused by the sun (*De la pellagre*), p. 151. See also Strambio, *Due dissertazioni sull'pellagra.*

28. "Pellagra," in *Tropical Diseases* (4th ed.; London and New York: Cassell, 1907), pp. 328–340.

Chapter 8. Sandwith's Experience

1. F. Pruner, *Topographie médicale du Caire avec le plan de la ville et des environs* (Munich: n.p., 1847), p. 67; and *Die Krankheiten des Orients vom Standpunkte der vergleichenden Nosologie* (Erlangen: Palm and Enke, 1847).

2. *Studii scientifica sull-Egitto* (Lucca: n.p., 1847), Part V, p. 334.

3. T. C. Allbutt, *A System of Medicine by Many Readers* (New York: Macmillan, 1897), III, 800–804.

4. F. M. Sandwith, "Pellagra in Egypt," *Journal of Tropical Medicine,* 1 (1898), 65–70.

5. F. M. Sandwith, "How to Prevent the Spread of Pellagra in Egypt," *Lancet,* 1 (1903), 723.

6. A. Marie, "Pellagrous Insanity among the Arabs in Egypt," *TNCP.*

7. *Encyclopaedia Britannica* (1963), VIII, 68.

8. *Le Fellah: Souvenirs d'Egypte* (4th ed.; Paris: Librairie Hachette, 1883). The copy of this novel that I have used was the property of

the first president of Cornell University, Andrew Dickson White. On the title page he penciled this note, dated March 3, 1889: "In About's best style—the whole admirably told, and throwing a strong light on modern Egypt."

9. F. M. Sandwith, "Introductory Remarks," *TNCP.*

Chapter 9. King Corn in the Ascendant

1. J. Gray, "A Case of Pellagra of the Insane," *American Journal of Insanity,* 21 (1864–1865), 223–227.

2. E. J. Wood, *A Treatise on Pellagra for the General Practitioner* (New York and London: Appleton, 1912), pp. 28–29. It is clear from Wood's writing that he wished to emphasize the occurrence of pellagra in the United States prior to 1900 and prior to the time of its recognition by the American medical profession at large. This attitude was shared by Dr. Claude Lavinder, who commented: "The disease has since 1864 till recently, 1906–7, either disappeared or been overlooked, or, which is more likely, the physician when first studying one of these puzzling cases and inclining to the diagnosis of pellagra has accepted too readily the assertion of all authorities that pellagra does not exist in the United States, and has therefore given another name to his case although his professional conscience may never have been satisfied" ("The Prevalence of Pellagra in the United States: A Statistical and Geographical Note," *PHR,* 24 [June 18, 1909]).

3. E. J. Wood and R. H. Bellamy, "Pellagra," *Bulletin of the North Carolina Board of Health,* 24 (1909), 83–91.

4. E. J. Wood, "The Appearance of Pellagra in the United States," *JAMA,* 53 (1909), 274–282.

5. J. W. Babcock, "Introduction, first session," *TNCP.*

6. J. W. Babcock, "How Long Has Pellagra Existed in South Carolina," *American Journal of Insanity,* 69 (1912), 185–200.

7. G. H. Searcy, "An Epidemic of Acute Pellagra," *JAMA,* 49 (1907), 37.

8. From the beginning of 1908, the South Carolina State Board of Health started active investigation of the pellagra problem. Dr. Lavinder of the U.S. Public Health Service was sent to Columbia to assist in the program, and here worked actively with Williams, who was then secretary of the State Board of Health in that city.

9. C. H. Lavinder, C. F. Williams, and J. W. Babcock, *The Preva-*

lence of Pellagra in the United States, Treasury Department, Public Health and Marine-Hospital Service of the United States (Washington, D.C., 1909).

10. The National Conference on Pellagra was not only convened by Babcock and his associates to allow interchange of ideas and experience but also to establish the National Association of Pellagra, which was charged with the task of preserving and protecting the health of the people of the United States from a scourge which threatened to become national. (See the emended "Constitution of the National Association of Pellagra," *TNCP,* pp. 7–11).

11. Babcock spoke to the assembled delegates as follows: "Governor Ansel has referred to me as having been the discoverer of pellagra in this country. Pellagra was discovered in this country many years before I made my observations upon it. It was discussed at a meeting of the asylum superintendents in Washington as far back as 1864. It was observed in Brooklyn, New York by Dr. Sherwell, an eminent dermatologist. It was observed twenty-two years ago, so I have been informed by Dr. Bass of New Orleans, by Dr. Bemis of that city. It has probably prevailed in this institution for a generation. Furthermore, Dr. Harris, of Georgia, made a notable observation upon pellagra in 1902, and the hero of our modern civilization, the country doctor, observed it several years ago, notably Dr. McConnell of Chester, S.C., also Dr. Wright of Lincolnton, N.C. and Dr. Bellamy of Wilmington. The disease was observed in the Alabama Asylum for the Colored Insane before observations had been made in the South Carolina Hospital, so that if you and the Governor will pardon me, I do not wish to be placed in the false position of making any claims as to having discovered or made any early observations upon pellagra, because such is not the case, and credit is due to all of the gentlemen whose names I have mentioned and perhaps there are others" (*TNCP,* p. 3).

12. F. M. Sandwith, "Introductory Remarks," *TNCP,* pp. 14–19.

13. E. J. Watson, "Economic Factors of the Pellagra Problem in South Carolina," *TNCP,* pp. 25–32.

14. "Personal Experience with Damaged Corn," *TNCP,* pp. 199–201.

15. Discussion of a paper by Dr. J. H. Taylor ("The Question of the Etiology of Pellagra"), *TNCP,* p. 195.

16. *Ibid.,* p. 194.

Chapter 10. Transmission of the Disease

1. For a laudatory but brief description of Sambon's career see S. R. Roberts, *Pellagra: History, Distribution, Diagnosis, Prognosis, Treatment, Etiology* (St. Louis: Mosby, 1912), pp. 250–260. See also E. J. Wood, *A Treatise on Pellagra for the General Practitioner* (New York and London: Appleton, 1912), p. 36.

2. L. W. Sambon, "Remarks on the Geographical Distribution and Etiology of Pellagra," *British Medical Journal*, 2 (1905), 1272–1275.

3. L. W. Sambon, *Progress Report on the Investigation of Pellagra* (London: Bale and Danielsson, 1910); reprinted from *Journal of Tropical Medicine and Hygiene*, 13 (1910), 18–27.

4. H. Garman, *A Preliminary Study of Kentucky Localities in Which Pellagra Is Prevalent*, Kentucky Agricultural Experiment Station Bulletin 159 (Lexington, 1912).

5. C. H. Lavinder, "Notes on the Hematology of Pellagra," *TNCP*, pp. 155–162.

6. H. J. Nichols, "Discussion," *TNCP*, p. 60. See also B. R. Tucker, "Pellagra, with the Analytical Study of Fifty-five Non-institutional or Sporadic Cases," *JAMA*, 56 (1911), 246–255.

7. J. H. Taylor, "The Question of the Etiology of Pellagra," *TNCP*, pp. 181–193.

8. "Pellagra in Illinois: Condensed Report of the Illinois Pellagra Commission," *AIM*, 10 (1912), 219–249.

9. "Pellagra: A Summary of the First Progress Report of the Thompson-McFadden Pellagra Commission," *JAMA*, 62 (1914), 8–12.

10. J. F. Siler, P. E. Garrison, and W. J. MacNeal, "A Statistical Study of the Relation of Pellagra to Use of Certain Foods and to Location of Domicile in Six Selected Industrial Communities," *AIM*, 14 (1914), 292–373.

11. *Hunger, U.S.A.: A Report by the Citizens' Board of Inquiry Into Hunger and Malnutrition in the United States* (Boston: Beacon Press; Washington, D.C.: New Community Press, 1968).

12. J. F. Siler, P. E. Garrison, and W. J. MacNeal, "The Relation of Methods of Disposal of Sewage to the Spread of Pellagra," *AIM*, 14 (1914), 453–474.

13. A. H. Jennings and W. V. King, "An Intensive Study of Insects

as a Possible Etiologic Factor in Pellagra," *AJMS,* 146 (1913), 411–440.

14. W. J. MacNeal, "Observations on the Intestinal Bacteria in Pellagra," *AJMS,* 145 (1913), 801–806.

15. J. F. Siler, P. E. Garrison, and W. J. MacNeal, "Further Studies of the Thompson-McFadden Pellagra Commission: A Summary of the Second Progress Report" (read before the joint meeting of the Section on Preventive Medicine and the Section on Pharmacology at the sixty-fifth Annual Session of the American Medical Association, June, 1914), *JAMA,* 63 (1914), 1090–1093.

16. C. B. Davenport, "The Hereditary Factor in Pellagra," *AIM,* 18 (1916), 6–15.

17. J. S. De Jarnet, "Pellagra, the Corn Curse," *TNCP,* pp. 288–293.

18. C. Voegtlin, "The Treatment of Pellagra," *JAMA,* 63 (1914), 1094–1098.

19. *Medical Reports of the Effects of Arsenic in the Cure of Agues, Remitting Fevers and Periodic Headaches* (London: Johnson, 1786).

20. Review of C. Lombroso, "Die Lehre von der Pellagra," *BJD,* 10 (1898), 419.

21. S. O. L. Potter, *Therapeutics, Materia Medica and Pharmacy* (12th ed.; Philadelphia: Blakiston, 1913).

22. C. H. Lavinder, *Pellagra: A Précis* (Washington, D.C., 1908), p. 18; J. J. Watson, "Discussion," *TNCP,* pp. 193–194.

23. A. Albert, *Selective Toxicity* (2d ed.; New York: John Wiley, 1960), 169–176; H. Eagle and G. O. Doak, "The Biological Activity of Arsenobenzenes in Relation to Their Structure," *Pharmacological Reviews,* 3, (1951), 107–143.

24. W. J. Dilling, *The Pharmacology and Therapeutics of the Materia Medica* (17th ed.; New York: Cassell, 1943), 110.

25. J. F. Siler and H. J. Nichols, "Aspects of the Pellagra Problem in Illinois," *TNCP,* 53–64.

26. "Salvarsan in Pellagra: Report of Cases Treated at the Georgia State Sanitarium in 1911," *JAMA,* 58 (1912), 1509–1510.

27. C. H. Lavinder, "Pellagra: Brief Comments on Our Present Knowledge of the Disease," *PHR,* 28 (1913), 2462–2463.

28. B. R. Tucker, "Pellagra, with the Analytical Study of Fifty-five Non-institutional or Sporadic Cases," *JAMA,* 56 (1911), 246–255.

29. "Treatment of Pellagra," *American Journal of Tropical Diseases and Preventive Medicine,* 3 (1916), 580; quoted by J. Goldberger and W. F. Tanner, "Amino-Acid Deficiency Probaby the Primary Etiological Factor in Pellagra," *PHR,* 37 (1922), 462–486.

30. G. N. Niles, *Pellagra: An American Problem* (Philadelphia: W. B. Saunders, 1912), 178–204; H. P. Cole and G. J. Winthrop, "Transfusion in Pellagra," *TNCP*, pp. 158–161.

31. D. H. Yates, "The Treatment of Pellagra by Static Electricity," *Journal of Advanced Therapeutics*, 33 (1915), 61–69; D. H. Yates, "Pellagra Successfully Treated by Electricity," *American Journal of Electrotherapeutics and Radiology*, 11 (1922), 217–219. See also the bibliography in E. W. Etheridge, "The Strange Hunger: A Social History of Pellagra in the South," Ph.D. dissertation, University of Georgia, 1966.

32. Pamphlets and clippings about the Dedmond Remedy Company, Box 150, National Archives, Washington, D.C.; used in Etheridge, "The Strange Hunger." See also E. W. Etheridge, *The Butterfly Caste* (New York: Greenwood Press, 1972), pp. 34–38; and "Pellagracide and Ez-X-Ba: Fraudulent Nostrums Sold as Cures of Pellagra," Editorial, *JAMA*, 58 (1912), 648–649.

33. *JAMA*, 61 (1913), 1828–1830.

34. *Pellagra*, pp. 196–204.

35. B. Scheube, "Die Pellagra," in *Die Krankheiten der warmen Länder* (Jena: Fischer, 1900), pp. 349–363.

36. J. J. Grace, "Some Uses of Static Electricity in Medicine and Surgery," *Lancet*, 1 (1915), 180–181.

Chapter 11. Goldberger Goes South

1. R. P. Parsons, *Trail to Light: A Biography of Joseph Goldberger* (Indianapolis: Bobbs-Merrill, 1943).

2. M. Terris, *Introduction to Goldberger on Pellagra* (Baton Rouge: Louisiana State University Press, 1964).

3. J. Goldberger, "The Etiology of Pellagra: The Significance of Certain Epidemiological Observations with Respect Thereto," *PHR*, 29 (1914), 1683–1686.

4. J. Goldberger, C. H. Waring, and D. G. Willets, "The Prevention of Pellagra: A Test of Diet among Institutional Inmates," *PHR*, 30 (1915), 3117–3131.

5. *Ibid.*

6. J. Goldberger, "The Transmissibility of Pellagra: Experimental Attempts at Transmission to the Human Subject," *PHR*, 31 (1916), 3159–3173.

7. J. Goldberger and G. A. Wheeler, "The Experimental Produc-

tion of Pellagra in Human Subjects by Means of Diet," *Bulletin of the Hygienic Laboratory*, No. 120 (1920), 7–116.

8. J. Goldberger, G. A. Wheeler, and E. Sydenstricker, "A Study of the Relation of Diet to Pellagra Incidence in Seven Textile-Mill Communities of South Carolina in 1916," *PHR*, 35 (1920), 648–713.

9. E. Sydenstricker, *Health and Environment* (New York: McGraw-Hill, 1933), p. 114.

Chapter 12. Blacktongue

1. M. F. Goldberger, "Dr. Joseph Goldberger: His Wife's Recollections," *Journal of the American Dietetic Association*, 32 (1956), 724–727.

2. W. J. MacNeal, "The Alleged Production of Pellagra by an Unbalanced Diet," *JAMA*, 66 (1916), 975–977.

3. J. G. Goldberger and G. A. Wheeler, "Experimental Blacktongue of Dogs and Its Relation to Pellagra," *PHR*, 43 (1928), 172–217.

4. R. H. Chittenden, *The Nutrition of Man* (New York: Stokes, 1907).

5. Goldberger and Wheeler, "Experimental Blacktongue"; A. Seidell, "Vitamines and Nutritional Diseases: A Stable Form of Vitamine, Efficient in the Prevention and Cure of Certain Nutritional Deficiency Diseases," *PHR*, 3 (1916), 364–370. Seidell was for many years technical assistant in the Hygienic Laboratory of the U.S. Public Health Service in Washington, D.C. His association with Goldberger undoubtedly stemmed from their common interests since both were concerned with the concept of pellagra as a vitamin-deficiency disease.

6. R. H. Chittenden and F. P. Underhill, "The Production in Dogs of a Pathological Condition which Closely Resembles Human Pellagra," *American Journal of Physiology*, 44 (1917), 13–66.

7. Hofer, "Der Typhus der Hunde," *Repertorium de Thierheilkunde* (Stuttgart), 13 (1852), 201–211. It is clear from the literature that *Typhus der Hunde* was a severe and widespread veterinary problem in Europe during the late nineteenth and early twentieth century. Various synonyms were used, including *Hundetyphus, Stuttgarter Hundeseuche, Gastroenteritis haemorrhagica,* and *Typhus canum.* Under the title "Typhus of Dogs," it occupies five pages of description in the second authorized American edition of a standard three-

volume text by Dr. Franz Hutyra and Dr. Josef Marek, *Special Pathology and Therapeutics of the Diseases of Domestic Animals* (Chicago: Eger, 1922), I, 225–230. Both authors were professors at the Royal Veterinary College in Budapest. Their exhaustive account begins: "Typhus of dogs is an acute infectious disease which periodically occurs in an epizootic form, in the course of which severe symptoms of a gastrointestinal inflammation are observed frequently complicated by ulcerative stomatitis [inflammation of the mouth] and severe nervous symptoms." Dr. Hutyra had a personal research interest in the "infectious" nature of the complaint, since he claimed that in all his cases of dog typhus he had succeeded in isolating intestinal bacteria ("a virulent proteus strain") from the intestinal lining, which after culture produced a severe gastroenteritis and death in normal dogs. The authors mention that mild Russian or bitter tea or a tablespoon of black coffee every hour has been advocated as treatment.

8. Klett, "The Stuttgart Dog Epizootic: Contagious Gastroenteritis and Ulcerative Stomatitis in the Dog," *Journal of Comparative Pathology and Therapeutics,* 13 (1899), 36–50 (trans. from Klett, "Die Stuttgarter Hundeseuche," *Deutsch tierarztliche Wochenschrift,* 7 [1899], 41–45, 49–52, 57–64, 69–71).

9. G. A. Wheeler, J. Goldberger, and M. R. Blackstock, "On the Probable Identity of the Chittenden-Underhill Pellagra-like Syndrome in Dogs and 'Blacktongue,' " *PHR,* 37 (1922), 1063–1069.

10. Spencer, "Is Blacktongue in Dogs Pellagra?" *American Journal of Veterinary Medicine,* 11 (1916), 325.

11. C. A. Cary, "Deficiency Diseases," *Journal of the American Veterinary Medical Association,* 56 (1920), 609–614.

12. M. B. Saunders, "Pellagra and the 'Sore Mouth' of Dogs," *New York Medical Record,* 98 (1920), 153–154.

13. Wheeler, Goldberger, and Blackstock, "On the Probable Identity of the Chittenden-Underhill Pellagra-like Syndrome in Dogs and Blacktongue."

14. J. Goldberger, W. F. Tanner, and E. B. Saye, "A Case of Blacktongue with Post-Mortem Findings," *PHR,* 38 (1923), 2711–2715.

15. C. Eijkman, "Eine Beri Beri-ähnliche Krankheit der Hühner," *Virchow's Archiv für pathologische Anatomie und Physiologie,* 148 (1897), 523–532.

16. G. Grijns, "Over Polyneuritis Gallinarum," *Geneesk tijdschrift voor Nederlansch-Indie,* 49 (1909), 216.

17. Goldberger and Wheeler, "Experimental Blacktongue of Dogs and Its Relation to Pellagra."

18. J. Goldberger et al., "A Further Study of Experimental Blacktongue with Special Reference to the Blacktongue Preventive in Yeast," PHR, 43 (1928), 657–694; M. I. Smith and E. G. Hendrick, "Some Nutrition Experiments with Brewers Yeast," PHR, 41 (1926), 201–207.

19. J. Goldberger et al., "A Study of the Blacktongue-Preventive Action of 16 Foodstuffs with Special Reference to the Identity of Blacktongue of Dogs and Pellagra of Man," PHR, 43 (1928), 1385–1455. While Goldberger was conducting his studies of blacktongue and of diets which would prevent this disease, Frank Underhill and Lafayette Mendel pursued similar studies in the Department of Physiological Chemistry at Yale. They produced a type of malnutrition similar to blacktongue by feeding dogs cracker meal, dried peas, and cottonseed oil, and then attempted to restore the dogs to health by adding various food supplements to their diets. Since the dogs at the time of refeeding were often reduced to a condition in which swallowing was almost impossible, it is not surprising that some animals died in spite of being given dried yeast, which Goldberger found so effective in preventing blacktongue. They also extolled the properties of carrots, carrot extracts, and carotene as restoratives; the efficacy suggests that their dogs had a mixed vitamin deficiency (Underhill and Mendel, "A Dietary Deficiency Canine Disease: Further Experiments on the Diseased Condition in Dogs Described as Pellagra-like by Chittenden and Underhill and Possibly Related to the So-called Blacktongue," American Journal of Physiology, 83 [1928], 589–633).

20. G. R. Minot and W. P. Murphy, "Treatment of Pernicious Anemia by a Special Diet," JAMA, 87 (1926), 470–476.

21. G. R. Minot et al., "Treatment of Pernicious Anemia with Liver Extract: Effects Upon the Production of Immature and Mature Red Blood Cells," AJMS, N.S., 175 (1928), 599–622.

22. E. J. Cohn et al., "The Nature of the Material in Liver Effective in Pernicious Anemia, II," JBC, 77 (1928), 325–358.

23. J. Goldberger and W. H. Sebrell, "The Blacktongue Preventive Value of Minot's Liver Extract," PHR, 45 (1930), 3064–3070.

24. The studies of the pellagra-preventive properties of Minot's liver extract were organized prior to Goldberger's death on January 17, 1929, and were in part carried out under his direction.

25. "The History of Pellagra, Its Recognition as a Disorder of Nutrition and Its Conquest," AJCN, 6 (1958), 409–414.

Chapter 13. Niacin Is Discovered

1. C. A. Elvehjem and C. J. Koehn, Jr., "Studies on Vitamin B₂ (G): The Non-identity of Vitamin B₂ and Flavins," *JBC*, 108 (1935), 709–728.

2. C. J. Koehn, Jr., and C. A. Elvehjem, "Studies of Vitamin G (B₂) and Its Relation to Canine Blacktongue," *JN*, 11 (1936), 67–76.

3. D. V. Frost and C. A. Elvehjem, "Further Studies of Factor W," *JBC*, 121 (1937), 255–273.

4. O. Warburg and W. Christian, "Co-ferment Problem," *Biochemische Zeitschrift*, 275 (1935), 464.

5. H. von Euler, H. Albers, and F. Schlenk, "Über die Co-Zymase," *Zeitschrift für physiologische Chemie*, 237 (1935), 1–2.

6. Frost and Elvehjem, "Further Studies of Factor W."

7. C. A. Elvehjem *et al.*, "The Isolation and Identification of the Anti-blacktongue Factor," *JBC*, 123 (1938), 137–149.

8. E. Jahns, "Üeber die Alkaloide des Bockshorn Samens," *Berichte der deutschen chemischen Gesellschaft*, 18 (1885), 2518–2523.

9. U. Suzuki, T. Shimamura, and S. Odake, "Über Oryzanin, ein Bestandheil der Reiskleie und seine physiologische Bedeutung," *Biochemische Zeitschrift*, 43 (1912), 89–153. Nicotinic acid had been prepared as a pure chemical substance in 1867, but it was neither considered as a nutrient nor used in medical practice (C. Huber, "Vorläufige Notiz über einige Derivate des Nicotins," *Leibig's Annalen der Chemie*, 141 (1867), 271.

10. C. Funk, "Studies on Beri-Beri; VII: Chemistry of the Vitamine Fraction from Yeast and Rice Polishings," *Journal of Physiology*, 46 (1913), 173–179.

11. C. Funk, "The Etiology of the Deficiency Diseases: Beri-Beri, Polyneuritis in Bird, Epidemic Dropsy, Scurvy-Experimental, Scurvy in Animals, Infantile Scurvy, Ship Beri-Beri, Pellagra," *Journal of State Medicine*, 20 (1912), 341.

12. P. J. Fouts *et al.*, "Treatment of Human Pellagra with Nicotinic Acid," *Proceedings of the Society for Experimental Biology and Medicine*, 37 (1937), 405–407.

13. D. T. Smith, J. M. Ruffin, and S. G. Smith, "Pellagra Successfully Treated with Nicotinic Acid," *JAMA*, 109 (1937), 2054–2055.

14. L. J. Harris, "The Vitamin B₂ Complex, VIII: Further Notes on

Monkey Pellagra and Its Cure with Nicotinic Acid," *Biochemical Journal,* 32 (1938), 1479–1481.

15. T. D. Spies, C. Cooper, and M. A. Blankenhorn, "The Use of Nicotinic Acid in the Treatment of Pellagra," *JAMA* 110 (1938), 622–627.

16. T. D. Spies, W. B. Bean, and R. F. Stone, "The Treatment of Subclinical and Classic Pellagra: Use of Nicotinic Acid, Nicotinic Acid Amide, and Sodium Nicotinate with Special Reference to the Vasodilator Action and the Effect on Mental Symptoms," *JAMA,* 111 (1938), 584–592.

17. Virgil Sydenstricker and his co-workers also contributed early evidence of the efficacy of nicotinic acid in the treatment of pellagra. From 1937 to 1938, they treated forty-five pellagra patients at the University Hospital in Augusta, Georgia, with nicotinic acid as an adjunct to a pellagra-producing diet without vitamin supplements. At first the dosage of nicotinic acid was entirely empirical. Later the treatment was standardized by giving six hundred milligrams daily for three days as a curative measure and following this by a maintenance dose of one hundred milligrams daily. Gastrointestinal symptoms showed definite improvement after twenty-four hours of treatment, mental symptoms cleared within two to five days, and genital lesions and dermatitis within one week (Sydenstricker *et al.,* "Treatment of Pellagra with Nicotinic Acid: Observations in 45 Cases," *Southern Medical Journal,* 31 [1938], 1155–1163).

18. "National Research Council, Food and Nutrition Board, Proceedings," 1 (1941), 220–229 (papers of Leonard Maynard).

Chapter 14. The Conquest of Pellagra

1. J. N. P. Davies, "The Decline of Pellagra in the Southern United States," *Lancet,* 1 (1964), 195–196.

2. H. K. Stiebeling and H. E. Munsell, *Food Supply and Pellagra: Incidence in 73 South Carolina Farm Families,* U.S. Department of Agriculture Technical Bulletin, No. 333 (1932).

3. E. Caldwell and M. Bourke-White, *You Have Seen Their Faces* (New York: Viking, 1937), 25–31, 76–81.

4. V. P. Sydenstricker, "The History of Pellagra, Its Recognition as a Disorder of Nutrition and Its Conquest," *AJCN,* 6 (1958), 409–416.

5. E. N. Todhunter, "Some Aspects of the History of Dietetics," *World Review of Nutrition and Dietetics,* 5 (1965), 32–78. See also "Council on Foods of AMA," *JAMA,* 113 (1939), 681.

6. R. M. Wilder and R. R. Williams, "Enrichment of Flour and Bread: A History of the Movement," *Bulletin of the National Research Council,* 110 (1944).

7. W. G. Figueroa *et al.,* "Lack of Avitaminosis among Alcoholics," *Journal of Clinical Nutrition,* 1 (1953), 179–199.

8. J. C. Drummond and A. Welbraham, *The Englishman's Food: A History of Five Centuries of English Diet* (London: Cape, 1939).

9. Todhunter, "Some Aspects of the History of Dietetics"; Committee on Cereals, National Research Councils of the Food and Nutrition Board, *Cereal Enrichment in Perspective* (Washington, D.C., 1958).

10. Committee on Cereals, *Outlook for Bread and Flour Enrichment: Review of Events during 1947–48* (Washington, D.C., 1948).

11. "National Research Council, Food and Nutrition Board, Proceedings," 5 (1945), 107–108.

12. Committee on Cereals, *Cereal Enrichment in Perspective.*

13. Figueroa *et al.,* "Lack of Avitaminosis among Alcoholics."

14. "The Food Problem in Georgia," ed. G. G. Dull, Report No. 2 of the Inter-Institutional Committee on Nutrition, Athens, Ga., 1970.

Chapter 15. Pellagra Revisited

1. W. J. Darby and A. Hassan, "William Hawkins Wilson: A Biographical Sketch," *JN,* 92 (1967), 3–9.

2. K. Thomas, "Über die biologische Wertigkeit der Stickstoffsubstanzen in verschiedenen Nahrungsmittel," *Archiv für Physiologie,* 219 (1909); "Biological Values and the Behavior of Food and Tissue Protein," *JN,* 2 (1930), 419–435.

3. W. H. Wilson, "The Diet Factor in Pellagra," *Journal of Hygiene,* 20 (1921), 1–59.

4. "Nutritive Properties of the Protein of Maize," *JBC,* 18 (1914), 1.

5. "Importance of Individual Amino Acids in Metabolism: Observations on the Effect of Adding Tryptophane to a Dietary in Which Zein Is the Sole Nitrogeneous Constituent," *Journal of Physiology,* 35 (1906–1907), 88–102.

6. Darby and Hassan, "William Hawkins Wilson"; F. M. Sandwith, "Is Pellagra a Disease Due to Deficiency of Nutrition?" *Transactions of the Society for Tropical Medicine and Hygiene,* 6 (1913), 143.

7. W. H. Wilson, Appendix I, in R. G. White, *Report on an Outbreak of Pellagra amongst Armenian Refugees at Port Said, 1916–17: Reports and Notes* (Cairo: Government Press, 1919).

8. *Egyptian Pellagra Commission 1918 Report of a Committee of Enquiry Regarding the Prevalence of Pellagra among Turkish Prisoners of War* (Alexandria: Goverment Press, 1918).

9. W. H. Wilson, "Report on Asylum Diets," in *Annual Report,* by Director of the Lunacy Division (Cairo: Government Press, 1919), Appendix I.

10. Wilson, "The Diet Factor in Pellagra."

11. W. H. Sebrell, "Joseph Goldberger," *JN,* 55 (1955), 3–12.

12. H. Chick and E. M. Hume, "The Production in Monkeys of Symptoms Closely Resembling Those of Pellagra by Prolonged Feeding on a Diet of Low Protein Content," *Biochemical Journal,* 14 (1920), 135–146.

13. J. Goldberger and W. F. Tanner, "Amino Acid Deficiency Probably the Primary Etiological Factor in Pellagra," *PHR,* 37 (1922), 462–485.

14. *Ibid.*

15. G. A. Goldsmith, "Niacin: Antipellagra Factor, Hypocholesterolemic Agent," *JAMA,* 194 (1965), 167–173.

16. W. A. Krehl *et al.,* "Growth Retarding Effect of Corn in Nicotinic Acid-Low Rations and Its Counteraction by Tryptophane," *Science,* 101 (1945), 489–490.

17. F. Rosen, J. W. Huff, and W. A. Perlzweig, "The Effect of Tryptophane on the Synthesis of Nicotinic Acid in the Rat," *JBC,* 163 (1946), 343–344.

18. H. J. Sarrett and G. A. Goldsmith, "The Effect of Tryptophane on the Excretion of Nicotinic Acid Derivatives in Humans," *JBC,* 167 (1947), 293–294.

19. R. W. Vilter, J. F. Mueller, and W. B. Bean, "The Therapeutic Effect of Tryptophane in Human Pellagra," *Journal of Laboratory and Clinical Medicine,* 34 (1949), 409–413.

20. G. A. Goldsmith, "The B Vitamins: Thiamine, Riboflavin, Niacin," in *Nutrition: A Comprehensive Treatise,* ed. G. H. Beaton and E. W. McHenry (New York: Academic Press, 1964), II, 161–198.

21. M. K. Horwitt, "Tryptophan-Niacin Relationships in Man:

Studies with Diets Deficient in Riboflavin and Niacin, together with Observations on the Excretion of Nitrogen and Niacin Metabolites," *JN,* 60 (1956), Sup. 1, pp. 1–43.

22. "Niacin."

Chapter 16. "H" Families and Other Conundrums

1. D. N. Baron *et al.,* "Hereditary Pellagra-like Skin Rash with Temporary Cerebellar Ataxia, and Other Bizarre Biochemical Features," *Lancet,* 2 (1956), 421–428.

2. W. Henderson, "A Case of Hartnup Disease," *Archives of Disease in Childhood,* 33 (1958), 114–117; H. Weyers and H. Bickel, "Photodermatose mit Aminoacidurie, Indolaceturia, und cerebralen Manifestationen (Hartnup-Syndrome)," *Klinische Wochenschrift,* 36 (1958), 893–897.

3. J. B. Jepson and M. J. Spiro, "Hartnup Disease," in *The Metabolic Basis of Inherited Disease,* ed. J. B. Stanbury, J. B. Wyngaarden, and D. S. Fredrickson (Toronto: McGraw-Hill, 1960), pp. 1338–1364.

4. M. D. Milne *et al.,* "The Metabolic Disorder in Hartnup Disease," *Quarterly Journal of Medicine,* 29 (1960), 407–421.

5. Carcinoid tumors are uncommon neoplasms arising from secretory cells normally found in the bronchial and intestinal tissues. Endocrinologically active substances, notably serotonin, are manufactured by the normal cells and are produced in abundance by rapidly growing or spreading tumors. The functioning tumor cells depress niacin production from tryptophan because the tryptophan is diverted into serotonin synthesis. Loss of appetite often limits the diet of patients with the carcinoid syndrome, and the combined effects of low niacin intake, malabsorption, and inadequate niacin production in the body can lead to pellagra. However, only six such cases have been recorded in the medical literature, perhaps because the symptoms have been overlooked (R. J. Castiello and P. J. Lynch, "Pellagra and the Carcinoid Syndrome," *Archives of Dermatology,* 105 [1972], 574–577).

6. I. J. Selikoff and G. G. Ornstein, "Chemotherapy of Human Tuberculosis with Hydrazine Derivatives of Isonicotinic Acid (Preliminary Report of Representative Cases)," *Quarterly Bulletin of the Sea View Hospital,* 13 (1952), 27–51.

7. J. P. Biehl and R. W. Vilter, "Effect of Isoniazid on Vitamin B$_6$ Metabolism: Its Possible Significance in Producing Isoniazid Neuritis," *Proceedings of the Society for Experimental Biology and Medicine*, 85 (1954), 389–392; H. B. Carlson *et al.*, "Prophylaxis of Isoniazid Neuropathy with Pyridoxine," *New England Journal of Medicine*, 255 (1956), 118–122.

8. E. Haber and R. K. Osborne, "Icterus and Febrile-Reactions in Response to Isonicotinic Acid Hydrazine: Report of Two Cases and Review of the Literature," *New England Journal of Medicine*, 260 (1959), 417–420; H. W. Berger and S. J. Berte, "Hypersensitivity to Isoniazid," *American Review of Respiratory Diseases*, 85 (1962), 100–104.

9. W. M. Honeycutt and D. H. Huldin, "Reactions to Isoniazid," *Archives of Dermatology*, 88 (1963), 190–194.

10. E. Witbind and I. Willner, "Clinical Experiences with Isonicotinic Acid Hydrazide," *Diseases of the Chest*, 23 (1953), 16.

11. R. B. McConnell and H. D. Cheetham, "Acute Pellagra during Isoniazid Therapy," *Lancet*, 2 (1952), 959–960; R. J. Harrison and M. Feiwel, "Pellagra Caused by Isoniazid," *British Medical Journal*, 2 (1956), 852–854.

12. P. A. DiLorenzo, "Pellagra-like Syndrome Associated with Isoniazid Therapy," *Acta Dermato-Venereologica*, 47 (1967), 318–322.

13. P. S. Shankar, "Pellagra in Gulbarga," *Journal of the Indian Medical Association*, 54 (1970), 273–275; W. S. Haynes, "Pellagra Occurring in Africans under Treatment for Pulmonary Tuberculosis," *East African Medical Journal*, 35 (1958), 171–180.

14. F. M. Sandwith, "Pellagra in Egypt," *Journal of Tropical Medicine*, 1 (1898), 63–70.

15. C. Gopalan, "Possible Role for Dietary Leucine in the Pathogenesis of Pellagra," *Lancet*, 1 (1969), 197–199.

16. B. Belavady, T. V. Madhavan, and C. Gopalan, "Experimental Production of Niacin Deficiency in Adult Monkeys by Feeding Jowar Diets," *Laboratory Investigation*, 18 (1968), 94–99.

17. C. Gopalan and S. G. Srikantia, "Leucine and Pellagra," *Lancet*, 1 (1960), 954–957.

18. Gopalan and his group are now convinced that pellagra may be associated with an amino-acid imbalance. On the basis of data from rat studies indicating that the amino acid isoleucine can counteract the metabolic effects of leucine, they gave isoleucine to sixteen patients with pellagra who were jowar eaters. All recovered, whereas sixteen

control subjects on the same diet who did not receive the amino acid supplement failed to improve (K. Krishnaswamy and C. Gopalan, "Effect of Isoleucine on Skin and Electroencephalogram in Pellagra," *Lancet,* 2 [1971], 1167–1169).

Chapter 17. The Spring Equinox

1. D. M. d'Oleggio, *Tratto teoretico-pratico delle malattie dell' insolato di primavera volgarimente dette della pellagra* (Venice: n.p., 1784).

2. J. M. Good, *The Study of Medicine,* ed. Samuel Cooper (6th American ed.; New York: Harper, 1835), pp. 110–112.

3. J. Goldberger, "Pellagra," ed. W. H. Sebrell, in F. Tice, *Practice of Medicine* (Hagerstown, Md.: Prior, 1931) IX, 205–231.

4. T. D. Spies, "Relationship of Pellagrous Dermatitis to Sunlight," *AIM,* 56 (1935), 920–926.

5. D. T. Smith and J. M. Ruffin, "Effect of Sunlight on the Clinical Manifestations of Pellagra," *AIM,* 59 (1937), 631–645.

6. E. J. F. Ford, "Hepatogeneous Light Sensitization in Animals," in *Comparative Physiology and Pathology of the Skin,* ed. A. J. Rook and G. S. Walton (Philadelphia: Davis, 1965), pp. 351–363; A. M. El Mofty, "Photodynamic Activity of Psoralens," in *Vitiligo and Psoralens* (Oxford: Pergamon Press, 1968), pp. 105–116.

7. M. Grzybowski, "A Peculiar, Pellagra-like Skin Sensitization to Light in Starving Persons," *BJD,* 60 (1948), 410–415.

8. J. J. Matignon, "De l'atriplicisme (intoxication par l'arroche)," *Chinese Customs Reports* (5th ed.; 1898), p. 1.

9. K.-Y. Yu, "Atriplicism: Report of Two Cases," *Chinese Medical Journal,* 49 (1935), 148–154.

10. K.-Y. Yu, "Observations on the Dermatitis Solaris in China," *Acta Dermato-Venereologica,* 3 (1957), 538–543.

11. L. Harber, personal communication.

12. G. F. Findlay, "Epidermal Diphosphopyridine Nucleotide in Normal and Pellagrous Bantu Subjects," *BJD,* 75 (1963), 249–253.

13. G. F. Findlay, L. Rein, and D. Mitchell, "Reactions to Light on the Normal and Pellagrous Bantu Skin," *BJD,* 81 (1969), 345–351.

14. Report on wild edible plants (unpublished), Ministry of Health, Education and Social Welfare, Maseru, Lesotho, 1971.

Chapter 18. In the Light of Present Knowledge

1. Jean Léon Gérôme (1824–1904) and George du Maurier, *père* (1834–1896), gave to an admiring public in Paris and London paintings and novels which were avidly discussed and enjoyed from the time they were produced until the First World War. Gérôme was a good draftsman and an inventive illustrator, but his paintings of idealized ladies of the harem have not regained their popularity in modern times. Du Maurier, *père,* better remembered as a caricaturist for *Punch,* wrote three novels, two of which were semiautobiographical. The first of these, *Peter Ibbetson* (1891), tells of his happy childhood, and the second, *Trilby* (1894), of life in the Paris art world. Both are preposterous stories and yet plausible. Our fathers and grandfathers liked their daydreams on canvas or between the pages of a book, just as they preferred to consider pellagra as affecting people they did not know or care about (*Encyclopaedia Britannica* [1910], XI, 901–902; VIII, 658–659).

2. L. V. Hankes *et al.,* "Tryptophan Metabolism in Patients with Pellagra: Problem of Vitamin B$_6$ Enzyme Activity and Feedback Control of Tryptophan Pyrrolase Enzyme," *AJCN,* 24 (1971), 730–739.

3. *Perspectives in Human Nutrition* (New York: Grune and Stratton, 1951), p. 64.

4. J. F. Potgeiter, S. A. Fellingham, and M. L. Neser, "Incidence of Nutritional Deficiency Diseases among the Bantu and Coloured Populations in South Africa as Reflected by the Results of a Questionnaire Survey," *SAMJ,* 40 (1966), 504–509.

5. P. J. Quin, *Foods and Feeding Habits of the Pedi* (Johannesburg: Witwatersrand University Press, 1959), chs. i–iii, x, xl–xlii.

6. P. J. Pretorius, "The Clinical Nature and Extent of Protein Malnutrition in South Africa," *SAMJ,* 42 (1968), 956–958.

7. G. H. Findlay and R. G. Park, "Common Skin Diseases in the Transvaal: An Analysis of 22,000 Dermatological Outpatient Cases," *SAMJ,* 43 (1969), 590; M. Dogliotti, "Skin Disorders in the Bantu: A Survey of 2000 Cases from Baragwanath Hospital," *SAMJ,* 44 (1970), 670–672.

8. M. L. Neser, "Can We Eradicate Malnutrition in South Africa?" *SAMJ,* 39 (1965), 1158–1163.

9. J. A. Munoz and M. M. Anderson, *Report on a Nutrition Survey Conducted in Basutoland from 1956 to 1960,* Project Basutoland 1 (Johannesburg: WHO Regional Office for Africa, 1962).

10. E. Linusson, "Nutrition Education in Lesotho," 1969.

11. E. Linusson, "Draft of Proposals to Reorganize the Permanent Bureau of Nutrition (P.B.N.)" (Lesotho, 1969).

12. C. M. H. Morojele, *1960 Agricultural Census, Basutoland* (Maseru: Agricultural Department, 1963).

13. W. R. Aykroyd, *Conquest of Deficiency Diseases,* Basic Study No. 24 (Geneva: WHO, 1970), pp. 28–34.

14. M. C. Latham, "Nutritional Problems of Tanganyika," *Proceedings of the 6th International Congress of Nutrition* (Edinburgh and London: Livingstone, 1964), p. 453.

15. M. C. Latham, "Nutritional Studies in Tanzania (Tanganyika)," *World Review of Nutrition and Dietetics,* 7 (1967), 31–71.

16. V. N. Patwardhan and W. J. Darby, *The State of Nutrition in the Arab Middle East* (Nashville, Tenn.: Vanderbilt University Press, 1972).

17. I. A. Abdou, "A Study of Pellagra in the Egyptian Region," *U.A.R. Bulletin of the Nutrition Institute,* 1 (1965), 61.

18. In a personal communication dated September 8, 1971, Gopalan not only commented on the occurrence of the disease among patients admitted to general hospitals, but also stated that pellagra was seen in mental institutions. He cited the fact that in one such city institution 8 per cent of the inmates were found to have symptoms and signs of pellagra during a winter survey.

19. Aykroyd, *Conquest of Deficiency Diseases.*

20. J. Trémolières, "La Nutrition, instrument de la médicine préventive en France," *Proceedings of the 7th International Congress of Nutrition, Hamburg* (New York and London: Pergamon Press, 1966), pp. 44–46. The disappearance of endemic pellagra from Italy after the Second World War has been confirmed in a number of nutrition surveys. Up-to-date information was supplied by Dr. F. Ronchi Proja, nutrition officer to the World Food Programme of the Food and Agriculture Organization in Rome. Her data came from recent discussions with officers of the Italian Ministry of Health, with the staff of the National Institute of Nutrition in Rome, and from reports of nutrition surveys of school children carried out between 1959 and 1969. Although these surveys were limited to school children from age six to eleven, the presence of pellagra in the rest of the population would have been discovered by the teams, because they lived in

the provinces for some weeks and discussed nutritional problems with the local authorities. Dr. Proja's husband, who was a public health officer with these teams, testified that endemic pellagra was nowhere to be found. Pellagra is seen sporadically among chronic alcoholics in Italy, but no statistical data are available on these cases. See O. Ferro-Luzzi, "Lo stato nutrizionale della comunita scolari italiane, IIIa: Lo stato di nutrizione dei bambini di tre colonie permanenti romane," *Quaderni della Nutrizione,* 22 (1962), 106–113; and O. Ferro-Luzzi and M. Proja, "Lo stato nutrizionale delle comunita scolare italiane, IVa: Lo stato di nutrizione degli scolari di due comuni rurali nell'Italia centrale," *ibid.,* pp. 114–118.

21. J. K. Brock, "Human Nutrition and the United Nations Agencies," in *Recent Advances in Human Nutrition* (Boston: Little, Brown, 1961), p. 439.

22. Endemic pellagra was still prevalent in certain regions of Yugoslavia, especially around Kosovo and Metohija, until ten or fifteen years ago. Cases can still be found in those areas, but the incidence of the disease has greatly decreased. Ratko Buzina, of the Institute of Public Health of Croatia, who supplied this information, is of the opinion that dietary inadequacy in these areas was the result of economic conditions; foods such as milk, cheese, and eggs were sold by peasants in the markets for cash, and inferior foods, including corn, were kept for home consumption. The decline in the incidence of pellagra in Yugoslavia is due not only to a higher standard of living but also to a dietary change: wheat has replaced corn as the staple cereal. According to Buzina, alcoholics with pellagra are still seen both inside and outside mental hospitals.

According to Aykroyd, pellagra was first observed in Rumania in 1836. In 1932, 55,013 cases were recorded, with 1,654 deaths. In a study Aykroyd and his co-workers carried out in four villages in the province of Moldavia in the 1930's, it was found that almost 10 per cent of the population suffered from pellagra every spring. At that time, about 75 per cent of the calories consumed by the people in these villages came from maize (W. R. Aykroyd, I. Alexa, and J. Nitzulescu, "Study of the Alimentation of Peasants in the Pellagra Area of Romania," *Archives roumaines de pathologie experimentale et de microbiologie,* 8 [1935], 29). In 1966, Nitzulescu wrote Aykroyd that pellagra had become rare in Rumania because of greater diversification in the diet and, as in Yugoslavia, a partial substitution of wheat for maize. Corn products had not been enriched with niacin.

23. Jean, or Jehan Meschinot (1415–1491), Breton poet and

steward to Duchess Anne of Brittany, was a disciple of the Burgundian chronicler Georges Chastelain (1415?–1475). Meschinot's principal work is *Les Lunettes des princes,* a long moral and allegorical poem, which was published posthumously in 1493. Bound with this work are twenty-five ballads jointly composed by Meschinot and Chastelain, which form a bitter satire on the life of King Louis XI of France. Quotations in the text are from these ballads and probably represent the work of Meschinot rather than that of his collaborator. (A. de la Borderie, "Jean Meschinot—sa vie et ses oeuvres, ses satires contre Louis XI," *Bibliothèque de l'École des Chartes,* 56 [1895], 99–140, 274–317, 602–638; "Jean Meschinot," *Grand Larousse Encyclopédique,* 1963, VII, 281; J. Huizinga, *The Waning of the Middle Ages* [Garden City, N.Y.: Doubleday, 1954], 56–67, 128–138).

24. G. Hunter, *Modernizing Peasant Societies: A Comparative Study in Asia and Africa* (London and New York: Oxford University Press, 1969).

Subject Index

Author Index

A PLAGUE OF CORN

Designed by R. E. Rosenbaum.
Composed by Vail-Ballou Press, Inc.,
in 10 point linotype Times Roman, 3 points leaded,
with display lines in monotype Bulmer.
Printed letterpress from type by Vail-Ballou Press
on P&S Offset, 60 pound basis.
Bound by Vail-Ballou Press
in Holliston book cloth
and stamped in All Purpose foil.

Library of Congress Cataloging in Publication Data
(For library cataloguing purposes only)

Roe, Daphne A
    A plague of corn: the social history of pellagra

    Includes bibliographical references.
    1. Pellagra—History. 2. Social history.
I. Title. [DNLM: 1. Pellagra—History. WD126 R698L   1973]
RC625.R64   616.3'009   72-12408
ISBN 0-8014-0773-7